the Lyle
official
ANTIQUES
review

DRAWINGS BY

PETER KNOX
STUART BARTON
JANE BARTON
ALISON MORRISON
NORMA TWEEDIE

the Lyle
official
ANTIQUES
review
1977

**Compiled by
Margo Rutherford**

Edited by Tony Curtis

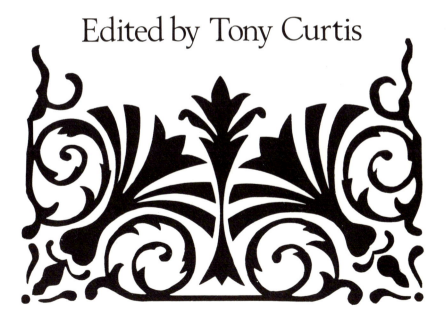

SBN 0902921-55-X

Copyright © Lyle Publications 1976   7th year of Issue

Published by Lyle Publications Glenmayne Galashiels Selkirkshire Scotland

PREFACE

1976 has been, in many ways and for many people, an alarming year financially. The list of calamities has been so long and so depressing that foreign visitors could well have been excused for expecting to find our streets knee-deep in ragged starvelings begging for crusts and coppers as a means of supplementing their fathers' strike pay or dole.

That may yet come but, for the time being anyhow, some sections of the community are still doing very nicely thank you. Not least among these are the auction houses and antiques dealers.

Right across the country, in cities and in villages, the answer is the same; 'Business is booming'. Even the most cautious and pessimistic of dealers are admitting it, albeit reluctantly, but can't spend too much time discussing this happy state of affairs because they have shops full of eager Germans, Dutchmen, Belgians, Americans, Australians, South Africans, New Zealanders, Japanese, etc., etc., falling over themselves to buy almost everything going with their pocketfuls of lovely cheap pound notes.

This really brings us down to what the antiques trade is all about. For years we have had dealers who, ticking over very nicely with their shops in the High Street and their trade deals, have stoutly declared

that, as dealers, they were primarily concerned with preserving Britain's Heritage - and if they managed to scrape an honest living in so doing, well fair enough. Quite right. But the majority of dealers are far more realistic in their approach to life and their chosen trade; they always have been. Most have always freely admitted that sentimental value can never be converted into pounds and pence. That an item is worth no more than someone is prepared to pay for it and that, in general, the person who is prepared to pay most is the person to whom the item will be sold.

Those are the rules by which the game is played, and the game is open to all comers.

Over the past year - and partly as a result of the 'come one, come all' situation which the falling pound encouraged, there have been steady increases in the values placed on just about all goods. Those of better quality have tended to show rather greater gains than the rest but the important factor as far as the trade is concerned is that the increase in values has kept comfortably ahead of inflation.

Dealers everywhere have noticed that good Georgian furniture is in increasing demand and, at the time of going to press, shows no signs of slacking off - indeed, there is evidence to suggest that it is tending to replace the lumps of Victoriana with which so many people were persuaded to fill their homes over the past few years.

Auctioneers, particularly, seem to have noticed that private buyers are on the lookout for serviceable Georgian pieces - chairs, bureau-bookcases, tables - and are well enough aware of their values to pay around shop prices for them. This means that, to a certain extent, dealers may be having to let such pieces go, sometimes being unable to buy them at prices which would allow reasonable profits on resale.

Domestic silver, too, has been the subject of increasing interest once again and here, also, the private buyers have tended to take the initiative, causing prices to rise to a degree. The feeling is, however, that old silver is still rather too dear for dealers and small collectors alike.

In some respects, this pinpoints an increasing tendency among members of the general public to be better informed than hitherto as regards the current values of all kinds of goods. They have been made very definitely aware of the investment value of antiques and, in consequence, tend to buy, and sell, goods far more knowledgeably than ever before - even, in some cases, withdrawing money from their Building Society deposits in order to pay for things which, they are reasonably certain, will show them greater dividends.

This is, of course, an extremely healthy trend for the trade, and will be welcomed by every antiques dealer worthy of the name. The more the public are aware of the values of antiques of all kinds, the more they aid the circulation of goods, the stronger the home trade will become against the export trade.

A secondary advantage to the average dealer is the more widespread acceptance among the general public that he is not a rogue continually on the lookout for gullible old ladies from whom he can prise heirlooms and treasures for a paltry few pounds - a slow-dying image which will probably tend to persist for as long as the trade tolerates its few tricksters - and as long as there are gullible people about.

The rapid growth of LAPADA, of course, should do much to improve the dealer's public image in this respect, and it is to be hoped that the Association will always employ a portion of its considerable talent toward this end. Membership of this very worthwhile organisation is growing steadily and there can be no doubt that, given continued support and enthusiasm, it will be of immense benefit to every legitimate antiques dealer and collector in the country.

For those who have not yet joined the association, it might be of interest to know that it offers considerable assistance to those selling goods overseas, and has recently negotiated particularily favourable shipping rates with one of the major lines.

As regards goods being bought by overseas dealers, country furniture (particularily pine) is still selling well to the Americans and Swedes especially - one South of England dealer had a £1,500 order from Macy's of New York earlier this year - and German dealers are tending to buy quantities of clocks in order to satisfy the demands of their customers. They are not, however, buying any old rubbish but are tending to pay good money for the right goods.

At home, apart from the interest in Georgiana, small collectables are reported to be doing well all over the country. Doubtless spurred on by the steady flow of articles encouraging collecting of this or that which have appeared in the glossies over the past couple of years, many more members of the general public are discovering the fascination of owning collections of all things small and antique.

Small ivories (including netzukes of course,) are doing well, though it is still possible to strike lucky at auction sales. Glass of all descriptions is also on the up, though with a number of youth groups seeking (and finding) large numbers of bottles on elderly rubbish dumps, there is likely to be no great increase in the prices of Victorian ginger beer bottles for years to come!

Kitchenware has enjoyed its predicted boom over the past year and should continue to do well for some time and, at the other end of the scale, jewellery shows definite signs of attracting a steadily increasing share of the investment market.

Still on the subject of small collectables, scientific instruments are attracting more attention than ever before, particularily those which, like brass microscopes, can be displayed to advantage around the home. Here, too, prices in provincial auction rooms are often surprisingly low.

Although, in the field of furniture it is that from the Georgian period which is attracting the most noticeable interest, almost all furniture in good condition is earning its living. The operative words here are 'in good condition'. Dealers all over the country are realising that, more than ever before, a good coat of polish is helping goods to sell but, going beyond this, there appears to be a definite rise in trade for quality restoration work. Earlier pieces with Victorian conversions are finding their way back into workshops in growing numbers to be put back into as near their original condition as possible - and still showing a profit at the end of the day!

The need for good quality merchandise - and the capital required to improve the quality of stock - added to the constantly increasing cost of overheads are, despite the current boom in sales, creating a number of problems for some of the country's smaller dealers. One practical solution, already adopted by quite a number of dealers and likely to become even more widespread, is the formation of Antiques Market conglomerates where, under a single roof, numbers of dealers can share the costs of advertising, insurance, rent, rates etc. without sacrificing control over their individual business activities.

Generally, the year ahead offers exciting prospects for the trade as a whole, with particular benefits likely to fall to those dealers who attack the problems of competitive marketing imaginatively and with determination.

TONY CURTIS

Acknowledgements

Phillips in Scotland
King & Chasemore
Tweeddale Press
Kelso Graphics
Annette Hogg
May Mutch
Constance Inglis
Lynn Hall
Josephine McLaren
Janis Moncrieff

All photographs and text of the arms were provided by Wallis and Wallis, 'Regency House', 1 Albion Street, Lewes, Sussex.

Printed by Apollo Press, Unit 5, Dominion Way, Worthing, Sussex.

CONTENTS

CONTENTS

CONTENTS

CONTENTS

SIXTEEN FOR THE ROAD

ESSENTIAL COMPANIONS ON ANY BUYING TRIP.

Sixteen specialist volumes, each crammed with over 100 pages of illustrations, descriptions, up-to-date- prices of antiques.

Handy, too; each beautifully bound, hard-cover book measures just under 6¼ by 4¼ inches to slip easily into a pocket. FANTASTIC VALUE AT ONLY £1.50 PER SUBJECT!

18

22

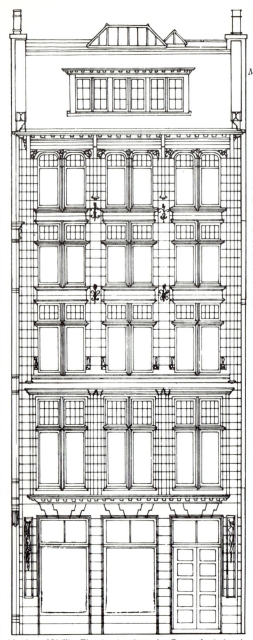

Woburn Abbey
Antiques Centre

The largest Antiques Centre under one roof in England, with over 40 independent shops and 50 established dealers, some of whom are members of the B.A.D.A., is situated in the magnificent South Court of Woburn Abbey.

We are pleased to offer the dealer and private collector a wide range of Antiques: Clocks, Porcelain and Glass, Paintings, Prints, Furniture, Jewellery, Georgian Domestic Silver, later silver, Bronzes, Works of Art etc., at competitive prices.

ALL ITEMS ARE VETTED BY A COMMITTEE OF ESTABLISHED DEALERS TO ENSURE THEIR AUTHENTICITY.

Within one hour's drive of London via M. 1, Exit 12 signposted Woburn Abbey). Trains from St. Pancras to Flitwick can be met by prior arrangement. Dealers admitted free and their park entrance refunded at the Antiques Centre. Visiting dealers' car park adjacent to the Antiques Centre.

OPEN EVERY DAY OF THE YEAR
Including Sundays and Bank Holidays

Easter to October 10 — 6 p.m. November to Easter 10 — 5 p.m.

WOBURN ABBEY ANTIQUES CENTRE, WOBURN ABBEY, BEDFORDSHIRE. MK 43 0TP

Telephone Woburn (052525) 350.

27

28

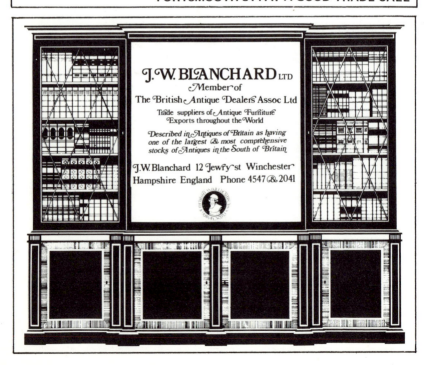
30

31

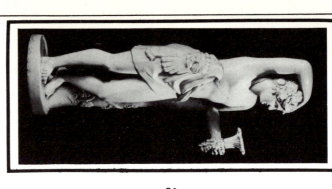

Terry Antiques

(TH Murphy)

Fine English Furniture
and Antiques of all descriptions

Continental Carriers

Importers and Exporters

175 Junction Road, London N19

Tel. 01-263 1219   01-889 2398

33

There are a great many antique shippers in Britain

British Antique Exporters Ltd. of Newhaven, Sussex. Thirteen years experience of shipping goods to all parts of the globe have confirmed his original belief that the way to build clients' confidence in his services is to supply them only with goods which are in first class saleable condition. To this end, he employs a full-time staff of over 40, from highly skilled packers, joiners, cabinet makers, polishers and restorers, to representative buyers and executives. Through their knowledgeable hands

but few, if any, who are as quality conscious as Norman Lefton, Chairman and Managing Director of

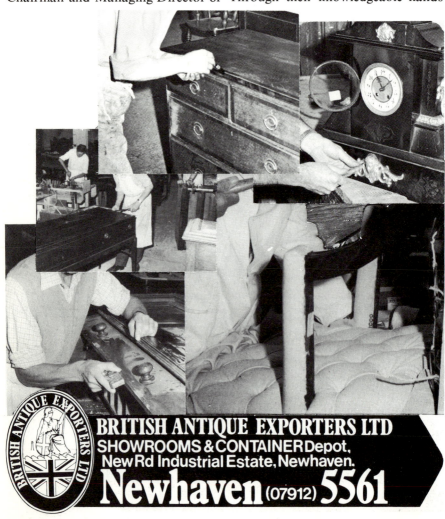

34

passes each piece of furniture before it leaves the B.A.E. warehouses, ensuring that the overseas buyer will only receive the best and most saleable merchandise for their particular market. This attention to detail is obvious on a visit to the Newhaven warehouses where potential customers can view what must be the most varied assortment of Georgian, Victorian, Edwardian and 1930's furniture in the area. One cannot fail to be impressed by, not only the varied range of merchandise but by the fact that each piece is in perfect condition awaiting shipment. As one would expect, packing is considered somewhat of an art at B.A.E. and David Gilbert, the factory manager, ensures that each piece will reach its final destination in the condition a customer would wish. B.A.E. set a very high standard and, as a further means of improving each container load Mr. Gilbert, who also deals with customer/container liaison, asks each customer to return detailed information on the saleability of each

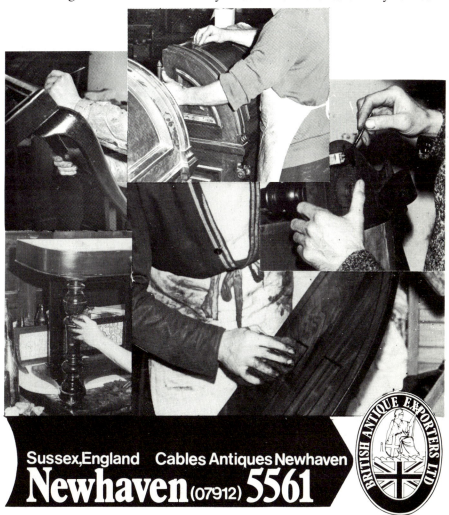

35

piece in the container thereby ensuring successful future shipments. This feedback of information is the all important factor which guarantees the profitability of future containers "By this method" Mr. Lefton explains, "we have established that an average £4,000 container will, immediately it is unpacked at its final destination, realise in the region of £6,000-£8,000 for our clients selling the goods on a quick wholesale turn-over basis". These figures are confirmed by the Chartered Accountant, Mr. A. E. C. Wheeler who whilst officially the Company Accountant is also very involved in promoting good customer relationships and could be called B.A.E.'s public relations genius. He is always ready to discuss the financial aspects of the shipments and proves a valued member of this highly successful Company. Other employees you will meet on a visit to Newhaven are Tracy Ware, who deals with documentation/customer liaison, Christine Pilote who is a buyer as well as generally looking after overseas visitors and Jenni Moring who specialises in container

36

selection and is on hand to deal with customer queries.

In any average 20-foot container, B.A.E. put approximately six really fine pieces, some 20 quality pieces, 20 "run of the mill" items and as many as 400 to 500 smaller pieces of bric-a-brac, all in eminently saleable condition.

Based at the south coast port of Newhaven – 10 miles from Brighton and on a direct rail link with London (only 50 minutes journey) the Company is ideally situated to ship containers to all parts of the world. The showrooms, restoration and packing departments are open to overseas buyers and no visit to purchase antiques for re-sale in other countries is complete without a visit to their Newhaven premises where a welcome is always found.

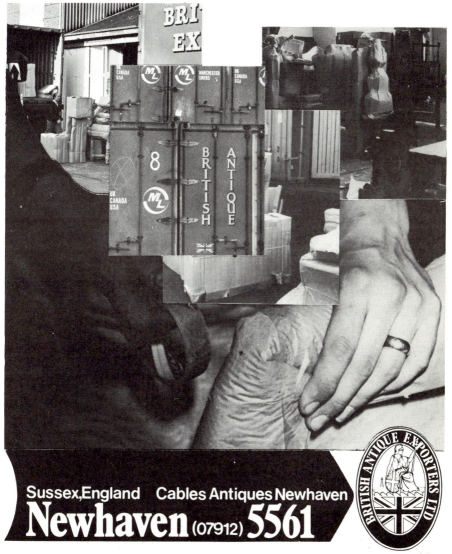

37

A selection of antiques

38

from a container load

39

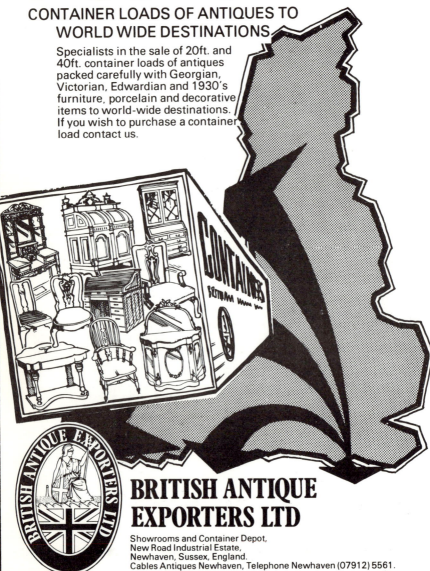
40

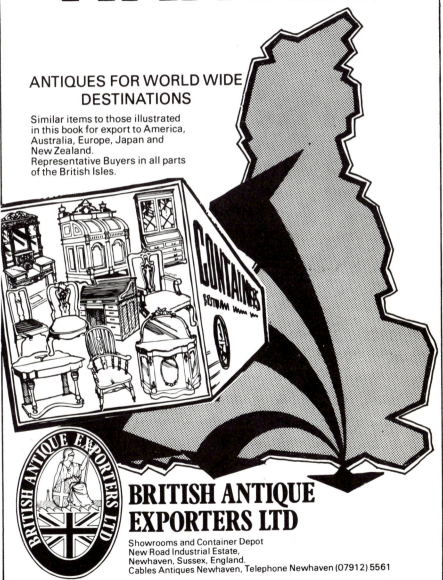
41

42

43

GOOD COMPANIONS

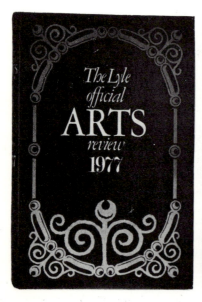 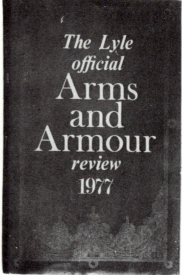

FOR THE REAL PROFESSIONAL.

Antiques, Arts, Arms and Armour - three essential fields of reference for every go-ahead dealer.   Equip yourself properly for the year ahead by adding these two beautifully produced companion volumes to your library.
Thousands of illustrations, descriptions, up-to-date prices.
Wonderful value at only £6.00 each.

The Lyle Official Antiques Review is published on the first of November of every year, enabling you to begin each new year with an up to date knowledge of the current trends, together with the verified values of antiques of all descriptions.

We have endeavoured to obtain a balance between the more expensive collector's items and those which, although not in their true sense antiques, are handled daily by the antique trade.

The illustrations and prices in the following sections have been arranged to make it easy for the reader to assess the period and value of all items with speed.

You will find illustrations for almost every category of antique and curio, together with a corresponding price collated during the last twelve months, from auction rooms and retail outlets throughout Britain.

When dealing with the more popular trade pieces, a calculation of an average price has been estimated from the varying accounts researched. As regards prices when 'one of a pair' is given in the description the price quoted is for a pair, for with the limited space we have at our disposal we feel only one illustration is necessary.

ANIMALIA

Tiger skin, with stuffed head, on felt mount. £105

Leopard skin with a stuffed head. £30

A stuffed kite on a cork base, 36cm. high. £100

Elephant's foot jardiniere with brass rim and interior. £32

A stuffed goshawk on a pedestal, 47 cm. high. £52

A Highland Light Infantry trophy of a ram with silver mounts. £50

Table ornament of seven stuffed birds on a tree branch under a glass shade. £18

Animal ashtray in shell work £5

Early 18th century
Papal Guard cuirass.
£300

Miniature suit of
armour in the 16th
century style, made
in the 19th century,
84cm. high.   £180

A Japanese half
suit of armour
bearing a gilt
monogram.
£425

A suit of 17th century
pikeman's armour.
£400

Italian suit of horseman's
three-quarter armour.
£1,200

A good suit of early
17th century pikeman's
armour.   £440

A Victorian other rank's white metal helmet plate of The 2nd Edinburgh Rifle Volunteer Corps. £46

A very rare cap badge of The Royal Marine Labour Corps, the globe within laurel wreath surmounted by a ship, bows-on. £10

A scarce Georgian officer's copper gilt shako badge for the Waterloo Shako. £48

A very rare cap badge of The Tyneside Scottish, circular belt bearing motto Quo Fata Vocant. £30

A very rare cap badge of The Middlesex Regimental Public Works Pioneer Battalion. £36

An officer's gilt 1861 pattern shako badge of The 44th Regiment of Foot. £78

A pre 1902 officer's gilt metal plate of The Army Vetinary Department. £36

A pre 1902 Victorian officer's silvered helmet plate of the Somerset Light Infantry 2nd Volunteer Battalion. £56

A post 1902 officer's gilt helmet plate of The Royal Irish Regiment. £48

A fine officer's silvered and blue enamelled 1855 pattern shako badge of The East Norfolk Militia.   £52

A post 1902 officer's helmet plate of The Duke of Cornwall's Light Infantry.   £26

A rare Victorian officer's large silvered shako grenade of The Royal Tyrone Fusiliers.   £52

A scarce Victorian plated officer's blue cloth helmet plate of The Dorsct Militia.   £32

An other rank's brass 1816 pattern shako badge of The Royal Jersey Militia.   £46

A good Victorian officer's gilt blue cloth helmet plate (1878-81) of the 20th Foot.   £46

A pre 1902 officer's gilt helmet plate of The North Staffordshire Regiment. £32

A Victorian officer's helmet plate of The Hertfordshire Yeomanry.   £40

A rare cap badge of The Tower Hamlets Rifles.   £34

BAROMETERS

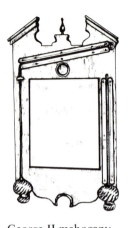

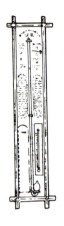

Fine barometer in rosewood, inlaid with mother-of-pearl. £235

George II mahogany angle barometer and thermometer in the form of a wall mirror, 102cm. high. £850

Admiral Fitzroy barometer in an oak case. £45

Early 18th century walnut stick barometer by S. Cade of Charing Cross, 37in. long. £500

Victorian carved oak aneroid barometer and thermometer. £52

Mahogany inlaid pediment barometer by Champion, Glasgow, 97cm. long. £140

Victorian inlaid banjo barometer by Lione and Samalvico of Holborn. £50

Oak pediment barometer and thermometer by J.M. Bryson, Edinburgh. £65

18th century banjo barometer with swan-necked pediment. £130

George III mahogany pediment barometer with carved shell ornament, 92cm. long. £80

Victorian barometer and timepiece in a carved oak rope and anchor pattern case. £24

Rosewood pediment barometer by Adie & Sons, Edinburgh. £160

Sheraton style inlaid mahogany pediment barometer by Davidson Dunse. £150

Large onion-topped mahogany wheel barometer with 10in. dial, made by 'Snow Ripon'. £125

Mahogany inlaid pediment barometer by Donevan, Edin., 97cm. long. £100

Rosewood onion-topped wheel barometer with painted scroll work, 37in. high, circa 1820. £110

BAROMETERS

An Admiral Fitzroy barometer and thermometer in an oak case. £44

Mahogany inlaid wheel barometer and thermometer of Sheraton design by A. Riva & Co. Glasgow. £70

Victorian carved wood aneroid barometer and thermometer. £22

Rare 18th century stick barometer in mahogany with ebony and boxwood stringing, silvered plate engraved 'Zappa Fecit', 38in. £195

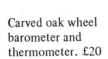

Rosewood wheel barometer, circa 1860. £95

Carved oak wheel barometer and thermometer. £20

19th century inlaid mahogany wheel barometer and thermometer by J. Gilmour, Glasgow, 94cm. high. £30

Victorian banjo barometer and thermometer in a rosewood case. £25

Fortin barometer by 'J. Hicks, London', mahogany back plate 50in. high. £350

Large mahogany wheel barometer by Snow Ripon, circa 1850, with a 10in. dial. £125

Mahogany wheel barometer by 'N. Barnuka, Bury', inlaid with ebony and holly paterae shells and edging, circa 1795. £175

18th century gilt framed barometer and thermometer. £220

Early 19th century mahogany barometer. £158

19th century mahogany banjo barometer and thermometer. £50

Fine quality large 19th century mahogany carved banjo barometer with clock. £300

Mahogany inlaid wheel barometer and thermometer by Gulletti, Glasgow. £65

BRONZE

Pair of French Art Nouveau gilt bronze Dutch figures with ivory faces and hands by 'La Monica'.£230

A pair of Louis Philippe bronze and ormolu candelabra.   £475

Japanese bronze circular jar and cover. £115

19th century bronze of a mare and foal signed Fratin, 16in. high.   £300

One of a pair of 19th century bronze cherubs.   £55

Onyx square jardiniere with cloisonne enamel mounts, 10ins.   £135

Pair of Art Deco gilded metal figures of dancers, 14½in. £95

Pair of fine bronzes, signed Salmson.
£500

Pair of Malayan bronze figures of a man
and a woman with a child, 7¾in. high. £32

A bronze dancing
figure of Isadora
Duncan, 18in. high.
£150

19th century bronze of a
horse and jockey, signed
P.J. Mene, 17in. high.
£760

Japanese
bronze vase.
£55

Pair of urn-shaped bronze vases and
covers with relief Bacchanalian
scenes, 22in. high.   £340

19th century bronze figures of
Mercury and Juno.   £220

BRONZE

Victorian bronze of a drunkard. £195

Bronze study of two dogs approaching a grouse, sgnd. P.J. Mene, 1847, 16in. long. £440

Bronze study of a native girl, signed Salmson, 53cm. £300

19th century bronze of 'Ulysses stringing his bow', 35ins. tall. £725

Pair of large bronze Marley horse groups, signed C.H. Crozatier, 23in. high. £320

One of a pair of bronze and ormolu figures of a Bacchante and companion, in the manner of Clodion. £4,000

Pair of 18th century bronze statuettes of gentlemen, 20in. £450

19th century bronze figure of a retriever signed E. Wunshe, 1ft 9in high. £725

Pair of Japanese bronze vases decorated with flowering trees and birds, 9½in. high. £50

Standing bronze figure of O. V. Topino.   £165

Bronze table gong supported by two carved elephants, 2ft 11in wide   £28

One of a pair of whippets by P.J. Mene.£460

Bronze female winged statuette, stamped J. S. Westmacott, dated 1852.   £60

Animalier bronze of a horse on a marble base, 22cm. long.   £750

19th century French bronze torchere, in the form of a boy holding an eight-light mount.   £3,600

Pair of bronze figures, circa 1850.   £110

Standard bronze measure with container, 1601.   £200

Victorian pair of spelter figures of cavaliers, 14½in.£14

Bronze belt mask from Benin, Nigeria, 6in. high £42

A late 16th/early 17th century bronze figure of a cheval ecorche, attributed to the Florentine Bolgna-Susini workshops, 92cm. high. £150,000

Bronze statue sgnd G. Marty, base inscription A. Cecioni, Firenze. £950

One of a pair of 19th century bronze vases. £50

Pair of 19th century bronze studies of Eastern warriors, signed Deniere, 14½in. £420

One of a pair of bronze double handled vases, 9in high. £50

19th century French bronze group of lovers, 61cm high. £400

Automobiles Ferman, a bronze figure of Daedelus on a marble base fitted with two inkwells by G. Colin, 1907. £320

Late 19th century coloured bronze bust of La Sibylle by E. Villanis. £420

Japanese bronze oblong box with bird head handles, 9½in wide. £30

Animalier bronze figure of an Arab stallion 'Ibrahim' by P.J. Mene, 31cm. high. £760

Chinese bronze wine vessel on triple legs. £42

Oriental bronze table bell, on carved and pierced ironwood stand. £28

Late 18th century pair of coloured bronze models of Red Indian chiefs by G. Kauba. £4,200

One of a pair of Regency bronze and ormolu three branch, four light candelabra. £305

One of a pair of French 'Egyptian' bronze and ormolu twin-branch candelabra. £355

Bronze Thai Buddha, 30in. high. £450

One of a pair of Thai bronze kneeling figures, 19th century, 79cm. high. £412

Figure of a young girl with hoop by Preiss. £400

Bronze figure of a discus thrower, 8½ins. high. £18

Preiss figure of a young boy with his hands in his pockets. £400

Bronze classical male figure, 13¼ins. high. £40

19th century bronze of a hunter on horseback, signed E. Drovet, on a rouge marble base, 16ins. wide. £230

19th century French bronze. £240

Bronze figure of a woman by Charles Sykes inscribed 'Phryne-Women', 1919. £100

Ivory and gilt-bronze figure of a running girl by F. Preiss. £750

Bronze figure of Daphne by Josephine Sykes, 1930, 22½ins. high. £100

Canadian bronze group 'Le Premier Bairer' by Alfred Laliberte, 46cm. high. £775

Early 19th century Kashmiri style figure of Buddha, 15ins. high £85

A classical bronze group of a goat and two figures of children, 26cm. high. £210

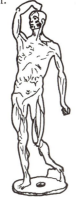

Late 16th century German bronze, 33cm. high. £5,000

Preiss figure of a girl skating, 14ins. high. £700

Bronze figure of a Grenadier Guard, 1815, on plinth, signed J.E. Boehm, stamped Elkington & Co., 18ins. high. £230

Signed Carrier gilt bronze figure of a mandolin player. £660

Bronze study of a stallion, signed P.J. Mene, 126cm. high. £230

Preiss figure of a standing girl in a casual dress. £750

BRONZE

Victorian bronze vase, 14in. high. £14

Pair of French bronze putti on chased ormolu bases, 27cm. high. £480

One of a pair of bronze pricket candlesticks, 15th century. £900

Tibetan bronze of Maitreya seated in Virasana with hands in Dharmacakra, circa 1600, 5in. £800

Art Nouveau bronze wall panel, 8½ x 5¾ ins. £18

Tibetan bronze of an abbot, circa 1800, 6¼in. £450

19th century Japanese bronze circular jardin-iere with bird and dragon in relief. £32

A bronze and ivory figure of a dancer by Chiparus, 38.5cm.£780

Japanese bronze circular jardiniere with birds and flowers in bas-relief, 40cm. diam. £92

One of a pair of bronze cheek-pieces from a horse's bit, Iranian, 14cm. square. £8,000

Japanese bronze bell of the Yayoi period, 62cm. high. £35,700

One of a pair of Japanese bronze bottle shaped vases, 37cm. high. £95

West Tibetan bronze seated figure of Kubera holding a mongoose vomiting jewels, 3½in. high. £250

Bronze Indian fisherman, 26¾in. £600

16th century Tibetan bronze of Sherab Seng-Ge, 7¼in. high. £350

10th century Javanese bronze bowl, 20.9cm. high. £6,300

Oriental bronze ewer with figures and animals in relief. £18

Indian bronze group of chieftain and three attendants on an oval cobra pattern base. £100

BRONZE

19th century Japanese bronze vase with kylon handles, 6½in. high. £10

'The Bathers' by F. Preiss. £1,000

19th century bronze vase with pierced cover 6 in. £10

Chinese bronze statuette of a deity in ceremonial dress, 14in. high.   £70

18th century Tibetan bronze of Kubera, 8in. high.   £800

18th century Chinese bronze buddha on a wooden stand, 27cm. high.   £55

Bronze statuette of King Henry VIII on black marble square base.   £36

Bronze statue of a bison by J. Haehnek, 12 in. long.   £125

17th century Nepal bronze of the Bodhisattva Avalokitesvara, 5½ in. high.   £600

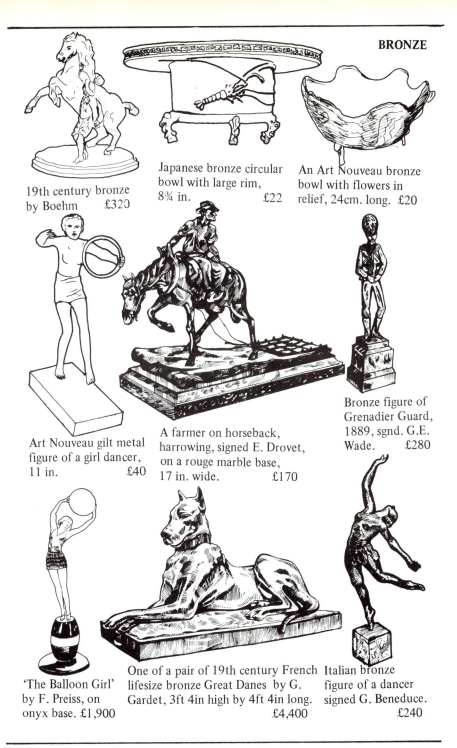

19th century bronze
by Boehm   £320

Japanese bronze circular
bowl with large rim,
8¾ in.   £22

An Art Nouveau bronze
bowl with flowers in
relief, 24cm. long. £20

Art Nouveau gilt metal
figure of a girl dancer,
11 in.   £40

A farmer on horseback,
harrowing, signed E. Drovet,
on a rouge marble base,
17 in. wide.   £170

Bronze figure of
Grenadier Guard,
1889, sgnd. G.E.
Wade.   £280

'The Balloon Girl'
by F. Preiss, on
onyx base. £1,900

One of a pair of 19th century French
lifesize bronze Great Danes by G.
Gardet, 3ft 4in high by 4ft 4in long.
                        £4,400

Italian bronze
figure of a dancer
signed G. Beneduce.
              £240

BUCKETS AND HODS

Victorian copper scoop coal scuttle with a swing handle.   £18

One of a pair of brass bound tubs, circa 1850. £95

One of a pair of grocer's display scuttles decorated in red and gold, circa 1820.   £145

19th century copper pail with swing handle.   £20

Circular copper log cauldron with brass handles and claw feet.   £22

Copper and brass bound oval coal pail with swing handle.   £30

Edwardian rosewood coal cabinet inlaid with boxwood.   £24

Copper coal scuttle, circa 1800.   £45

19th century stained wood and brass bound coal pail with brass handle.   £22

19th century copper
coal helmet.   £38

Late 18th century
brass bound maho-
gany plate bucket.
£180

19th century brass
coal helmet with a
swing handle. £32

Victorian brass coal
vase and cover with
handles, on three
paw feet.   £20

A Pontypool coal
bin.   £78

Art Nouveau design
copper circular coal
vase, 56cm. high.
£32

Copper circular jar-
diniere with brass
lions masks and
paw feet, 32cm.
high.   £28

18th century maho-
gany brass bound
bucket.   £195

Late Victorian oak
coal box with brass
fittings.   £18

CADDIES AND BOXES

Mahogany inlaid sarcophagus shaped tea caddy. £22

Walnut and brass bound portable writing desk. 19½ in. £28

17th century silver mounted tortoiseshell jewellery casket. £350

Victorian leather bound workbox with brass mounts and paw feet. £14

Two of six black japanned tea canisters, decorated with Chinese gilt design, 17 in. high. £40

Tortoiseshell two division tea caddy strung with pewter 15.5cm wide. £48

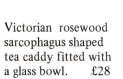

Victorian rosewood sarcophagus shaped tea caddy fitted with a glass bowl. £28

Early 18th century Austro-Hungarian octagonal casket containing twelve gilt decorated glass bottles, 26.5cm wide. £460

An alabaster oblong cigarette box on gilt metal paw feet, 16cm. wide. £10

A tortoiseshell and mother-of-pearl tea caddy, 20 cm. wide. £60

A tortoiseshell and silver mounted casket, 15.5 cm. wide. £78

George III tea caddy veneered in rolled paper, 18 cm. wide. £85

Japanese, late Edo period robe-chest (hasami-bako) lacquer with metal mounts, 58.5 cm. wide. £2,310

Chinese black lacquered box, 15 in. wide £18

Indian carved ebony square shaped jewel casket with mosaic panels, 9 in. £90

Sheraton mahogany tea caddy, 19 cm. wide. £45

A George III mahogany knife box, 37 cm. high. £65

George III hexagonal caddy. £85

CADDIES AND BOXES

Rosewood tea caddy inlaid with mother-of-pearl. £70

Sheraton period partridgewood tea caddy, circa 1800. £38

Carved oak oblong bible box, 2ft 2in. wide. £32

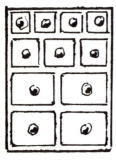

Pinewood spice drawers with brass pulls, circa 1820, 14½ in high x 11½in x 7in. £56

A small 18th century Continental ebonised cabinet of drawers with mirror fronts, 23cm. wide. £48

Japanese black lacquered octagonal work box with hinged cover, 15½in. wide. £35

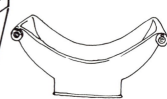

One of a pair of 19th century inlaid mahogany half circle boxes, 22cm diam. £32

Large tea caddy in figured mahogany, 21in. high. £110

George III mahogany cheese dish with scroll ends, 42½cm. wide. £32

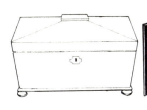

Rosewood sarcophagus box and cover, 12½in. wide. £10

Indian ivory veneered small cabinet, 18th century, 66cm. wide. £550

Victorian inlaid rosewood writing case with fitted interior. £38

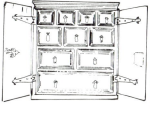

An old oak cabinet of ten small drawers formerly belonging to Queen Mary, from Holyrood Palace. £220

Outstanding George III mahogany apothecary's cabinet on bracket feet, with old bottles, pestle and mortar, 15in. high, circa 1795. £320

Victorian inlaid oak smoker's cabinet, 39cm. high. £26

Sheraton period satinwood inlaid octagonal tea caddy with paperwork and glazed panels, 17cm. wide. £130

Victorian oak log box with embossed copper lid, 79cm. wide. £34

Victorian rosewood sarcophagus shaped tea caddy with a glass bowl. £42

CADDIES AND BOXES

Oak table desk with original handles, circa 1700, 36cm. wide. £450

19th century Chinese export lacquer chess and backgammon board complete with ivory chessmen. £150

Yew wood two division tea caddy inlaid with mother-of-pearl, 22cm. wide. £60

Writing box with green leather writing surface and compartments. £7

Fine Japanese lacquer-work box and tray. £3,360

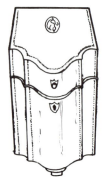

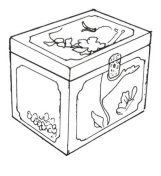

Small square Oriental box in the Komai style, late 19th century. £85

Late 18th century inlaid mahogany knife box with serpentine shaped front. £42

Japanese lacquered box decorated with flowers. £15

19th century Continental walnut chest, 48in. wide. £300

George III fruit-wood tea caddy in the form of an apple. £125

Rosewood two division tea caddy strung with boxwood, 21cm. wide. £40

Part of a set of six green japanned tea canisters, 17in. high. £40

Pair of George III mahogany knife boxes, 15in. high. £150

19th century Japanese lacquer box. £90

Chippendale octagonal mahogany bonnet box, circa 1760, 58cm. wide. £375

Japanese lacquered box, 13½in. wide. £22

CADDIES AND BOXES

Lever Brothers 'Plantol' soap, circa 1900.   £3

Lever Brothers 'Lux' soap flakes, circa 1910.   £2

Miniature tin of Andrews Liver Salts produced by LNER trains, circa 1930.   £3

Lever Brothers 'Lifebuoy Soap', circa 1910.   £2

Rowntrees toffee tin, circa 1930.   £8

Mackintosh's toffee shop, circa 1930 £6

Mahogany cheese coaster with gilt decoration. £80

Ivory tea caddy with rosewood stringing. £140

19th century Japanese lacquered portable writing desk decorated in gilt, 44cm. wide.   £36

Small tortoiseshell tea caddy, 12cm wide.   £40

Tortoiseshell two division tea caddy inlaid with mother-of-pearl, 22cm wide.   £60

Tortoiseshell two division tea caddy, 17.5cm wide. £75

Sheraton mahogany caddy inlaid with roses. £90

Walnut portable writing desk. £22

A large confectionery tin by John Buchanan, Glasgow, 8¾in. wide, circa 1890. £6

Lever Brothers 'Sunlight Soap', circa 1890. £2

Huntley and Palmer tin decorated with printed paper, circa 1900. £10

W & R Jacob biscuit tin in the form of a Jacobean log box. £8

One of a set of three George III tea caddies by W. Vincent, 25.7oz. £960

Caleys Jazz-Time toffee tin, circa 1920. £5

Ivory and tortoiseshell box, early 19th century. £50

Sheraton fiddle back mahogany two division tea caddy inlaid with marquetry, 17.5cm wide. £90

Tortoiseshell two division tea caddy with ivory feet, 18.5cm wide. £40

George III inlaid satinwood caddy with silver mounted glass containers. £150

CADDIES AND BOXES

Serpentine fronted tortoiseshell tea caddy. £38

Tortoiseshell two division tea caddy strung with pewter and applied with mother-of-pearl, 20cm wide. £40

Tortoiseshell two division tea caddy inlaid with mother-of-pearl, 8in. wide. £60

Sheraton fiddle back mahogany tea caddy, 11.5 cm wide. £50

Victorian Tunbridge ware glove box with geometric design. £20

George III fruitwood tea caddy, 10.5cm high. £120

19th century mahogany sarcophagus shaped tea caddy, 23 cm. wide. £28

Walnut oblong tea caddy with domed cover. £22

Mahogany oblong tea caddy with satinwood shell motifs, 7½in. £18

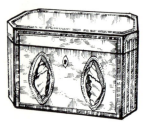

Sheraton yew wood two division tea caddy, 19cm. wide. £55

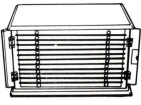

Mahogany coin cabinet of twelve drawers, 12 in. £32

Two division mother-of-pearl caddy on ivory feet. £75

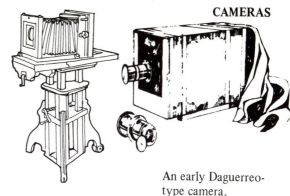

An Armanox high-speed miniature press camera and case. £360

A whole plate studio camera and stand, circa 1900. £200

An early Daguerreo-type camera. £2,200

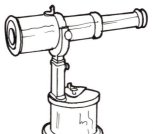

Dry plate camera by 'J. Lancaster and Son, Birmingham'. £48

A rare buttonhole ferro-type camera, circa 1890. £300

19th century mahogany and brass dry plate camera engraved 'Patent Thornton Pickard'. £85

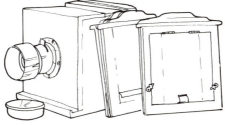

A plate camera by Bausch and Lomb. £22

A good wet plate camera, circa 1860. £400

Old plate camera. £10

A highly stylised brass lady, twenties, 9in. x 5½in. £110

A French bronze 'cockatoo' car mascot signed Bourcart, 6½ins. high. £25

A caricature bulldog puppy inscribed on the collar 'Telcote Pup', 6in. x 4¾in. Twenties. £90

Labrador's head with game in mouth, sgnd. C.H. Paillet, thirties, 3½in. x 3in. £80

Desmo horse and jockey, circa 1937. 5½in. x 5in. £80

Fin with thermometer, circa 1920, 4in. x 4½in. £28

Desmo aquaplane with mobile propeller, circa 1937, 5½in. x 2in. £95

A brass caricature policeman, sgnd. H. Hassall, circa 1911. £85

American stylised bird, mid-thirties, 7¼in. x 8in. £120

'The Essex Man', circa 1928, mounted on radiator cap, 3½in. x 5in. £65

Silver-plated camera motoring mascot. £350

Red-Ashay's boy, English, circa 1930, 3in. x 5in. £160

Bulldog on chain, French, circa 1923, 4¾in. x 4in. £150

Mobile brass aeroplane with rotary engine and propeller inscribed 'Robt. Beney & Co.' 4in. x 6½in., circa 1915. £100

A stylised rearing horse, circa 1930, 2½in. x 4in. £42

A 'Spirit of Ecstasy' mascot by C. Sykes, for Rolls Royce 1911/34, 4½in. x 3½in. £100

Stylised swan within oval silhouette, circa 1935, 8in. x 3½in. £40

Greyhound in motion, twenties, 5in. x 3in. £25

Red-Ashay's bird in flight, English, tinted bulb in base, circa 1930, 8in. x 8½in. £180

'The Spirit of Triumph' by F. Basin, twenties/ thirties, 6in. x 7in. £160

A solid bronze 'Old Bill' mascot, circa 1919, sgnd. Bruce Bairnsfather. £40

Vulcan brass car mascot of a blacksmith standing beside an anvil, 5ins. high. £32

A chrome stag's head car mascot mounted on a radiator cap, 4in. high. £22

A skull and cross-bones mascot, 3in. x 3in., circa 1915. £160

CARVED WOOD

Ogoni mask from south-east Nigeria, 24cm. high. £350

Face mask from Baule, Ivory Coast, 32.4cm. high. £850

Guro, Ivory Coast mask, topknot bound in a hair-clip consisting of four leather pouches, 30.5cm. £400

Early 19th century Venetian carved wood jardiniere. £760

A carved walnut panel depicting 'The Adoration', 1.2m x 1.04m. £1,450

Carved walnut table ornament, 2ft. high. £25

Bassa mask from the Monrovia area, Liberia, 25.4cm. high. £250

Flemish early 17th century carved oak figure of the head and shoulders of a man, 25in. high. £475

Ibibio, from south-east Nigeria, the marks on the fore-head represent scarification. £1,000

African mask, probably Balumbo or Masango, from the southern Gabon, 28cm. high. £650

Unusual and fine mask from the Ivory Coast, 40.7cm. high. £950

A carved wood mask from the Congo, 13in. high. £20,000

A Marquesian islander's carved hardwood club, 54¼in. long. £670

Bati carved walnut head of a man with flower head-dress, 11in. high. £12

Early 19th century masonic spoonrack in fruitwood, 23in. high. £95

Gelede mask from Yoruba, Western Nigeria, 19.1cm. high. £350

One of a pair of North German oak polychrome figures of the Virgin and St. John, circa 1220.£36,000

Mbuya mask, Katunda style, Eastern Pende, Zaire. £450

CARVED WOOD

19th century elm bellows.   £16

19th century Balinese mask of wood with baked on colours.£27

Regency mahogany circular jardiniere, attributed to Gillows of Lancaster, 61cm. £750

A Singalese painted wood panel, 87cm. high.   £42

Pair of Regency period blackamoor figures, 98cm. high.   £820

16th century carved oak beam.   £330

Early wooden knitting sheath in elm.   £4.50

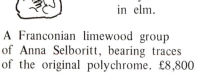

A Franconian limewood group of Anna Selboritt, bearing traces of the original polychrome. £8,800

Art Deco carved walnut standing figure of a nude girl, stamped N.J. Forrest, 1926.   £40

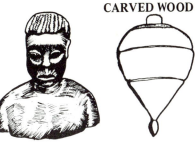

Walnut bellows, with carved landscape 'Auld Brig O'Doon'. £20

Pair of Nigerian carved teak busts of a man and a woman, 8½in. high. £12

Victorian children's wooden spinning top. £2

Old lightwood carving of an African female crouching figure, 10in. high. £27

One of a pair of oak wall bracket shelves, 21in. £18

Rare 18th century carved wood figure of a blackamoor, 30in. high. £295

Pair of oak candlesticks with barleysugar twist stems and brass drip pans. £5.50

Cameroon grasslands bushcow mask, 58.5cm. long. £280

Pair of Victorian butter pats. £2.50

CARVED WOOD

One of a pair of yew wood thumb screws. £19

16th century wood carving of a beast's head. £50

Yew wood string holder. £9

19th century wooden needle case and thread spool. £5

Late 19th century child's wooden wheelbarrow, 3ft. long x 1ft. 7ins. wide. £25

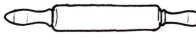

Victorian rolling pin. £3.50

One of a pair of Adam giltwood wall candle sconces. £110

Renaissance carved wood panel. £75

19th century carved wood figure of a cobbler. £44

One of a pair of
yew wood goblets.
£10

Two Continental wicker
oval military despatch
cases, different, 18th
century.   £70

Polished oak and brass
Huntsman's Whip Rack,
circa 1870.   £68

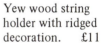

Set of William IV grain measures in wood. £75

Yew wood string
holder with ridged
decoration.   £11

An Indian carved teak
panel with a figure of
an elephant in high
relief, 69cm. x 52cm.
          £45

Pokerwork photograph frame,
8ins. high, circa 1910.   £7

Japanese lacquer panel,
29ins. x 19½ins.   £28

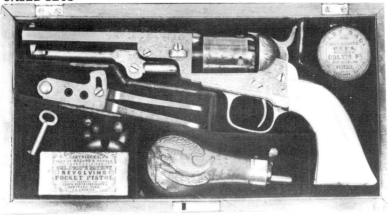

A fine 5-shot .31in. model 1849 Presentation Engraved Colt Pocket single action percussion revolver.   Overall length 9¾ in., blued octagonal barrel 5in. hand engraved 'Saml Colt' on top flat.   £1,800

A fine quality double barrelled 14-bore percussion sporting gun by T.E. Mortimer, 47in, damascus twist browned barrels 30in, engraved 'T.E. Mortimer, Edinburgh, late St. James St, London'.   £500

A good 5-shot .31 single action Colt pocket percussion revolver, 9½in, octagonal barrel 5in. stamped.   'Address Saml Colt, New York City.' £410

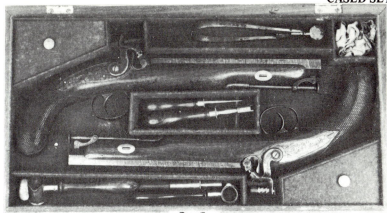

A good pair of 16-bore back action percussion holster pistols by W Richards & Co., 13½in., browned octagonal twist barrels 7½in., engraved 'W. Richards & Co. London £450

A fine and desirable 12-bore double barrelled percussion sporting gun by Charles Lancaster, 48in., browned twist barrels 31in., London proved, with 'C.L.' and '2018' £540

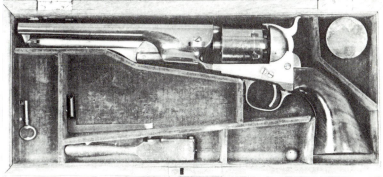

A fine 6-shot .36in. model 1861 single action, round barrel Colt Navy percussion revolver. Overall length 13in., blued round barrel 7½in., stamped 'Address Col. Saml Colt, New York, U.S. America'. £1,375

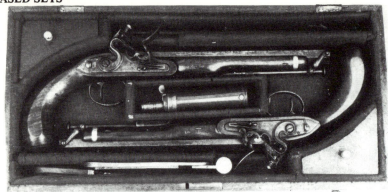

A good and desirable pair of 16-bore officers' flintlock holster pistols by Wogdon and Barton, 14½in, octagonal twist barrels 9½in. engraved 'Wogdon & Barton London' in script on top flats.   £1,050

A rare 6-shot .36 London-made Colt 1851 model navy single action percussion revolver, 12½in, barrel 7½in, single line London address, No 25906 on all parts, London proofs, steel trigger guard and backstrap. £650

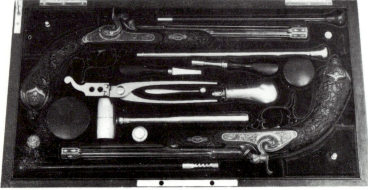

A magnificent pair of 48-bore percussion target pistols by Mathes Freres Btes a Paris, made for 'Exposition Universelle Paris 1878'.   Overall length 16in, fluted brightly blued barrels 8¾in with twelve groove rifling. £4,700

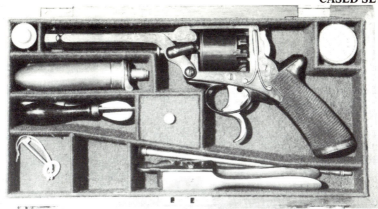

A 5-shot 54-bore double action double trigger Tranter percussion revolver, 12in, octagonal rifled barrel 6in, Birmingham proved, engraved 'Cogswell & Harrison, 223 and 224 Strand London'. £370

A good .45 Westley Richard's Patent breech loading monkey tailed percussion rifled carbine, No. 2254, 42in, blued barrel 25in, Birmingham proved, stamped 'Whitworth Patent .450, .483, 2254 etc'. £400

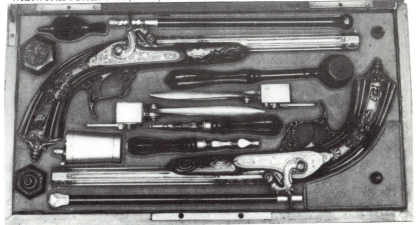

A fine quality pair of 36 bore gold inlaid French percussion target pistols. Overall length 15¾in, fluted octagonal barrels 10in, with twelve groove rifling. £2,600

BELLEEK

A small 19th century Belleek jardiniere. £40

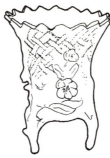

A Belleek flared cylindrical vase on three branch feet, 14cm. high. £16

Belleek porcelain jardiniere with birds and flowers in high relief 20in. high. £48

BOW

Bow dish of kidney shape painted in the style of James Giles, circa 1760, 10¾ins. wide. £200

18th century Bow teapot with damaged handle. £10

Early Bow sauceboat, the squat body with shaped rim, circa 1752, 9ins. wide. £190

Bow figure of 'The Indiscreet Harlequin', circa 1750, 7ins. high. £620

Bow sparrow beak jug painted in polychrome with flowers, 4ins. high, circa 1760. £45

Bow bocage figure group of a lady in an arbour, 9ins. high. £180

CANEWARE

Caneware Krater vase, about 1820. £450

CANEWARE

Caneware jug, about 1795.
£200

CANTON

One of a pair of Canton porcelain pilgrim bottles with double handles, painted panels of figures, flowers and birds, 12½ins. high.   £120

Canton celadon ground plate mounted in ormolu, 24cm. diam.   £15

One of a pair of Canton lidded vases, circa 1830, 15ins. high.
£145

A 19th century Canton porcelain bowl, the interior panels of figures in landscapes and flowers in red, blue and yellow, 16¼ins. diam.   £80

Canton vase decorated with figure scenes, 19.5cm. high.   £22

One of a pair of Canton famille rose elephant candlesticks.   £300

CAUGHLEY

Small fan-shaped asparagus-
server in Caughley porcelain,
circa 1780-90. £20

Caughley cream jug in
underglaze blue, circa
1780, 3¼ins. high. £26

Caughley porcelain
egg-drainer and 'waster',
circa 1780-90. £25

CHELSEA DERBY

Chelsea Derby bucket-
shaped jug with wishbone
handle, 3½ins. high. £70

A 19th century Chelsea
Derby vase, with patch
marks and incised
numerals, 11ins. high.

Chelsea Derby jug
decorated with green
and gilt floral swags,
circa 1770, 4¾ins.
high. £130

CHELSEA £75

Set of Chelsea figures of the elements with gold anchor marks,
9ins. high. £600

Chelsea triangle period acanthus leaf, moulded cream jug, circa 1746.
£850

Chelsea raised anchor 'Peach' shaped cream jug, circa 1750.
£1,500

Pair of Chelsea vases of flattened baluster shape, circa 1760, 8ins. high.
£780

Chelsea dish decorated with flowers, birds and bees in polychrome, circa 1756.   £800

Chelsea porcelain teapot and cover, 17.8cm. wide.
£6,090

Rare Chelsea blue and white bowl of octagonal form with galleried rim, circa 1750, 4¾ins. high.
£540

Chelsea triangle 'Goat and Bee' jug, circa 1745, 3¾ins. high.   £900

Rare Chelsea scent bottle moulded in the form of a cluster of strawberries, circa 1760, 2¾ins. high.
£380

Chelsea group of 'The Music Lesson', 5½ins. high.
£5,500

Ch'ien Lung famille rose charger, 15in. diam. £175

Export tureen modelled as a seated goose, Ch'ien Lung, 15¾in. high x 12¾in. wide. £22,050

Saucer dish of the early Ch'ien Lung period (1736-95) in Canton enamel. £160

A celadon ground 'famille rose' vase of the Ch'ien Lung period. £1,650

Chinese, Ch'ien Lung period porcelain figures of European man and woman, 42.5cm. and 41cm. high. £5,269

Chinese porcelain vase of the Ch'ien Lung period, decorated with coloured enamels, 16cm. high. £16,800

Ch'ien Lung period two handled censer with a frieze of the eight immortals, 11in. wide. £95

Ch'ien Lung period (1736-95) porcelain tureen and cover, 36.8cm. wide. £9,450

Blue and white porcelain potato ring, Ch'ien Lung, 8½in. diam. £24

Ch'ien Lung octagonal armorial plate, 6in. diam.   £36

Ch'ien Lung period famille rose goose tureen, 41cm. high.
£10,000

One of a pair of shallow bowls with iron-red grained wood decoration, Ch'ien Lung, 5¼in. diam.   £180

Ch'ien Lung famille rose figure of a court lady, 41cm. high   £850

Two of a set of four Ch'ien Lung plates, being two shallow plates and two deep soup bowls, 9in. diam. £195

One of a pair of cloisonne enamel beaker vases of the Ch'ien Lung period, 42cm.
£1,200

Pair of blue and white porcelain leaf-shaped dishes, Ch'ien Lung, 7½in. long.   £34

Ch'ien Lung powder blue ground porcelain vase and cover, 25in. high.   £480

Ch'ien Lung period blue and white pilgrim vase, 51cm. high.   £7,000

CHINESE

Nankin tureen and cover, circa 1900. £250

A Ch'ien Lung figure of a crouching Buddhistic lion, 11¾ins. high. £50

Chinese teapot with applied floral decoration and gargoyle spout, made about 1760 for the Dutch or French market. £180

Chia Ch'ing famille rose bowl enamelled with the 'Immortals from the Isles of the Blest', 56cm. diam. £880

Figure of a recumbent water buffalo, Chia Ch'ing/Tao Kuang, 23cm. long. £997.50

One of a pair of late 18th century Chinese vases decorated with squirrels amidst vines, bearing the character marks of Wan Li, 20ins. high. £720

Pair of 18th century Chinese covered vases in porcelain with celadon glaze mounted in gilt bronze, 41cm. high. £28,350

Chinese 18th century blue and white porcelain jug, 8½ins. high. £160

19th century Chinese interior painted snuff bottle, 6cm. high. £7

Chinese bowl decorated with figure scenes in polychrome and gilt, 28.5cm. diam., chipped. £22

One of a pair of Chinese blue and white jardinieres, 1830. £220

Pair of blue enamelled porcelain models of dogs, 4ins. high, Chinese, 19th century. £18

Chinese famille rose bowl decorated with figures, 29.5cm. diam., cracked. £16

Baluster shaped blue and white porcelain vase, Chinese 18th century, 9¼ins. high, wooden stand and cover. £50

14th century Chinese jar and cover in porcelain painted in underglaze blue, 33.6cm. high. £160,000

One of a pair of round blue and white Nankin vases, 24ins. high. £300

CHINESE

19th century Chinese circular jardiniere painted in underglaze blue, 37.5cm. diam. £42

Chinese grey and green speckled hardstone figure of a horse. £80

18th century Chinese export porcelain Masonic tankard. £325

An extremely fine Chinese underglaze blue vase. £700

Chinese 18th century snuff bottle made of bird beak, 7.5cm. high. £280

Pair of 19th century export figures of an Emperor and Empress. £390

COALBROOKDALE

Coalbrookdale vase. £75

Coalbrookdale two-handled cabinet cup, cover and stand, 5½ins. tall. £95

Coalbrookdale flower-encrusted vase. £420

A Coalport plate from an
attractive set of twenty-
four, each painted with a
different scene of game birds
by P. Simpson, signed, 9ins.
£1,450

A Coalport jug
printed in dark
blue, 21.5cm.
high.   £110

Coalport plate from
a service presented to
the Tsar of Russia in
1845 by Queen
Victoria.   £750

Henrietta, circa 1750,
china figure by Coal-
port, 7ins. high.
£98.50

Coalport teapot, circa 1840-45,
with elaborate rococo twirls at
handle base, lid and spout. £35

One of a pair of
Coalport vases
painted by John
Raudall.   £980

Coalport tureen with
acanthus decoration,
circa 1820.   £28

Coalport style pot
pourri jar with a
'Church Interior'
panel in polychrome,
11cm. high.   £22

One of a pair of 19th
century Coalport
porcelain circular two-
handled sauce tureens,
6½ins. high.   £130

COMMEMORATIVE

Commemorative mug showing Lord Roberts of the Boer War, earthenware.   £6

A rare London Delft plate commemorating John Wilkes' controversial 45th issue of 'The North Briton', in 1763.   £520

Mug to commemorate the Peace Treaty of the First World War, made by Chelson, England.   £5

Pearlware blue-printed two-handled loving cup, circa 1837-38, 6¾ in. high.   £170

A rare commemorative Bragget pot of large size, possibly by Ralph Simpson, circa 1700, 7¼ in. high.   £1,250

Mug to celebrate the opening of Miller Park, Preston.   £35

A rare commemorative puzzle jug, the sides painted in pink lustre, circa 1816, 7ins. high.   £200

Earthenware Coronation mug of Queen Victoria.   £550

Earthenware mug for the nursery, the portrait of present Queen as a child, marked Crown Ducal ware.   £20

Earthenware mug with black transfer of a cricketer, dated 1924-25. £20

China commemorative mug, 1916. £4

Cream earthenware mug to commemorate the Coronation of Edward VIII marked T. Goode & Co.Ltd. £15

First period Worcester mug of Granby the Brave, a popular hero of 1760's. £600

Two-handled Great Exhibition mug, dated 1851, showing two child workers. £9

Pottery jug with black Jackfield type glaze, 1897. £5

Victorian Diamond Jubilee mug in porcelain with green transfer. £15

Plate made to celebrate the opening of the Coal Exchange in 1849. £400

Mug to commemorate the marriage of the Duke of York and Princess Mary. £30

DELFT

London Delft mug
decorated in blue
and white, dated
1684.   £550

One of a pair of early
18th century blue
and white Dutch
Delft plaques, 16.7cm.
across.   £480

One of a pair of late
19th century blue
and white Delft style
candlesticks.   £15

Dutch Delft narrow necked
baluster bottle in blue and
white, circa 1750, 14in.£120

Late 18th century
Dutch Delft group
of double salts,
30cm. wide. £300

18th century Liverpool
Delft bottle in blue and
white, 24cm. high. £150

Delftware polychrome
plate, circa 1760. £35

One of a pair of 18th
century English Delft-
ware wet drug jars.
                £300

Delft 'Adam and Eve'
charger, damaged.
                £250

Bristol Delft polychrome
flower brick, circa 1740.
£700

Dutch Delft baluster
shaped jar decorated
in blue and white,
circa 1690.   £160

Bristol Delft tile
depicting Heaven
and Hell, 5in. sq.
£15

One of a pair of
Dutch Delft
baluster shaped
vases, 42cm.
high.   £48

Dutch Delft polychrome
plate with a shaped
edge, 19.5cm. diam. £350

19th century Dutch
Delft blue and white
clock case, 12in. high.
£65

Rare London Delft plate,
9in. diam., circa 1740.
£480

Dutch Delft ewer in
the shape of a monkey,
circa 1750.   £2,400

Delftware plate with
blue painting and red
rim, circa 1750. £25

DELFT

18th century English Delft blue and white barber's bowl. £1,200

Pair of 18th century Delft drug jars. £150

Delftware polychrome dish decorated in blue, iron-red and green, circa 1710. £295

English Delft charger with figure of William III, 13¾ in. high. £336

London Delft dry drug jar, 7½ins. high, first half 18th century. £150

17th-18th century London Delft barber's bowl, 10in. diam. £320

London Delft wet drug jar, first half of 18th century, 8in. high. £130

Bristol Delft punchbowl. £1,600

London Delft 'Sack' bottle inscribed in blue, 5in. high, 1651. £500

18th century Delft
plate painted with
flowers in under-
glaze blue, 23cm.
£6

Pair of 18th century
Delft drug jars with
handles.   £150

Rare blue, 1750,
Dutch Delft bar-
ber's shaving bowl.
£145

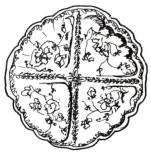

English Delft blue
dash charger depict-
ing General Monck,
circa 1665.   £825

17th-18th century London
dry drug jar, painted in
tones of blue, 7in.   £560

English Delftware, four
division sweetmeat dish
on three feet, Liverpool,
about 1750-60.   £130

Lambeth Delft
armorial jug
dated 1673,
24.5cm. high.
£3,400

Lambeth Delft cup,
dated 1715, and
initials I.H.F.
450gns.

English Delft pottery
coronation mug of
Charles II, dated
1661. 2,700gns.

DERBY

Derby teapot decorated with a traditional Imari pattern. £75

Derby figure of a seated boy holding a dog, 5½in. high. £55

Bloor Derby Group of traveller astride a goat carrying basket, 5in. £95

Set of four Derby child figures depicting Europe, Asia, Africa and America, 5½in. high. £580

Large Derby jug painted with exotic birds, 8½in. high, circa 1760. £400

Pair of Derby figures depicting Fire and Water, 6½in. high. £180

Part of an early 19th century crown Derby Imari part tea and coffee service, 53 pieces in all. £235

One of a pair of Derby candlestick figures, about 1770. £375

Derby desk set comprising pen tray, ink well, sponge pot and pounce pot, 20cm. wide. £55

Bloor Derby figure of a lady seated in a chair, 5½in. high. £110

Part of a Derby dessert service painted with fruit, nuts, flowersprays and insects. £4,200

Derby 'Admiral Rodney' jug, 9¼ in. high. £200

Pair of Derby figures depicting a 'Sailor' and his 'Lass', circa 1760, 9½in. high. £420

Derby baluster shape jug with chinoiserie decoration, 3½in. high. £95

DOULTON

Doulton tureen with floral decoration, circa 1900. £12

Pair of Royal Doulton mugs of 'Micawber' and 'Captain Cuttle', 10.5cm. high. £6

Doulton plate with amusing culinary shield. £15

Doulton stoneware tea set decorated by Hannah Barlow and dated 1875. £75

Royal Doulton art pot about 1902-22, 7½ins. high x 8½ins. deep. £12

A pair of Doulton stoneware vases, decorated by Hannah Barlow. £165

Doulton (Lambeth) art pot, about 1880-91, 8½ins. high x 10ins. deep. £35

19th century Dresden group of Harlequin and a companion, after Kandler, 8ins. high. £110

Large Dresden ewer moulded in high relief with mermaids, seahorses and Neptune. £220

19th century Dresden comport on four scrolled feet, 21ins. high. £520

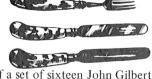

Part of a set of sixteen John Gilbert fruit knives and forks with Dresden handles in porcelain, about 1870. £160

One of a pair of Dresden lemon ground ovoid vases and covers, 24½ins. high. £1,100

19th century Dresden pen box with hinged cover, 17.5cm. long. £28

One of a pair of Dresden style vases with pierced covers, 32.5cm. high. £32

19th century Dresden group of a boy standing beside a female who is feeding birds, 6ins. high. £110

Pair of Dresden candelabra with the crossed swords mark, 9½ins. high. £260

19th century Dresden pierced and flower encrusted comport, 17½ins. high. £210

ENGLISH

Deep Royal blue box
with the message
'Esteem the Giver'
£48

Earthenware vase
painted in clear
enamels with figures
in kimonos.   £320

Liverpool earthenware
lead glaze jug, circa
1700.   £60

An alabaster sculpture
of a boy, 21ins. high.
£130

Part of the 100-piece
Leake Okeover dinner
service, 18th century.
£57,645

Rectangular shaped baluster
vase with celadon glaze, fitted
for electric light, 30cm. high.
£30

Polished hardstone
chinoiserie clock
garniture.   £150

Ormolu decorated
plaque from the
Great Exhibition,
1851.   £7.50

English Lambeth jug
with the Arms of the
Cordwainers Company
1673, 24.5cm. high.
£3,400

Small Victorian majolica jardiniere, 7ins. diameter. £3

Blue and white china cheese dish and cover, circa 1890. £5

Jug showing the famous brass quintet of the Distin father and sons, in Parian ware, about 1850, 14ins. high. £300

Unglazed stoneware figure of an old man by Joseph and Pierre Mougin. £60

English porcelain jug and two tumblers, circa 1880. £8

Art Deco figure of a boy in Turkish dress. £110

Victorian basin jug decorated with hand painted floral designs. £8.50

A porcelain Amstel part cabinet set. £300

Victorian milk jug with a pewter lid. £7

ENGLISH

Bristol jug decorated
with swags of flowers
in polychrome, 4¾ins.
high.   £105

Coadstone plaque.
£500

Rare semi-circular
bulb pot and cover,
24.8cm. wide.
£315

One of a pair of Brownfield's
Geisha flower vases, 11ins.,
printed with date code for
October 1899.   £95

White apothecary
pottery jar with
gold lettering
'Leeches', 10ins.
high.   £120

A good, late 18th century
model of a squirrel in the
style of Ralph Wood.
£300

Vase, aggrandised by
laying on lines and
slip ware to imitate
marble, about 1775.
£1,250

Late 19th century
jardiniere, 14½ins.
high x 17ins. deep.
£45

One of a pair of beaker
vases in underglaze
blue on a cracked ice
ground, 30cm. high. £15

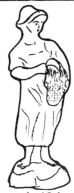

Rare early 19th century yellow ground figure of summer, probably Yorkshire, 6¾ins. high. £120

Wafer-thin Queensware dish decorated in puce, about 1725. £125

Early 17th century Westerwald puzzle jug, 18.3cm. high. £210

English porcelain figure of a seated hound, by the 'Girl-in-a-Swing' factory, circa 1750, 10.8 cm. high. £3,600

Early 19th century figures of a Turk and his companion. £40

Transfer printed Liverpool tureen and stand by Richard Chaffer, circa 1760. £250

Cassolette, aggrandised by the laying on lines and splashes of slipware to imitate marble, about 1775. £1,250

Victorian hanging art pot by the Watcombe Pottery Co., about 1867-1901, 7ins. high x 9ins. deep. £22

13th-14th century Medieval jug of baluster form in a mottled green lead glaze, 12½ins. high, probably Surrey. £340

ENGLISH

Small hand-painted box, inscribed with a motto, made in Bilston.   £77

William Moorcroft teapot 1898, painted with blue poppies.   £60

Bough pot, aggrandised by laying on lines and splashes of slipware to represent marble, about 1775. £1,250

Bird-shaped bonbonniere from Bilston, beautifully coloured.   £415

Early 19th century porcelain cup and saucer, painted with flowers.   £9

Porcelain perfume bottle with silver cap, bird and flower decoration in blue, rust and yellow.   £8

English china money box in the form of a pear.   £18

Fine set of figure groups symbolical of the seasons, 19th century.   £840

An Ault jardinière designed by Christopher Dresser.   £45

Copeland and Garrett tureen and stand, circa 1860.   £30

Art Deco teapot in shape of a car.   £24

Miniature porcelain watering can with raised and painted flowers. £6

Pottery teapot dated 31st March 1786 and marked with a 'C'. £95

Pottery duck tureen. £68

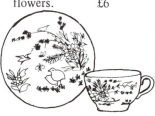

Worcester tea cup and saucer, circa 1765. £100

One of a pair of Victorian ribbon plates, 22 cm. diam. £9

Dairy shop's pottery milk bucket, named 'Pure Milk', 12ins. high, circa 1850. £68

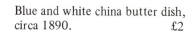

Part of a set of twelve plates and three comports, with polychrome decoration. £250

Blue and white china butter dish, circa 1890. £2

Barr, Flight and Barr feather painted part tea and coffee service, late 18th/early 19th century. £750

Tea bowl and saucer, made in England around 1780. £40

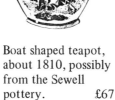

Crown Devon pottery cheese cover.   £7

Boat shaped teapot, about 1810, possibly from the Sewell pottery.   £67

Basket-shaped box with metal handles.   £80

One of a pair of creamware figures of Hamlet and Ophelia, glazed in green and brown.   £1,600

19th century De Morgan tile.   £20

Martin Brothers mask jug, 6¼ins. high.   £385

Prattware two-handled mug.   £37

An attractive 'London decorated' Nantgarw plate, 1813-20, 9½ins. diam.   £340

A rare Wrotham Tyg by George Richardson dated 1649.   £1,600

19th century gourd shaped vase in underglaze blue, 30cm. high. £10

Flamboyant green, yellow, gold and white teapot, dates to within three years of 1843, made by Samuel Alcock. £28

Victorian plate in blue rust and ochre bearing initials M.G., and dated 1527, 28.5cm. diam. £20

Illustrated cup and saucer by Adam Buck, 1830. £3.50

Morgan Smith tile. £10

A Neiderville parian figure of a shepherd boy with dog, 67 cm. high. £85

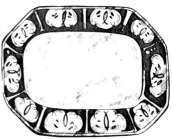

Stone china turkey dish by Knight, Elkin and Co., circa 1830. £23

One of a pair of Ringtons square-shaped tea caddies transferred in blue, 10cm. high. £9

Isnik dish by Frank Brancywn. £15

FAMILLE ROSE/VERTE

17th century Arita plate enamelled in the Kakiemon palette, 23cm. diam. £620

A Sampson 'famille rose' gravy boat decorated with flowers and a heraldic device, 21cm. wide. £24

Chinese famille rose plate, circa 1830, 15½ins. diam. £200

One of a pair of Victorian baluster vases in the famille verte palette, 37.5cm. high. £38

18th century famille rose fish tank, 23ins. diam. £2,700

One of a massive pair of famille rose vases, 36ins. high. £2,500

One of a pair of 18th century famille rose saucer dishes, 9ins. diam. £56

Famille rose coffee cup and saucer decorated with flowers. £8

Famille rose plate, 18th century, 9ins. diam. £32

Belgian faience dish consisting of four interlocking vine leaves in green with black veins, circa 1760. £870

French oval porcelain casket. £310

19th century French oval porcelain jardiniere. £360

Mid-16th century French pottery ewer, decorated with stamped and inlaid designs, 34cm. high. £44,000

A Cunerville sauceboat with two jugs. £24

French earthenware model of a young lady, signed J. Gille, Paris, 36½ins. high. £440

Hand painted faience plate, circa 1780. £165

Late 19th century Marseilles faience sauce tureen decorated with flowers. £45

French bowl decorated with diaper banding and sprigs of flowers in blue and gilt, 25cm. diam. £50

19th century German group of three dancing girls, 26cm. high.   £8

German polychrome relief carving of a Nativity scene, 2ft. 3ins. x 3 ft.   £4,900

One of a pair of Berlin vases.   £470

A pair of German porcelain figures of dogs, 12ins. long.   £95

19th century German fan-shaped trinket box, with hinged cover, 3.5cm. wide.   £18

A pair of late 19th century Lichte china cycling figures, 12¾ins. high.   £160

Pair of Ludwigs Berg figures after Kandler, 6ins. high.   £90

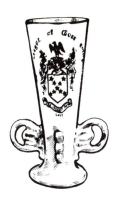

Staffordshire tyg by Goss.   £35

Rare Goss Toby jug, 6¾ins. high.   £70

Goss model of Campbelton Cross, 145mm. high.   £75

A Goss style Robert Burns cottage.   £22

Bideford mortar, by Goss.   £5

Shakespeare's house, 78mm. long.   £27.50

Goss penguin, 88mm. long.   £65

Wall pocket of a cherub impressed W.H. Goss.   £85

The Goss 'Sandbach Crosses' model.   £380

IMARI

17th century
Imari charger,
54cm. diam.
£880

Pair of Imari octagonal
baluster vases and covers,
70cm. high.   £2,000

19th century
Japanese Imari
plate, 22cm.
diam.   £6

19th century Japanese
Imari octagonal
jardiniere and cover,
32cm. wide.   £95

One of a pair of large
Imari chargers.

£370

Late 17th century
Arita dog decorated
in black, iron red
and turquoise green,
23cm. long.   £920

An Imari fluted
baluster vase
decorated with
flowers, 30.5cm.
high.   £38

Pair of Japanese Arita vases,
late 17th century, porcelain
decorated in underglaze blue,
46cm. high.   £1,470

17th century
Japanese Arita
vase.   £360

A large Deruta jug jar, early 16th century, 34cm. high.
£1,000

Deruta lustre dish about 1510.
£2,900

16th century Urbino alberello of waisted form, 17.5cm. high.
£600

Italian Nive pottery tureen and stand, circa 1880.
£80

Italian marble figure of La Compaicenza by Alphonse Carabi, dated 1883.
£740

15th/16th century Faenza drug jar of inverted baluster shape, 37cm. high.
£520

Castel Durante dish painted in blue, green, ochre and yellow, circa 1540, 23cm. diam.
£460

Capo di Monte figure of a sempstress by G. Gricci.
£20,000

Rare Urbino Istoriato dish of Cardinal's hat form, 26cm. diam.
£2,940

JAPANESE

19th century Japanese china vase, 12¼ ins. high. £20

Pair of Japanese vases decorated with domestic scenes. £400

One of a pair of 19th century vases of fluted Ku shape, 24cm. high. £58

Japanese lacquer tray with raised border decorated to simulate a tree stump. £440

Late 17th century Japanese porcelain bottle, painted in Ko-Kutani style, 42cm. high. £9,000

Pair of Japanese vases, decorated with red and black ground lacquer panels, 35¼ ins. high. £1,350

One of a pair of Victorian Ku shaped vases, 22.5cm. high. £52

Blue and white porcelain vase of the K'ang Hsi period.   £48

Chinese teapot of the K'ang Hsi dynasty about 1680, decorated in famille verte.
£160

Blue and white porcelain ginger jar, K'ang Hsi period, 8½ins. high, wooden cover.   £60

Famille Verte seated figure of Kran Ti , K'ang Hsi period , 13 ins high .   £1200

K'ang Hsi blue and white porcelain dish depicting the Chinese Taoist Pu-Tai.
£1,200

Blue and white porcelain vase of the K'ang Hsi period.   £48

Blue and white porcelain vase of the K'ang Hsi period.   £34

K'ang Hsi blue and white bulbous vase.
£400

K'ang Hsi shallow bowl, circa 1700.
£15

Liverpool helmet-shaped jug painted with polychrome flowers, 2¾ins. high. £60

Liverpool teapot enamelled in black and gilding, Herculaneum factory, circa 1805. £20

Small Liverpool sparrow beak jug, 3½ins. high. £35

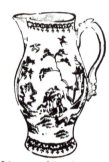

Liverpool creamware jug, transfer printed in black, circa 1785. £85

Liverpool jug in underglaze blue by Seth Pennington, circa 1785. £85

Blue and white Liverpool coffee pot, circa 1785. £58

Liverpool jug in under-glaze blue by Richard Chaffer, circa 1760. £125

Liverpool teapot and cover with artichoke finial, 5¾ins. high, circa 1770. £180

Liverpool mug printed in sepia, Herculaneum factory, circa 1833. £50

18th century Leeds pottery teapot and teaware. £150

One of a pair of early 19th century vases of compana shape, probably Leeds, decorated on a pink lustre ground, 6¼ins. high.   £360

LONGTON HALL

Longton Hall sauceboat moulded with overlapping cos lettuce leaves, circa 1758, 5½ins. wide.
£260

Longton Hall tea bowl and saucer, circa 1750.   £170

Longton Hall coffee cup, circa 1758-60.
£45

Longton Hall leaf-shaped jug crisply moulded with green and yellow vine leaves, 3½ins. high, circa 1754. £400

Longton Hall jug decorated with bouquets of flowers, 8ins. high.   £600

Miniature toy pot, about 1775-80, made by Lowestoft factory, 6.4cm. high. £150

Commemorative Lowestoft mug of cylindrical form, circa 1775, 4½ins. high, restored. £620

Charming Oriental teapot from the Lowestoft factory, about 1775. £185

Lowestoft pear shaped jug and cover, circa 1780. £110

Rare pair of Lowestoft pugs on flat bases, circa 1780, 2¼ins. high. £1,000

Lowestoft jug with kick-back handle, and pink border, 3¼ins. high, circa 1785. £50

Lowestoft tea bowl and saucer decorated in the Chinese style £32

Lowestoft milk jug with blue and white 'Fence pattern' decoration, 4¼ins. high, circa 1775. £40

Jumbo punch pot made by the Lowestoft factory, about 1770-75, 21cm. high. £265

Edwardian silver lustre teapot and stand. £4.50

A rare silver resist pot pourri, circa 1810, 4¾in. high. £320

Silver resist jug of large size, 6½in. high, circa 1810. £95

One of a pair of silver resist vases, probably Leeds, circa 1810, 6½in. £130

Early 19th century silver lustre pottery figures of Apollo and Diana, 10½in. high. £140

Early 19th century figure of a lion passant, covered in mottled pink lustre, 12 in. long. £700

Small yellow ground jug of ovoid form decorated in silver resist lustre, 3½in. high, circa 1810. £170

Sunderland lustre plate, 'Thou God See'st Me'. £24

Rare late 18th century figure of a cat, the press moulded body splashed overall in bright pink lustre, 6½in. high. £800

LUSTRE

Silver resist jug printed in underglaze blue with scenes, 3½in. high, circa 1810. £220

Copper lustre kettle of compressed globular form, 9in. high, circa 1825. £100

A Maling lustre jardiniere decorated with fruits and foliage, 22.5cm. diam. £24

Rare lustre lamp and cover, probably Coalport, circa 1800, 9½in. high. £680

A rare pair of Leeds pink lustre figures of a 'Shepherd' and 'Shepherdess', circa 1810, 7¾in. high. £300

Victorian copper lustre jug painted with a band of flowers in polychrome, 10.5cm. high. £10

Silver resist jug with sepia print decoration, 4¼in. high, circa 1810. £440

One of a pair of Leeds silver lustre candlesticks, 9in. high, circa 1810. £260

Wedgwood copper lustre incense burner and cover, early 19th century, 6in. tall. £820

Pink lustre cream jug and sugar bowl, marked 'Maling'. £10

A Sunderland ware bowl, with transfer printed panels of the Cast-Iron Bridge over the River Wear, 12½ins. diam. £40

A rare Sunderland pink lustre set of the seasons, impressed Dixon, Austin and Co., circa 1820, 9ins. high. £1,100

MASONS

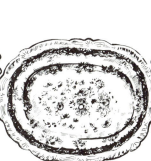

Large Masons ironstone tureen of Chinese shape, 32cm. wide, circa 1815. £120

Masons ironstone serving dish, circa 1813. £20

Masons ironstone tureen, circa 1830. £65

MEISSEN

German, Meissen, porcelain thimble decorated in schwarzlot and gold, by I. Preissler, early 18th century, 2.4cm. high. £3,818

Meissen cup and saucer. £45

Meissen thimble, decorated in schwarzlot and gold by I. Preissler, 2.4cm. high. £4,123

Pair of Meissen figures of green parrots modelled by J. Joachim Kaendler, 17½in. high. £4,500

Two Meissen figures of street sellers by J.J. Kaendler, 1745. £620

One of a pair of Meissen peony flower dishes, 1746 pattern. £420

Early 19th century Meissen tureen, 43cm. wide. £85

Meissen figure of a Narzison by P. Reinicke, circa 1744. £520

Part of a Meissen dinner service with crossed
swords and dot mark. £1,110

Pair of 19th century Meissen
groups. £430

Pair of Meissen figures each
supported by a conch shell
posy vase. £150

Mid 18th century
Meissen figure of
a dancer, 18.5cm.
high. £300

One of a pair of mid
18th century Meissen
wine coolers, 23.7cm.
high. £550

Meissen coffee pot
painted in Kakiemon
palette, 23cm. high,
circa 1735. £800

Meissen figure of
a swan, 2¾in high.
£180

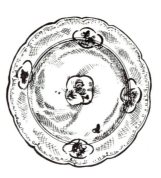

Meissen plate with crossed
swords mark, circa 1750.
£225

Meissen vase and
cover, 61cm. high.
£260

Meissen thimble deco-
rated with fruit and
inscription 'J' y pense',
2cm high.   £600

19th century Meissen reclining male and
female figures, 11½ in. wide (repaired).
£75

German, Meissen, porcelain
figures of Beltrame and
Columbine 'The Spanish
Lovers' by J.J. Kaendler,
1741, 17.8cm.   £2,308

An early Meissen
Hausmaler milk
jug and cover by
B. Seuter.£1,550

Late Meissen group of Count
Bruhl's tailor after the
smaller model of 1737.
Mid 19th century.   £400

Tureen from late Meissen, onion pattern service. £1,200

Marcolini Meissen mirror frame. £620

One of a pair of Meissen cock and hen teapots and covers, modelled by J.J. Kaendler, 21.5cm. £2,730

Pair of Meissen figures of Chinese man and woman. £400

One of a pair of Meissen flower-encrusted vases, circa 1850. £1,000

Meissen group of figures in 18th century costume with three putti, 36cm. £410

19th century Meissen winged figure on a pedestal base, 9in. £75

19th century Meissen figure group, 15in. high. £320

MING

19th century Ming style squat baluster vase, 39cm. high. £95

Chinese Ming 'Dog of Fo', 6¼ins. high. £450

A rare Ming polychrome wine ewer and cover, 9¾ins. high. £48,000

MINTON

Minton tureen with domed cover, circa 1868. £30

Minton biscuit porcelain figure of a seated girl, called 'Sense of Smelling', about 1840, 5½ins. high. £75

Minton sardine dish and cover decorated in polychrome, 23.5cm. wide. £24

Pair of 19th century vases and covers in the Sevres manner, probably Minton, 11½ins. high. £640

Minton porcelain plaque by M.L. Solon in pate sur pate, 7¼ins. x 6¼ins. £650

Pair of Minton vases painted by W. Mussill, 1876, 15ins. high. £260

Minton bust of William IV, 4in. high. £25

Minton bone china figure of Don Quixote, 4¾in. high. £175

Minton bone china figure of a girl leaning against a candlestick, 9in. high, about 1840, design number 192. £200

Minton Parian figure of Colin Minton Campbell, about 1875, 19in. £80

Minton earthenware figure of a monkey holding fruit, about 1860. £150

Minton figure of 'Dorothea' design number 189, about 1855, 14in. £40

Minton figure of a naked girl seated on a leopard, circa 1855, 8in. high. £75

Pair of Minton figure candlesticks. £175

Minton earthenware figure of a sea horse with shell, about 1855, 14in. £80

A Minton pate-sur-pate
moon flask.   £147

Minton earthenware figure
of a man with a wheelbarrow
draped with hop branches,
about 1870, design number
413, 13½ins. high.   £100

Minton art pot, dating
between 1895-1900 in
a single shade of mint
green, 8½ins. high   £23

Attractive Art Nouveau
Minton jardiniere, about
1900-08, 12½ins. high
x 14½ins. deep.   £75

Minton figure of a 'Guitar
Player and Harper', circa
1835.   £225

Parian bust of the Duke
of Wellington by Minton,
11ins. high, 1853.   £50

One Minton pate-sur-pate
vase with cover, 15½ins.
tall.   £775

Pair of Minton figures
depicting 'Science' and
'Fine Art', 14½ins. high,
circa 1870.   £200

Minton figure of a child
taking off shoes, 3½ins.
high, circa 1840.   £35

Newhall teapot, pattern 436, circa 1795. £55

Newhall jug decorated with sprigs of flowers, 4½ins. high. £30

Silver- shaped teapot of the Newhall factory, marked with the number 195, dating it to 1787-90. £62

Newhall part tea and coffee set of 38-pieces decorated in red rust and blue. £260

Rare Newhall water jug with hand painted Coat of Arms and landscape, circa 1810. £80

Newhall cream jug with deep blue ground, circa 1800. £25

Newhall shaped helmet jug with pink border on the inner rim, circa 1790. £35

Chinese bowl of the Yung Lo period (1403-24), porcelain decorated in underglaze blue, 37.8cm. wide. £100,000

One of a pair of bottle-shaped Oriental vases in polychrome and gilt, 28.5cm. high.   £22

One of a pair of late 19th century Oriental baluster vases painted with terrace scenes, 31cm. high.   £28

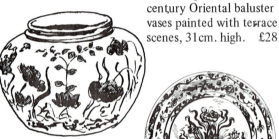

Chinese porcelain jar of the Ch'eng Hua period, decorated in underglaze blue, 10.3cm. high. £75,600

Famille rose saucer dish decorated with equestrian warriors from the Yung Ch'eng period.   £460

16th century Annamese saucer dish painted with underglaze blue. £1,000

19th century Oriental teapot decorated with landscapes in rust, blue and gilt, 15.5cm. wide.   £40

One of a pair of Oriental baluster vases painted in underglaze blue, 35cm. high.   £35

A Tao Kuang hexagonal tureen and cover painted in underglaze blue, 21cm. wide.   £72

Early 19th century Pinxton bowl on
a waisted foot, 6½ins. diam.   £75

Early 19th century Pinxton cup and
saucer painted with a landscape
medallion.   £95

Pair of Pinxton crocus pots and covers decorated in green,
brown and gilt, 19.5cm. wide.   £900

PLYMOUTH

Plymouth porcelain
figure of a toper,
15cm. high, circa
1770.   £450

Pair of Plymouth figures of boy
military bandsmen, 11ins. and
10½ins. high.   £300

Rare Plymouth vase
with polychrome
decoration, circa 1770.
                      £215

POT LIDS

An 1851 Exhibition pot lid 'Peasant Boys'. £660

Rare pot lid with a narrow foliate border, maker Robert Feast. £180

Pot lid 'Pet Rabbits'. £600

Landing the Fare, Pegwell Bay. £35

An original drawing by Jesse Austin for a pot lid prototype, 4ins. diam., inscribed 'H.R.H. The Prince of Wales visiting the Tomb of Washington'. £145

Rare pot lid with a scene in Trinidad. £380

RIDGEWAY

Ironstone hexagonal tureen by William Ridgeway, circa 1820. £65

A Ridgeway tobacco jar, cover and stand decorated with panels of landscapes, 38cm. high. £38

RUSKIN

RUSKIN

Ruskin eggshell
pottery bowl,
circa 1910.
£50

Ruskin flared cylindrical
vase with yellow lustre
glaze, 30.5cm. high. £20

A Ruskin cylindrical-
shaped vase with
orange lustre glaze,
25cm. high. £28

SALTGLAZE

Saltglaze, scale ground, teapot and
cover painted in famille rose palette,
circa 1755, 4½ins. high. £320

Saltglaze teapot and cover with
coloured sprays on a mottled
pink ground, circa 1760,
5ins. high. £190

18th century saltglaze
teapot with painted
and relief decoration,
3½ins. high. £155

18th century spherical
saltglaze teapot and
cover decorated with
a female figure,
4½ins. high. £200

18th century saltglaze
teapot decorated in
the Chinese style,
3¼ins. high. £130

SALTGLAZE

Important saltglaze group of lovers.   £4,600

Rare saltglaze, blue ground, teapot and cover of globular form, circa 1760, 3¾in. high.   £820

Coloured saltglaze pear shaped jug, circa 1760, 7in. high.   £300

Saltglaze stoneware spirit flask of Queen Victoria, 12¼in.£160

Saltglaze teapot and cover of diamond section with crabstock handle, circa 1760, 5½in. high.   £600

Saltglaze stoneware flask of the Duke of York.   £80

Saltglaze cream jug enamelled in brilliant palette, circa 1760, 3¾in. high.   £480

Coloured saltglaze teapot and cover, circa 1760, 4¾in. high.   £220

London saltglaze stoneware commemorative tankard of cylindrical shape, dated 1741, probably Fulham.   £150

Saltglaze mug of bell shape, the jewelled coloured enamels depicting a continuous scene, circa 1760, 2½in high.　£360

Saltglaze ermine spot teapot.　£600

One of a pair of saltglaze cups, the lower half moulded with gadroons, circa 1760, 3in. high.　£460

English saltglaze figure of a piper, about 1740-45, 19cm high.　£2,000

Saltglaze miniature 'King of Prussia' teapot on an ermine spot ground.£480

Saltglaze stoneware spirit flask of Old Tom by Oldfield & Company.　£75

Rare saltglaze porringer of small size in the white, circa 1745, 4in. wide.　£300

Saltglaze punch pot and cover painted with Bacchus.　£700

Saltglaze coffee pot and cover of slender pear shape, circa 1760, 8¼in high.　£320

SALTGLAZE

18th century saltglaze teapot painted with a male figure playing the flute to a lady, 3¾ins. high. £240

Turquoise ground saltglaze cream jug. £720

Saltglaze purple ground teapot and cover of globular shape, circa 1760, 3½ins. high. £300

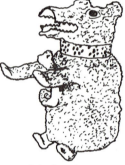

A coloured saltglaze mug decorated in famille rose style. £480

Mid-18th century English Staffordshire 'Pew Group' in white and brown, 18.4cm. high. £13,650

Saltglaze bear jug and cover, with outstretched paws, being attacked by a dog, circa 1740, 9¾ins. high. £260

Coloured saltglaze teapot and cover, enamelled in famille rose palette, circa 1760, 5ins. high. £340

Amusing saltglaze camel teapot, about 1750. £400

Saltglaze sauceboat, the oval body moulded in relief, circa 1755, 7ins. wide. £420

19th century Satsuma
figure of a school girl,
72.5cm. high. £1,000

Pair of Satsuma vases mounted
on elephants, 15cm. high. £12

Satsuma moon flask
decorated with figure
scenes, 45.5cm. high.
£16

19th century Satsuma
jardiniere decorated
with figure scenes,
27.5cm. high.   £34

One of a pair of Satsuma
baluster vases decorated
with heads, 24cm. high.
£50

19th century Satsuma
jardiniere decorated
with figure scenes,
26cm. diam.   £32

One of a pair of Satsuma
hexagonal baluster-shaped
vases decorated with a
peacock amidst shrubs,
24.5cm. high.   £45

Satsuma baluster vase
and cover decorated
with figured landscape
panels, 58cm. high. £62

19th century Satsuma
flared cylindrical vase
on three feet.   £12

SATSUMA

Satsuma saki cup,
19th century. £3

SEVRES

Satsuma baluster
vase decorated
with a figure panel,
30.5cm. high. £10

Satsuma saki cup,
19th century, with
detailed flowers on
a cream background.
£3

Sevres parian bust
of Marie Antoinette,
on a blue and gilt
glazed plinth, 31cm.
high. £75

A Sevres casket modelled
as an open fan, 33cm. wide.
£480

Sevres-pattern yellow-ground
ormolu-mounted bowl with
red printed mark, circa 1850,
20ins. wide. 500gns.

Top of 19th century French
gilt salon table in the Louis
Quinze manner, set with
Sevres porcelain plaques.
£3,800

Sevres vase and cover
with matching bleu-de-roi
pedestal. £2,100

Circular two-handled
tureen, cover and
stand from the Sevres
ornithological service.
£33,600

An important Sevres porcelain vase in the Louis XVI manner, signed C. Labarre, 3ft. 4ins. high. £2,250

Sevres bleu lapis divided jardiniere, 1758, 10¾ins. wide. £2,730

Sevres vase, porcelain. £1,300

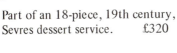

Part of an 18-piece, 19th century, Sevres dessert service. £320

Pair of Sevres vases. £660

One of a pair of Sevres-pattern vases decorated with Napoleonic scenes by Despres, 55½ins. high. £7,000

A pair of 19th century French china and ormolu mounted vases in the Sevres style, 33½ins. high. £1,950

Sevres-pattern blue ground ormolu mounted vase. £1,500

SLIPWARE

Slipware dish probably by William Taylor. £3,600

Rare slipware teapot decorated in 'Sgraffiato' technique. £900

Moulded slipware dish by John Simpson. £1,050

A rare slipware dish by Ralph Toft, decorated with a girl. £7,500

Late 18th century slipware baking dish with a trellis design, 14½ins. wide. £200

SPODE

Blue printed Spode tureen, circa 1830. £45

Spode, blue and white egg stand. £8.50

19th century Spode milk jug. £9.50

One of a pair of Spode Felspar decorated dishes, circa 1820. £120

Spode ware octagonal ashet. £15

Staffordshire jug inscribed 'Victoria Regina proclaimed 20th June 1837', puce printed, 5½ins. high. £220

Unrecorded Staffordshire pottery country house. £55

Staffordshire teapot and cover modelled in the form of a truncated tree stump, probably by Enoch Wood, 5¼ins. high. £300

Antique Staffordshire figure of a horse with a lion. £95

Rockingham figure of John Listar as Billy Luckaday, circa 1826, 15.2 cm. high. £2,000

One of a pair of Staffordshire dog ornaments, 32cm. high. £17

Green and white Staffordshire pottery spirit barrel, named in gilt 'Unsd Gin', 13ins. high. £48

Scent bottle made in South Staffordshire around 1780. £89.25

Staffordshire porcelain pastille burner cottage, circa 1840. £52

Staffordshire white pottery spirit barrel titled 'Brandy', circa 1850, 12½ins. high. £58

Staffordshire pottery figure of a zebra. £38

Small 19th century Staffordshire mug with pink lustre decoration. £4

STAFFORDSHIRE

Staffordshire portrait figure of Marshall Arnaud. £90

Staffordshire dairy shop window display sign of a cow, named 'Milk Sold Here'. £75

Staffordshire portrait figure of Queen Victoria and Princess Royal. £66

Staffordshire figure of Boy on a Goat. £30

Pair of Staffordshire doves perched on bushes, 25.5cm. high. £14

Staffordshire pottery figure of Queen Victoria. £60

Staffordshire group of fortune tellers. £28

Figure, possibly representing Mlle Alboni as Cinderella, sitting in a pumpkin coach drawn by a prancing horse. £350

Staffordshire figure of 'Tom King', 23cm high. £22

Unrecorded Staffordshire figure of Wm. Shakespeare. £48

Staffordshire theatrical group, circa 1850. £32

Unrecorded Staffordshire figure of Milton. £58

Staffordshire group of a boy and girl under a tree, 29cm. high. £20

Pair of early 19th century Staffordshire figures of Tom Cribb and Molineaux, 21.5cm. high. £720

Staffordshire portrait figure of a transpontine actress, 9½ in. £28

Staffordshire figure of a lion tamer with three lions and a leopard, 15cm. high. £120

Staffordshire figure 'The Lion Slayer', 43cm. £10

Staffordshire sheep, circa 1840. £10

STAFFORDSHIRE

Staffordshire soup bowl, circa 1825.
£3

Staffordshire Gothic Castle. £19

Early Staffordshire dish dated 1773.
£525

Early Staffordshire baluster cream jug with scroll handle, 2½in. high.£577

Staffordshire teapot with William IV silver design. £7.50

Early 18th century Staffordshire stag's head cup. £28

One of a pair of tea caddies, similar to enamel work carried out in Staffordshire. £2,475

A tobacco jar, with a tavern scene, in 19th century Staffordshire. £100

Staffordshire unpainted vase about 1780.
£85

154

Rectangular table snuff box, South Staffordshire about 1770.   £450

Staffordshire jug with portraits of William IV and Queen Adelaide, 6in. high, puce printed.   £90

Staffordshire willow pattern cup and saucer, circa 1860.
£3

Vase decorated with Chinese figures, probably made in Staffordshire.£1,250

King William III,English Staffordshire pottery, circa 1770-75, 39.3cm. high.   £5,800

One of a pair of Staffordshire pink lustre goblets, circa 1820, 4½in. high.
£85

Staffordshire hen dish, 18cm. wide.
£12

Art Deco pot by Thomas Forester & Sons Ltd., Staffs, about 1930, 7½in high x 8½in deep.
£36

Staffordshire figure of a lion on canary yellow ground, early 19th century, 3in. wide.£140

STONEWARE

An early pewter banded stoneware inkwell.   £94

A handsome Victorian vinegar barrel, in sand-coloured ironstone with a raised Coat of Arms.   £68

Stoneware spirit barrel, with a brass tap, circa 1840.   £24

A Bernard Leach stoneware vase.   £340

19th century stoneware quart jug.   £18

Han dynasty stoneware vase, shaped after a bronze model.   £3,000

Stoneware spirit flask moulded on each side to show Rice, an American entertainer, 8ins. high.   £50

A Doulton stoneware vase by Arthur Barlow, dated 1875.   £340

Stoneware spirit flask, depicting Daniel O'Connell.   £85

A large model of
a Tang horse,
20½ins. high.
£3,000

Glazed buff pottery figure
of a mounted lady attendant,
Tang dynasty, 36cm high.
£4,410

Tang dynasty three
colour glazed pottery
figure of a harnessed
horse, 50.8cm. high.
£6,250

VIENNA

Vienna rectangular dish
with fish-shaped handles,
decorated in monochrome
enriched with gold, circa
1730.   £2,500

Vienna porcelain plaque depicting
Columbus' return from his voyage
to the New World, 16ins. diam.
£450

One of a pair of
'tobacco leaf' plates
with red anchor marks
of the Cozzi factory,
23cm. diam.   £800

Vienna garniture with blue ground
and coloured figures on gilding,
late 19th century.   1,000 gns.

Vienna urn-shaped tureen
decorated with blue and
red roses, tulips and
forget-me-nots.   £89

Wedgwood stepped conical vase with grey glaze, signed Keith Murray, 18cm. high. £5

Black Egyptian ware inkstand by Wedgwood and Bentley, about 1768-80. £1,150

Unusual bamboo teapot made by Wedgwood in 1871. £90

Wedgwood flower holder of bucket shape covered in a mottled pink lustre, flecked with orange, 4.1/3 in. high, circa 1810. £360

A pair of Wedgwood and Bentley basalt pottery wine ewers, 41.3cm. high. £5,460

Late 19th century Wedgwood black jasper Portland vase. £65

Black Egyptian ware vase by Wedgwood and Bentley, about 1768-80. £900

19th century Wedgwood majolica fish dish. £3.50

A Wedgwood three-colour urn and cover. £400

Wedgwood creamware tea-pot and cover, decorated probably by D. Rhodes, 8½in., impressed mark. £150

Wedgwood and Bentley blue jasper plaque with half-length figures of Pan and the Faun, about 1775. £520

Wedgwood Queensware tureen decorated with overglaze decoration, circa 1790. £350

Jasper dip Wedgwood vase, about 1860, 25.5cm. high. £210

A Wedgwood copy of the Portland vase. £18,000

A Wedgwood Whieldon coffee pot, with fine green, grey-blue, man-ganese and yellow glazes. £520

Wedgwood fairyland lustre baluster vase decorated with elves, pixies and bats, 26.5cm. high. £190

One of a pair of Wedgwood earthen-ware plaques by S. Bateman, 1886. £280

Black basalt 'Etruscan' vase, probably Wedgwood and Bentley, circa 1770, 10¼in. high. £150

Small early sparrow beak Worcester jug with scroll handle, circa 1753.   £400

Worcester teapot, marked Barr, Flight and Barr, 1807-1813.   £110

Early Worcester fluted jug with rococo handle, circa 1752.   £720

Royal Worcester sweetmeat dish moulded in the form of shells, 11cm. high.   £10

'The Tea Party', a Royal Worcester limited edition model by Ruth van Ruyckevelt.   £1,700

A Worcester ovoid pot pourri vase with lid, painted with fruit.   £155

lst period Worcester 'Root pattern' jug, 3½in. high, circa 1756.   £1,500

Piece from the Royal Worcester service painted by Frank Roberts.   £5,090

lst period Worcester finely ribbed jug, circa 1758, 3¼in. high.   £120

1st period Worcester cabbage leaf jug, 7in. high, circa 1770. £100

Worcester teapot, about 1751-83, in printed porcelain. £88

Cream jug with similar decoration to Worcester porcelain. £577

Worcester porcelain vase with bird decoration. £63

Pair of late 19th century Royal Worcester male and female Japanese figures, 16in. high, dated 1871 and 1875. £330

Nightingale and Honeysuckle by Dorothy Doughty, No. 291. £825

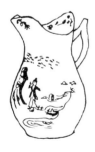

1st period Worcester jug with a wishbone handle, 3.2/3in.high. £420

18th century strapwork basket the centre depicting exotic birds and sprays, 6½in. diam. £110

1st period Worcester feather moulded jug with an elaborately jointed handle, 3in. high, circa 1760. £120

lst period Worcester sucrier and cover, 5in. diam. £46

Grainger & Co., Worcester oval tureen and cover decorated with birds and butterflies, 36cm. wide. £35

lst period Worcester teapot and cover in underglaze blue, 6½in. tall. £300

1st period Worcester coffee cup and saucer painted in a Kakiemon palette. £90

An attractive garniture of three Grainger Worcester pot pourri vases with pierced covers, circa 1815, 13½in. and 10¾in. high. £580

One of a pair of Royal Worcester diabolo shaped vases, marked 1900, 9½in. high. £85

One of a set of four Worcester shallow dishes, 10in. wide, two damaged. £380

Worcester bottle decorated in underglaze blue, circa 1770. £210

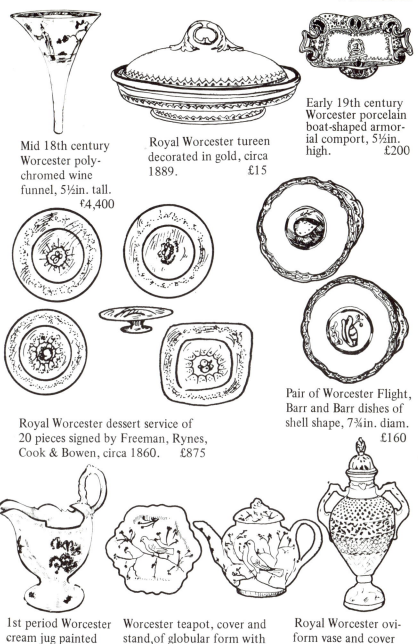

Mid 18th century Worcester poly-chromed wine funnel, 5½in. tall. £4,400

Royal Worcester tureen decorated in gold, circa 1889. £15

Early 19th century Worcester porcelain boat-shaped armor-ial comport, 5½in. high. £200

Royal Worcester dessert service of 20 pieces signed by Freeman, Rynes, Cook & Bowen, circa 1860. £875

Pair of Worcester Flight, Barr and Barr dishes of shell shape, 7¾in. diam. £160

1st period Worcester cream jug painted with a spray of flowers. £140

Worcester teapot, cover and stand, of globular form with flower knop, 5¼in. high, circa 1770. £850

Royal Worcester ovi-form vase and cover with pierced decor-ation, 17cm. high. £100

WORCESTER

Worcester sucrier and cover with flower knop, circa 1770, 14½in. high.
£440

Vase, Worcester porcelain.
£31.50

Rare Worcester 'Wigornia type' cream boat of hexagonal flared form, circa 1753, 2½in. high.   £260

Royal Worcester plaque by C. Baldwin, 38in. diam.   £650

Pair of Royal Worcester figures of draped classical ladies, 10¼in.
£170

1st period Worcester saucer dish in underglaze blue, 7½in. diam.   £28

Worcester moulded barrel shaped jug, circa 1765
£115

lst period Worcester moulded sparrow beak milk jug and cover, 4¾in. high.   £120

Barrel shaped Worcester jug, circa 1770, 3in. high.   £85

1st period Worcester jug, 3¾in. high. £250

Early Worcester hexagonal creamboat, enamelled in colours, circa 1752, 4¼in. long. £620

1st period Worcester 'Chelsea ewer' shaped jug with rococo handle, 3½in. high, circa 1762. £240

One of a pair of Worcester blue seal stands, circa 1770, 7¾in. wide. £300

Royal Worcester limited edition of Cock Robin in Autumn woods. £1,400

1st period Worcester, interlaced strapwork basket, 6½in. diam. £150

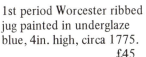

1st period Worcester ribbed jug painted in underglaze blue, 4in. high, circa 1775. £45

Worcester teapot and cover depicting 'The Beckoning Chinaman', circa 1755, 6¼in. high. £220

1st period Worcester blue and white cabbage leaf jug, 11½in. high, circa 1770.£140

19th century French ebonised bracket clock by A Furet, Paris, 51cm high. £150

18th century bracket clock by P. Rimbault of London. £3,600

Late 17th century kingwood quarter repeating bracket timepiece by J. Windmills, London, 1ft. 1½ins. high. £2,800

Table clock by T. Tompion, circa 1700, with ebonized wood case, 30.5cm high. £12,000

Late 17th century bracket clock by J Knibb, London, case of ebonised wood, 33.5cm. high. £12,500

Late 18th century mahogany cased bracket clock by E. Edlyne of London. £620

3-train bracket clock on 8 bells. £420

Mahogany mantel clock with domed cover and brass handle, 14in. £65

Early 18th century gilt-metal clock with musical/repeat movement by W. Webster, Lon., 47cm. £19,000

Verge bracket clock with passing strike, by J Wilson. £475

Two-train hour repeating bracket clock by Haddack of Bath in a mahogany case. £355

George II ebony bracket clock with two train movement by C. Halsted, London. £420

An ebonised bracket clock by C. Du Chesne, London, 42cm.£2,250

18th century mahogany bracket clock by Bryant & Son, London, 19½in. £500

Small mahogany verge timepiece alarm, signed Grant, Fleet St., London. £950

Verge bracket timepiece by J. Hewlett of Bristol. £675

18th century bracket clock. £650

Mahogany cased eight-day bracket clock, 18in. high. £1,250

BRACKET CLOCKS

Regency bracket clock by Elliot, on scroll feet. £350

Early 19th century bracket clock by J. Harper, London, 18½in. high. £320

Regency bracket clock by Grant, with brass inlaid mahogany case. £350

George III mahogany bracket clock by J. Prichard, with calendar aperture, 1ft.10½in. £900

Mid Victorian bracket clock in ebonised case with ormolu mounts. £520

19th century bracket clock by J. McCabe. £300

George III ebony bracket clock with two train movement and calendar aperture by Morgan Harbert, London. £640

Rare yew wood bracket clock by John Halifax, London, 11¾in. high. £3,400

Mahogany and brass inlaid mantel clock by Hampton & Sons, London, 34cm. high. £40

A late 18th century brass travelling clock by M. Karls-baad, 18cm. high.
£500

Victorian carriage clock with enamel and brass dial and fluted pillars, 13cm. high.
£115

Small French brass repeating carriage clock by Drocourt.
£360

Engraved gorged case carriage clock with strike, repeat alarm, and original lever escapement. £1,175

Japanese brass clock contained in a hardwood cabinet with glazed panels, 12.5cm. high. £640

French cylinder movement carriage clock circa 1910, 14cm. high.
£90

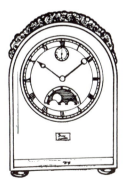

19th century French repeating carriage clock.
£400

English carriage clock by Jump, London, dated 1885, with striking movement and hour repeat. £6,000

A calendar carriage timepiece with an enamel dial, 6in. high. £420

CARRIAGE CLOCKS

French strike repeat carriage clock with alarm, circa 1890, in a cloisonne enamel case, 24cm.   £1,100

French strike repeat carriage clock with alarm, circa 1880, 16.5cm.   £335

French carriage clock with alarm, circa 1920, 10cm. high.   £110

Brass carriage clock with repeat by Archard of London, 16.5cm.   £2,000

An unusual twin carriage clock incorporating a barometer, by Spaulding & Co., Paris.   £150

French grande sonnerie with alarm by Drocourt, circa 1880, 17.1cm. high.£2,500

French timepiece with fusee movement, circa 1880, 14cm. high.   £675

Repeating alarm French carriage clock, 8in. £780

English striking carriage clock sgnd. Barwise, London, circa 1845.£4,500

Brass carriage clock, French, eight day repeating movement with alarm, No.2034. £390

English strike repeat carriage clock by Dent, London, in a Gothic case, 21cm. high. £6,000

19th century minute repeating French carriage clock by Hunt & Roskell.£2,500

French carriage clock by Leroy et Fils, circa 1870, 15cm. high. £1,950

Miniature French timepiece in silver, hallmarked 1899, 11.5cm. high. £185

French carriage clock, circa 1840, 12.5cm. high.£750

Large French carriage clock with an enamel chapter ring, 8ins. high. £500

Ebonised chronometer by T. Coombe, Brighton. £500

Miniature French time-piece by Leroy et Fils, circa 1880. £1,500

CARRIAGE CLOCKS

Engraved striking and repeating alarm carriage clock, circa 1850. £565

19th century baroque French carriage clock by Japy Freres. £520

A French brass oval carriage clock by Drocourt, 15cm. £900

Grande sonnerie alarm carriage clock with circular enamel dial. £1,000

An enamel mounted grande sonnerie carriage clock, 7in. £1,500

Late 19th century French brass carriage clock with alarm. £125

French strike, repeat, carriage clock with alarm, circa 1850. £850

Repeating carriage alarm clock, 6½in. high. £400

Small gilt metal carriage clock sgnd. Leroy et Fils, 4in. £820

Modern English
carriage clock by
W.J. Huber,
16.5cm.   £70

Breguet carriage
clock.   £5,000

American musical alarm
carriage clock in a brass
and tin case, 15cm. £65

An alarm carriage
clock, the circular
enamel dial with red
and black numerals.
                    £600

Singing bird carriage
clock with alarm by
Japy Freres.£2,500

French carriage clock
with grande sonnerie
and alarm, circa 1875,
15cm. high.   £900

An enamel mounted
carriage clock with
Corinthian columns by
Maurice & Co.   £880

French strike repeat
carriage clock, circa
1880, 18cm. high.
              £450

French striking clock
by Leroy et Fils,
circa 1845, 13cm.
              £685

Small white marble and ormolu mounted French striking clock by Vincent, circa 1860, with pair of matching candelabra sidepieces, 11ins. high x 7ins. wide x 4ins. deep. £475

19th century French polished hardstone and chinoiserie clock garniture. £150

A black slate clock set, inlaid with marble, and with white enamel circular dial. £35

19th century rouge marble and ormolu mounted striking clock with matching sidepieces, 11ins. high. £325

Finely chased rococo style ormolu French striking clock by Mougin, circa 1860, with matching sidepieces, 14ins. high x 11ins. wide x 8ins. deep. £550

Brass garniture de cheminee with coloured enamel mounts on French clock, 11ins. high, and pair of urn-shaped vases, 8½ins. high. £190

A 19th century French ormolu and champleve enamel garniture. £1,150

19th century French gilt metal and white marble garniture de cheminee. £700

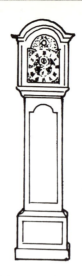

Mahogany regulator by Ellicott, 6ft. 3ins. high. £1,320

Inlaid mahogany longcase clock with painted enamel arched dial (glass door missing) £155

Mahogany three train brass fused eight day clock by James Gardner. £1,500

Early eight day arch dial longcase clock, 8ft. 2ins. high. £1,950

18th century stained oak longcase clock with eight day striking movement by Thomas Rea of Walton. £280

George III mahogany longcase clock with brass dial by Allan Fowlds. £485

A watch timepiece in miniature mahogany inlaid longcase, 40cm. high. £47

Marquetry longcase clock by Davis of Windsor. £1,300

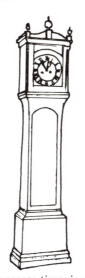

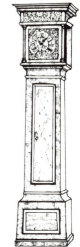

Early 19th century mahogany longcase clock heavily inlaid, striking on eight graduated bells.
£1,000

Longcase timepiece of quality by John Grant of London, 1790 in mahogany case. £575

North Country mahogany clock with painted face, 7ft. 2ins. high.
£198

Longcase clock by Thomas Land in a yew wood case with brass dial.
£1,450

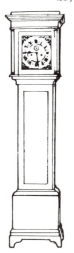

18th century inlaid and crossbanded oak longcase clock with 12in. engraved brass dial by Dickinson. £282

18th century carved oak longcase clock by Jas. Fletcher, Ripponden, circa 1760. £360

Longcase clock by Markham of London. £1,200

18th century black lacquered clock by Edward Bodenham.
£475

177

GRANDFATHER CLOCKS

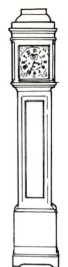

18th century long-case clock, plaque engraved Windmills, London.   £780

George III mahogany longcase clock by Vulliamy, London.   £2,000

Walnut marquetry longcase clock by W. Speakman.   £2,100

Oak longcase clock with musical movement by L. Holbin. £660

Mahogany long-case clock with painted dial by Jn. Dickman, Leith.   £65

Early 19th century longcase clock by Sam. Wichell.£1,150

18th century black lacquered longcase clock by R. Howard of Brentford. £520

Pagoda top longcase by J. Williams, circa 1770, with five pillar movement.£1,150

A walnut long-case clock sgnd. J. Knibb, circa 1690. £2,600

Early Dutch marquetry clock by F. Hauk, Rotterdam. £2,700

Walnut longcase clock sgnd. Windmills, London, with five pillar movement. £800

Victorian free-standing pedestal clock fitted with thermometer and barometer, 59½ins. high. £800

18th century long-cased clock, inscribed 'T. Talbot, Nantwich'.£1,600

Mahogany longcase clock with arched dial by G. Womesley. £340

Mid 18th century longcase clock, sgd. F. Conall of Lutterworth. £900

17th century marquetry longcase clock by C. Gould. £2,000

GRANDFATHER CLOCKS

Oak longcase clock by M. Lyon, Lanark. £300

Walnut marquetry longcase clock with eight day movement. £2,995

Thomas Mudge equation timepiece in mahogany case. £8,300

Black lacquer longcase clock by T. Moore, Ipswich, 1720-1789. £475

17th century marquetry longcase clock by W. Weir, London. £1,050

Mahogany longcase clock with brass circular dial by J. Bryson, Dalkeith. £200

18th century eight-day clock by J. Wyld of Nottingham. £545

Chiming longcase clock of Jacobean design, 89in. high. £520

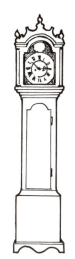

18th century burr walnut longcase clock by J. Chater, London. £1,250

Mahogany longcase clock, circa 1775, sgnd. in the arch James Chater, London. £795

Late 19th century inlaid mahogany clock, by Wm. Greenwood, Leeds. £560

Red Japanned clock, signed Diego Evans, London.£950

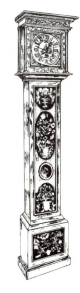

Longcase clock by H. Hurt, London, 12in dial.   £795

Green lacquer longcase clock by A. Dunlop, circa 1720.£975

George II mahogany longcase clock inscribed 'Thomas Brown'.   £780

George II longcase clock in a fine floral marquetry case. £1,800

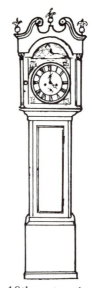

A 'Yorkshire' longcase clock by W. Massey of Nantwich. £200

Mahogany long-case clock inscribed Sic-Est Vita Hominis. £160

Late 18th century in-laid mahogany longcase clock with swan necked pediment and enamel arched dial. £220

Victorian mahogany longcase clock by G. White, Glasgow. £160

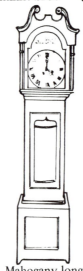

A 17th century walnut, willow and laburnum oyster veneered long-case clock. £2,500

Mahogany longcase clock with painted enamel arched dial by J. Sparke, Nairn. £170

18th century oak carved clock by T. Traunter of Salop, 6ft 10½in. £285

Eight-day oak-cased clock by Bevan of Brecon. £225

Oak grandfather clock, painted dial, by A. Mathewson, Kilconquhar, circa 1810, 80in. £345

Mahogany cased longcase clock by J. Nottle of Okehampton. £420

Louis Philippe boulle clock, ormolu mounted. £2,900

Chiming longcase clock of late 18th century design, 96in. high. £600

A mahogany longcase clock of eight day duration, by George of Fishguard. £170

Regulator longcase clock by G. Harvey of Edin., circa 1825, in mahogany case, 84in. high. £575

Inlaid mahogany longcase clock, five pillar movement with strike-silent regulation. £425

18th century design chiming longcase clock with satinwood inlay, 96ins. high. £600

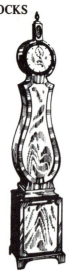

Late 18th century longcase clock by George Mawman, Beverley. £350

George III regulator inscribed 'Cragg, Southampton'. £2,000

Walnut longcase clock by E. Speakman, London, 7ft 6in. high. £1,200

A mahogany longcase clock, with swan neck cresting by John Hamilton, Glasgow, 7ft. 2ins. high. £300

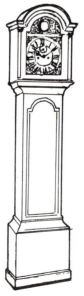

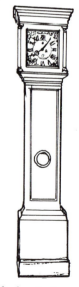

Late 19th century chiming longcase clock of Jacobean design, 89in. £520

Figured mahogany longcased clock, eight day, circa 1770, 81in. £560

18th century longcase clock by Dan Pallet, London, 7ft 9in. £290

Black ebonised clock by T Newman, Dublin, circa 1700, 11in. dial. £900

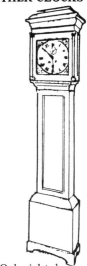

Mahogany longcase clock with arched dial, by J. Templeton, Maybole. £240

18th century walnut cased longcase clock by F. Conall of Butterworth, 7ft. £900

19th century mahogany cased grandfather clock with a square dial. £85

Oak eight day brass faced longcased clock by J. Snelling, Alton, circa 1770. £525

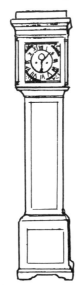

Eight-day red lacquer longcase clock by Brace of Chepstow. £870

18th century eight-day walnut longcase clock, by S. Bradley Jnr., Worc. £795

Mahogany longcase clock by W Theobold of Burneside. £200

17th century marquetry clock by R. Haughton Londini Fecit, five pillar movement. £2,250

19th century Chinese fire clock, 6.25 cm. long.   £340

English watch movement in a gilt bronze case, 9 in. high, of Louis XV style.£100

French ormolu mantel clock in rococo case with enamel chapters, 17cm. high.   £250

19th century French lighthouse clock with square base, 9½ in.   £390

French brass mantel clock with domed hood surmounted by an urn, 44 cm. high   £190

Louis XV bracket clock with boulle decoration.   £2,000

Mahogany inlaid lancet type mantel clock with French movement, 13 in. high.   £36

Regency mantel clock by Elliot on scroll feet.   £350

Edwardian inlaid mahogany mantel clock with a domed pediment, 8½ in. £14

19th century cased mantel clock inscribed Hollister, 15½ in. high. £270

Plaster model of Windsor Castle painted in polychrome, inset with a clock, 22 cm. wide. £5

Silver desk clock by Parkinson and Frodsham, London, hallmarked 1893. £260

Louis XV style gilt metal mantel clock with coloured enamel inlay, 49 cm. £240

19th century French boulle bracket clock by Thurel a Paris, 47in. high. £870

19th century boulle mantel clock surmounted by a figure of 'Time'. £590

French ormolu 'snake ring' clock. £980

19th century mahogany cased mantel clock inscribed Ed. Lohder Snr. London, with engraved back plate and fusee movement, 14½ in. high. £280

Louis XVI boulle clock by Jacques La Doux of Amiens. £1,000

MANTEL CLOCKS

Edwardian inlaid mahogany mantel clock £20

Victorian inlaid mahogany mantel clock with serpentine shaped pediment, 11½ ins. wide £20

Late 19th century walnut mantel clock with silverized and brass dial, 16ins.high £34

Bronze and gilt French bull clock. £600

Gilt metal mantel clock with an 18th century movement by Graham, 36cm. high £6,600

Late Meissen clock case of architectural form, 13ins. high £240

19th century French ormolu striking clock by Japy Freres, 14ins. high £395

Ormolu and white statuary marble mantel clock by Raingo Freres, Paris, circa 1800. £1,650

18th century gilt metal hexagonal striking table clock with verge escapement £1,100

Mahogany cased two-train mantel clock by Shepheard of Plymouth circa 1815 £295

French bronze and ormolu mantel clock inscribed 'Renoir Paris'. £460

Rare German itinerant clockmaker figure, carrying a clock on his chest 13¾ high late 18th cent. £650

Early 19th century French mantel clock by Garrigues of Paris £365

19th century French ormolu and white marble mantel clock by Leroy, Paris, 22in. high. £270

Mid 19th century white marble and ormolu mounted striking pillar clock, 17 ins. high £295

Victorian mahogany cased clock with repousse brass mounts, acorn finial and musical chiming movement, 52cm. high. £85

Regency mantel timepiece sold with a pair of pastille burners. £400

An ormolu mantel clock by Robert Philp of London, 41 cm. high £2,000

Two train hour repeating clock by J. Meek of London, circa 1810.
£325

Gilt metal mantel clock in drum case with a female classical figure to side on alabaster base and giltwood stand.
£100

Edwardian mahogany carved mantel clock by Walker & Hall, 12in. high.
£40

19th century Louis XV style mantel clock, 14in. high.
£60

Regency mahogany clock by J. Murray with repeating movement, 1ft. 10in. high.
£300

George III mahogany balloon clock by J. Radford.
£400

Edwardian mantel clock in a walnut case.
£11

Victorian cuckoo clock in ebonised and decorated case, 16in. high.
£178

Walnut mantel clock with silverised and brass dial, 16in. high.
£38

A small 19th century plated timepiece on a wooden stand.   £22

Silver triple cased quarter striking chaise watch by J. Cox, hallmarked 1809.   £1,250

19th century mahogany balloon case clock by W. Thomson of Leith.   £120

19th century French mantel timepiece, 8in. high.   £40

Black and coloured marble mantel clock with French movement, 12½in. high.   £10

A Carl Faberge silver gilt and mousse enamel boudoir timepiece. £2,000

Red tortoiseshell style striking mantel clock with gilt metal mounts.   £165

American mantel clock in carved wood case.   £26

19th century ormolu mounted French clock.   £300

Ornate ormolu and veneered Louis XV style bracket clock. £1,050

A Charles X ormolu mantel clock, 37cm. high.   £740

French boulle mantel clock by Miroy, Paris, 17½in. high. £250

Small French ormolu timepiece in rococo style, circa 1820, 10in. high.   £165

18th century Dutch table clock in tortoiseshell and silver case, 13cm. high. £2,500

Gilt metal mantel clock with 18th century movement by Graham, 36cm. £6,600

Edwardian inlaid mahogany mantel clock with eight day French movement.   £28

Alabaster mantel clock with gilt metal dial and fluted pillars, 11in. high. £24

Mantel timepiece in oak inlaid case. £12

A combined timepiece, barometer and calendar in a silver mounted case. £14

Late 18th century bisquit de Sevres mantel clock, movement sgnd. Felix Sandox, London, ormolu panels and feet, 11in. £190

George III neo-classic bronze and ormolu mantel timepeice by T. Hawley. £425

19th century French ormolu striking mantel clock, 20½in. £395

Victorian walnut mantel clock with a silverised and brass dial, 16in. £34

French striking clock by Howell et Cie and Vincenti of Paris, circa 1850, 14in. high. £450

French champleve enamel clock. £320

Black marble mantel clock, 15in. high. £15

Mid 18th century gilt metal hexagonal striking table clock, signed Rellames, London. £1,320

An early 17th century chaise clock watch by J. Barberet, Paris, 10cm. diam. £5,000

Late 19th century French marble and ormolu clock. £125

Early Victorian novelty timepiece of painted pressed tin. £290

Louis XV boulle clock and bracket by N. Baltazar of Paris. £2,000

17th century Augsburg clock by Georg Schmidt. £10,556

19th century French gilt bronze mounted boulle mantel clock. £320

19th century French ormolu and cloisonne enamel mantel clock, 17½in. high. £520

Late 18th century boulle clock by Perache. £525

19th century French clock designed for the Turkish market. £200

Brass skeleton clock with silverised and pierced dial, 13¾in. high. £140

An unusual skeleton timepiece surmounted by Prince of Wales feathers, 1ft.½in. high. £430

19th century six-pillar fusee skeleton timepiece, in glass shade, 11½in. high. £245

Small mid 19th century English skeleton timepiece, with five spoke wheels and skeletonised barrel. £225

York Minster type skeleton clock on a rose marble base, 1ft.10½in. high. £800

English double fusee skeleton clock of Lichfield Cathedral pattern. £495

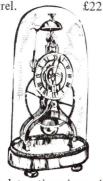

Skeleton timepiece with greatwheel deadbeat escapement, 14½in. high. £650

A three month skeleton timepiece inscribed Volpone Wynatt, 2ft.2½in. high. £1,450

Mid 19th century striking and repeating English skeleton clock, by Pearce & Sons. £750

195

SKELETON CLOCKS

A rare chiming skeleton clock by James Condliff with annular chapter ring, 2ft. 1in. high. £3,000

A fine and large chiming skeleton clock by Penlington and Hutton, Liverpool, 1ft. 11ins. high. £4,000

Skeleton clock by Hatfield and Hall, Manchester, 12½ins. high. £460

An ivy leaf skeleton timepiece, with finely fretted frame. £250

An unusual skeleton clock by Hy Marc, Paris, 1ft. 9ins. high. £500

A fine striking skeleton clock, with engraved frame. £370

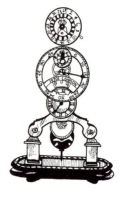

Skeleton timepiece signed Rippin, Spalding, 1ft. 4ins. high. £500

Lichfield cathedral-type skeleton clock, 1ft. 6½ins. high. £550

Skeleton timepiece signed Joyce, London, 1ft. 4ins. high. £750

A 17th century brass lantern clock by William Stevens of Godalming. £520

Wing lantern clock by William Moore of Brantford, circa 1680. £1,150

A brass lantern mantel clock with engraved dial, 39cm. high. £140

Brass lantern clock by Jonathan Chambers, with 7in. dial. £950

A Wing lantern clock with a 6½in. dial, signed Thomas West, London, 1ft. 3½ins. high. £760

Brass lantern clock, dial engraved Rick Rayment, 16ins. high. £220

Lantern clock by T. Birch, London, with anchor escapement. £600

Late 17th century lantern clock with verge escapement and long pendulum. £375

Balance wheel lantern clock by H. Scobell, runs on two weights and two pulleys, signed in corners of dial plate, circa 1630. £1,000

WALL CLOCKS

Late 18th century mahogany weight-driven wall clock with silvered dial. £335

German made late Victorian clock. £50

An attractive Vienna timepiece with brass pendulum. £195

Late Victorian mahogany-cased wall clock by Reiner of London, with painted iron dial. £70

Mahogany-cased wall clock with iron dial by William Martin, circa 1840. £80

London silvered dial mahogany verge wall clock by Thornton, circa 1790. £365

Small eight day tavern timepiece, circa 1790, in a lacquer case, 42ins. long. £365

Attractive and well-figured walnut striking Vienna regulator. £185

Well-figured full-length walnut Vienna regulator, with gridiron pendulum. £100

A Liberty silver and enamel clock, Birmingham 1905, its borders decorated with stylised leaves, 8ins. high. £500

Dial of a Quare and Horseman musical clock, case in poor condition. £2,100

A Victorian walnut and floral marquetry wall clock with enamel dial, 75cm. high. £50

English wall clock by John B. Cross, circa 1840. £150

Mahogany wall clock with convex dial and glass. £115

Ebony-veneered wall clock by Handley and Moore, London, circa 1820, with anchor escapement. £250

17th century Friesan wall clock. £520

French ormolu cartel clock, circa 1840, 4ft. 5½ins. high. £750

Unusual Japanese wall clock in ebonised case, 20ins. high. £500

A gold and enamel key-
less cylinder watch set
with rose diamonds.
£380

A rose diamond set fob
watch suspended from
a diamond and gem
set griffin brooch. £190

Late 19th century
silver and niello
hunting cased key-
less lever watch.
£110

Modern watch, the
teardrops of coral
and onyx divided
by a trail of dia-
monds, all set in
18 ct. gold.£3,600

18ct. gold pocket
watch on 9ct. gold
chain with
sovereign. £156

Modern watch of onyx
and diamonds set in
18ct. gold. £6,450

French gold watch
by Leroy decorated
with foliage and
diamonds, circa 1785.
£2,250

Gold and enamel
pair-cased quar-
ter repeating
cylinder watch
with chatelaine.
£4,200

Sporting watch
with niello
decoration,
circa 1890.
£265

Wristwatch by Petit
of Paris in 18ct. gold
set with rubies,
diamonds, emeralds
and turquoises.
£6,850

Gold and enamel key-
less lever watch, the
damascened move-
ment with compen-
sation balance.   £280

Fob watch by
J.F. Bautts and
Cie of Geneva.
£550

Gold and enamel verge watch by Charles Leroy of Paris, circa 1780. £520

18th century silver Oignon watch with a calendar dial. £700

A chaise watch by Cabrier, London in a silver case, circa 1740. £1,900

Pocket-watch by T. Tompion, the case hallmarked 1709, 5.6cm. diam.£4,300

A gold cased quarter repeating duplex watch by Leplastrier of London, hallmarked 1823. £360

Pair-cased silver pocket watch by Tarts of London, circa 1760, rococo case signed 'Mauris Fecit'.£375

A repousse gold pair-cased verge watch by Swayne of London, hallmarked 1727. £1,200

Swiss gold watch set with paste and decorated with three coloured gold, circa 1775. £800

Austrian silver and enamel table watch inscribed 'Luis Schudulin a Wien'. £700

An early pocket chronometer by Wright, London 1784, No. 2228. £3,700

Austrian watch in an 18 carat gold mandolin case decorated in champ-leve enamel, circa 1820. £2,900

Silver pocket watch by 'D.D. Neweren, London', circa 1760, enamel dial. £250

Pair-cased silver pocket watch by 'Cabrier, London', case by Cochin, circa 1750. £785

A gilt metal cased pedometer and com-pass by Fraser, circa 1800. £140

Gold and enamel half hunting cased keyless cylinder watch by Pater Philippe of Geneva. £360

A gold and enamel quarter repeating verge watch by Gudin of Paris, hallmarked Paris 1777. £1,100

A gold verge watch by Dubois et Fils with polychrome enamel dial plate, circa 1790. £420

William IV pair-cased silver pocket watch by G. Coxon of Oldbury, hallmarked for 1836, verge movement.£180

Gold minute repeating split seconds keyless lever chronograph by Audemars Piquet of Geneva £1,100

A gold quarter repeating verge watch by Vacheron and Constantin of Geneva circa 1820 £600

Gold pair-cased verge watch by Baronneau of Paris, mid 17th century. £4,200

Gold cased keyless mystery watch signed Mysterieuse, Brevete, S.G.O.G £520

Gilt metal verge clock watch by Edmund Price of London with brass crank key, circa 1720 £600

18 carat gold cased keyless lever chronograph by Ulysse Nardin £280

An unusual 19th century cylinder watch with engraved floral architectural decoration £320

Early 19th century detached double roller lever watch hallmarked 1822 £750

A gold keyless lever chronograph from the late 19th century £130

Gold pocket watch, Swiss, circa 1800, by Coulin of Geneva, in plain gold case, 5.3cm. diameter. £250

A minute repeating lever watch by Dent in a gold case set with rose diamonds, 1866. £580

Late Victorian man's pocket watch in good working order. £10

Early 19th century independent seconds quarter repeating cylinder watch by Lepine of Paris. £900

A gold pair-cased watch by Eardley Norton of London, circa 1790. £150

Victorian silver pocket watch in chased case. £22

A gold hunting cased lady's keyless cylinder watch. £300

A gold Massey lever watch by M.I. Tobias of Liverpool, circa 1830. £270

A gold quarter repeating virgule watch, circa 1840. £680

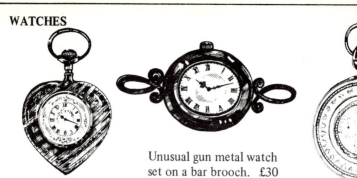

Unusual gun metal watch
set on a bar brooch.   £30

Heart-shaped silver watch
decorated with alternate
stripes of engraved silver
and plain pink gold over-
lay.   £75

Early 19th century French
sedan-chair clock in a gilt
metal case, 5ins. high.
                                      £250

French pocket watch
by Giradier, in pinch-
beck case with painted
dial and paste border.
                          £620

Gold and black enamel
lever dress watch by
Longines.   £210

Silver pair cased
watch by Ninyan
Burleigh.   £360

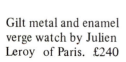

Gilt metal and enamel
verge watch by Julien
Leroy of Paris. £240

A silver triangular keyless
lever watch by Schwab
and Brandt of Switzerland.
                              £455

Pendulum watch by
Madelainy a Paris,
circa 1680, 1.9ins.
diam.   £22,000

One of a pair of late 19th century Chinese cloisonne bears. £190

Pair of Japanese metalware quails in copper, Shakudo and gilt, 12cm. high. £404

18th century bronze and Chinese enamel figure of Kwan Yin, 56cm. £520

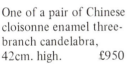

One of a pair of Chinese cloisonne enamel three-branch candelabra, 42cm. high. £950

One of a pair of early 19th century cloisonne vases, 15ins. high. £900

Large 19th century Japanese cloisonne enamel dish, 36ins. diam. £620

Japanese Art Nouveau Zeit Geist cloisonne vase, with damaged base, 46cm. high. £105

One of a pair of turquoise cloisonne enamel oval-shaped bowls, 26cm. wide. £190

19th century Japanese cloisonne enamel vase, the blue ground decorated with trees, 18ins. high. £50

COPPER AND BRASS

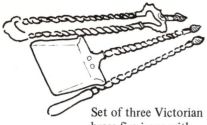

Set of three Victorian brass fire irons with spiral handles.   £30

Two Eastern brass circlets.   £14

Georgian brass shoe horn. £7

Brass pie trimmer and wheel, circa 1830.   £5

Unusual set of three copper and brass spirit measures, circa 1850, one gallon, 10½in. high, three gallons, 16in. high, five gallons, 19in. high.   £194

Set of three copper cider measures with iron handles.   £16

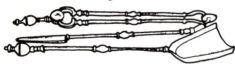

Victorian set of brass fire implements.   £40

19th century brass fender with pierced foliage design.   £42

Cook's copper cream skimmer with wrought iron handle, circa 1790.   £19

Brass circular chestnut roaster with iron handle.   £12

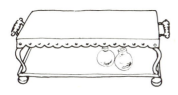

Edwardian double handled copper plate warmer. £16

Brass skimmer with pierced handle. £8

Four various copper lids. £8

18th century brass skimmer. £27

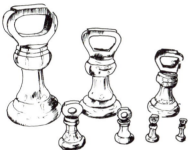

Cast-brass bell-shaped butcher s scale weights, circa 1850, graduated sizes from 7lb-½oz. nine in all. £68

Finely detailed Adam period door knocker, 9 ins. high £27

Victorian copper pan with a brass handle, 7in. diam. £8

Tibetan copper and brass horn with chased plated mounts, 5ft. 8in. £55

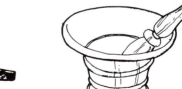

Irish bellows in brass and mahogany. £35

Small brass mortar and pestle. £9

COPPER AND BRASS

Brass octagonal box with handle on the cover, pierced. £5

Oriental copper circular tray with wavy border. £16

Eastern brass bell and brass wall bracket. £9

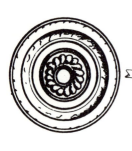

Eastern copper jug and cover. £14

18th century Nepalese copper and silver figure of Vajravarahi, 6¼ ins. high. £750

Victorian brass urn shaped jardiniere with embossed rosettes and festoons, 15ins. high. £40

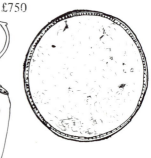

17th century Flemish brass alms dish, 42cm diam. £230

Georgian copper kettle with acorn lid. £40

Large copper circular tray with fluted border. £20

Brass circular kettle
with amber handle.
£24

Copper circular double
handled pan, 19½in.
£44

Victorian brass
dog door poster.
£14

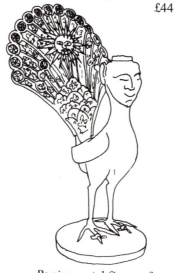

Eastern copper
jug and cover.
£14

Persian metal figure of
a simurgh, 19th century,
48cm. high.   £945

19th century brass
letter clip by Merry,
Phipson & Parker.
£6.50

One of a pair of
Oriental copper
and brass vases.
£40

19th century footman
with griddle.   £65

One of a pair of
Victorian brass
double handled
vases, 11in. £50

COPPER AND BRASS

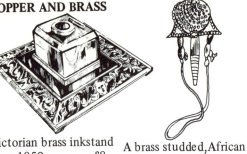

Victorian brass inkstand circa 1850.   £8

A brass studded, African chief's pectoral ornament. £20

Victorian brass pin case.   £5

One of set of four brass cannons, complete with their wooden framed carriages.   £240

Brass cash box with handle on the cover, 11½ins. £48

English, shaped front brass club fender with lion mask and green leather studded seats, circa 1865.   £225

19th century brass inkstand on four animal supports, 6ins. wide.   £28

Brass water jug with Art Nouveau decoration, circa 1900.   £8

Brass pestle and mortar, around 1890.   £23

Brass 'man in the moon' dish, circa 1905.   £4

Victorian brass oblong
snuff box. £5

Late 17th century
Flemish brass alms
dish with jelly mould
centre, 41 cm. diam.
£320

Cast and wrought iron
footman, circa 1820,
12 ins. long. £68

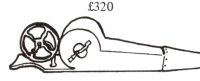

19th century oak and brass mounted
fire blower. £26

Chased brass bible box in book form,
7¾ins. wide. £12

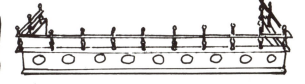

Victorian brass
stamp box. £2

Victorian brass fender with rail, 177cm. wide. £60

Steel and brass coffee
grinder made by A.
Kenrick & Sons,
21½cm. high. £29.50

Indian brass circular
jardiniere with
animal masks and
ring handles, 36cm.
diam. £18

Victorian copper
and brass kettle.
£14

COPPER AND BRASS

19th century copper jelly mould.   £21

Late 17th century six sided brass footwarmer, 13cm. high.   £200

Oriental copper and silverised jug with dragons head handle, 13in. high.   £26

Brass 'Humming Bird' surmounted with a pincushion.   £30

Pair of copper preserving pans.   £80

Georgian brass goffering iron, circa 1835. £20

Victorian copper kettle.   £22

Stylish brass jardiniere about 1900, with three supports and pierced-work band round the body.   £18

One of two Eastern copper and brass jugs and domed covers different.£20

Victorian copper
watering can. £14

Oriental copper and
brass jug.   £18

One of a pair of Indian
repousse brass circular
jardinieres with ring
handles, 28cm.   £34

One gallon copper
spirit measure,
dovetail seams, circa
1850.   £48

18th century Nepalese bronze
of Hayagriva in Yab-Yum,
6¼ in. high.   £375

Brass standard
measure, circa
1820.   £75

Copper and brass
five gallon measure
with iron handle.
          £30

Regency period ormolu
reel stand with the ori-
ginal reels.   £35

Four gallon copper
measure.   £55

CANDLESTICKS

Pair brass table candlesticks with spiral stems, 11in. high. £7

Brass chamber stick with a drip pan. £9

Pair of brass candlesticks on octagonal base, 10in. high. £10

One of a pair of brass table candlesticks with baluster stems, 12¼in. high. £22

Pair of Georgian brass candlesticks with petal shaped bases, circa 1740. £100

A Flemish brass candlestick, circa 1500, 21cm. high. £440

18th century brass oil lamp. £15

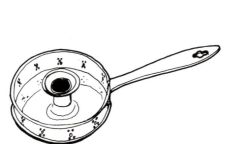

One of a pair of brass chamber candlesticks with handles. £11

One of a pair of Victorian miniature brass candlesticks. £9

One of a pair of moulded brass table candlesticks on oval bases, 11in. high. £12

One of a pair of superb Persian brass candlesticks with hand-engraved Arabic inscriptions, 14½ in. high, circa 1680. £265

One of a pair of brass candlesticks with open spiral stems, 12in. high. £16

One of a set of four brass altar candlesticks, 46cm. high. £80

Ormolu candelabrum for two lights on a marble base, 14½in. high. £7

Roman brass oil lamp. £17

Tall brass candlestick on circular base, 18½in. high.£12

One of a set of four 19th century Scandinavian candelabra, 3ft.8in. £600

One of a pair of George I brass candlesticks with knopped stems.£190

A mandarin robe of terra cotta silk. £115

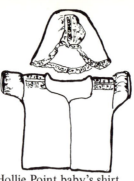

A Hollie Point baby's shirt and bonnet edged with Buckingham lace, 17th century. £52

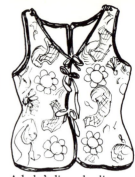

A lady's linen bodice with yellow silk quilting from the early 18th century. £170

Small examples of 19th century Honiton lace. £6

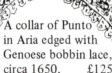

A collar of Punto in Aria edged with Genoese bobbin lace, circa 1650. £125

German fan painted with the 'Rape of the Sabine Women', circa 1730. £130

Officer's scarlet coatee of the Royal American Regiment. £250

Victorian officer's uniform of the 1st Volunteer Battalion. £175

19th century uniform of the Papal Guard. £210

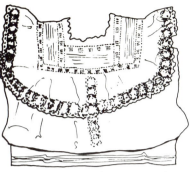

Boy's riding jacket of brown worsted with blue satin waistcoat, circa 1785.   £80

Late 19th century lace trimmed embroidered nightdress.   £10

Coat of red silk trimmed with Venetian beads, by Fortuny, 1923.   £230

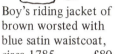

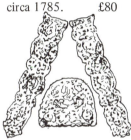

Pair of 17th century point d'Angleterre lappets and bonnet back.   £105

One of a pair of very decorative pierced leather boots, 11ins. long.   £24

Military sporran of the Seaforths with plated mounts.   £30

Open robe of dark brown cotton, printed with fireworks, circa 1785.   £70

.Black velvet court dress uniform of tail-coat, trousers hat and sword belt. £12

Uniform of the 3rd Madras Lancers.   £200

DAGGERS

A Caucasian dagger kindjal, broad, plain double edged blade 17½in, with deep central fuller, ivory and horn grips decorated with niello and Eastern silver mounts.   £42

An old jade hilted khanjar, ribbed, curved blade 8¼in, the hilt of white mutton fat jade inset with many coloured stones.   £65

A Turkish dagger bichaq, single edge blade 7½in. inlaid in silver on both sides for entire length with inscriptions; 2 piece ivory grips, white metal backstrap.   £42

A European maine gouche basket hilt dagger c. 1700, double edged blade 14¼in, of flattened diamond section, semi-basket guard with looped patterns, ovoid pommel.   £100

An Indo-Persian dagger khanjar, wavy blade 9in, etched with King, Queen and birds inhabiting foliage, ribbed hilt of translucent mutton fat jade. £60

A Persian jambiya, curved blade 10in, of watered steel with central rib, marine ivory hilt with plain silver mounts with beaded edges, in its leather covered wooden sheath with two simulated eastern silver mounts.   £95

A silver mounted Burmese dha dagger, blade 8½in, the bone hilt carved in the form of a grotesque seated demon, the hilt overlaid with Eastern sheet silver, with some decoration.   £72

A good niello and silver mounted Caucasian dagger, curved blade 11½in, with central fuller, the hilt with leopard head pommel entirely overlaid with eastern silver embossed with foliate and niello decoration.   £340

A Nazi Red Cross dagger, plated mounts in its metal sheath. £70

An Indo-Persian dagger kard, single edged black and white watered blade 10in, gold damascened at forte with foliage and diaper, walrus ivory grip, in its black leather covered sheath.   £56

A good Nazi Luftwaffe officer's 1st pattern dagger, by Eickhorn, plated mounts, wire bound blue leather covered grip, in its metal sheath with plated mounts with original hanging chains and belt clip.   £66

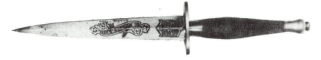

A scarce World War II Commando dagger, 'The Field Service Fighting Knife'.   Tapering blade 3¾in. by Wilkinson Sword.   Etched with officer's name 'A.W. Parish' within foliate scroll.   £32

Character baby doll marked W. Weyh, with blue eyes and closed mouth, 11in. £70

Poured wax doll stamped Frederic Aldis, 20in. tall. £180

Kesner lady doll with articulated arms and legs, 24in. tall. £85

Schoenau and Hoffmeister doll with blue eyes, 26in. tall, circa 1909. £55

German character doll with pouting mouth. £700

Doll by Schoenau and Hoffmeister wearing a navy blue school gymslip. £55

Kammer and Reinhardt celluloid character doll. £50

Simon and Halbig china faced doll. £49

Dark-haired Parian doll with original dress, circa 1865, 11½in. long. £100

Wax two-faced doll stamped Deutsches Reichs-Patent U.S.P., circa 1870, 16in. £200

Bisque headed English baby doll, circa 1914. £30

Bisque china Schoenau Hoffmeister doll, circa 1905, 15in. tall. £85

Bisque headed Bebe, 10in. high. £750

Lady Victoria Rose bisque head and shoulder portrait doll. £500

Bisque headed Bebe Bru. £1,600

Joll's house lady doll, 6in. high, circa 1860. £18

Parisienne bisque headed doll with pale blue eyes. £520

Dark-haired Parian doll, circa 1850. £275

DOLLS

Bisque-headed Bebe Bru. £1,600

Late 19th century coloured doll with black high heeled boots. £28

Victorian doll impressed 'Fabrication Francaise al and Cie Limoges Cherie 5', 19ins. high. £78

Bisque-headed doll with glass eyes, circa 1875, 10½ins. long. £85

French doll impressed S.F.B.J., overstamped 'Tete Jumeau' body marked 'Bebe Jumeau' (1897) 24ins. tall. £145

Parian doll with moulded hair and blue eyes, circa 1870, 12ins. high. £125

German doll made by Armand Marseille, mould No. 1894, 16ins. tall. £44

Doll's house boy doll, 3½ins. high, circa 1860. £20

Victorian doll with wax covered face. £20

Bisque-headed bebe doll. £400

German doll with kid body made by Armand Marseille (1900) 20ins. tall. £60

German doll made by Herm. Steiner (1912) 16ins. long. £38

Bisque-headed doll with painted blue eyes, circa 1875. £30

Jumea phonograph doll. £1,000

German doll made by Alt. Beck and Gottschalk (1910) 26ins. tall. £80

German doll (1920's) 24ins. tall, head made by Heubach for Seyfarth and Reinhart. £70

Doll's house doll of a man, 7ins. high, circa 1860. £30

Doll made by Simon & Halbig, circa 1905 £65

ENAMEL

Oviform enamel box, the lid painted with a landscape, 1¾in. high. £110

Bilston enamel box with light blue base and white lid. £16

Circular enamel patch box modelled as a spaniel dog on a powder blue cushion, 1½ in. diam. £210

Enamel scent bottle of flask shape with ormolu dove stopper, 3¾in. high.£210

One of a pair of Chinese cloisonne enamel cranes. £400

Enamel scent bottle of flask shape, 4in. high. £260

Oval enamel patch box, the lid painted with a shepherd and shepherdess, 1¾in. wide. £90

Unusual enamel collector's piece, called a bougie holder. £90

Oval enamel patch box, the lid painted with shipping by a quay, 2in. wide. £100

Enamel egg-shaped nutmeg grater in yellow and white. £30

Magnificent deep blue enamel rectangular Battersea box. £435

Round snuff box from Bilston around 1775. £320

Enamel scent bottle case of rectangular form, painted with floral sprays, 2½in. high. £170

One of a pair of Chinese cloisonne enamel quail. £150

Enamel scent bottle of rectangular form with ormolu flower stopper, 3in. high. £120

Circular enamel patch box modelled as a cat on a lilac cushion, 1½in. diam. £145

Bilston enamel box, with white lid and blue base. £24

Oval enamel patch box, modelled as a lion, 2in. wide. £260

London and Lancashire copper plate. £30

London Assurance mark, 11in. diam. £28

Central Insurance Company plate. £30

An engraved brass Lloyds Insurance Agency sign. £40

Sun Fire Office, 1710. £25

Early 19th century seven point star firemark of the Suffolk and General County Amicable Insurance Office (1799-1848). £540

Manchester Fire and Life Assurance Company plate. £30

A rare Hand in Hand company
firemark. £90

National Insurance Company
of Ireland. £22

Phoenix Assurance
Company lead mark.
£85

County Fire
Office plate.
£30

Royal Exchange
Assurance plate.
£80

Royal Exchange mark. £45

Farmers Insurance Company
copper plate. £28

FLASKS

A rare copper pistol flask with embossed Colt revolver, overall length 4¼in. £52

A fine, early 19th century, Continental powder horn with gilt metal mounts. Spring loader, plunger, charger unit, turned base plate with hanging ring, 8½in. £40

A good copper pocket pistol powder flask, 'Shell and Bush', brass charger unit. £21

A good bag-shaped copper powder flask, 5½in. £50

A scarce Austrian leather powder flask, 9in. brass 'eye glass' charger stamped 'Beetz Wien', each side of 'eye glass' is adjustable to 3 positions, 2 brass suspension rings. £30

A scarce 3 way copper powder flask of oval section from a cased pair of flintlock duelling pistols c. 1790. 5in. overall. £40

A large embossed copper powder flask, 8in. common-top. £32

A rare nielloed silver-mounted Russian Cossack powder flask, 7¾in. wooden body carved in gourd shape. £200

A good leather covered powder flask for a cased rifle, 8¾in, white metal Hawksley top. £40

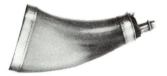

A good curved translucent horn pistol flask, of flattened form, brass mounts, overall 4¾in. £14

A good bag-shaped copper powder flask, 4¼in, common top. £40

A scarce leather 'cuir-boulli' French powder flask, 9in fluted demi-pear shaped body. £40

A good plain copper powder flask by J. Dixon & Sons, Sheffield. £29

A gun sized copper powder flask, 8in, patent top. £50

A gun sized copper powder flask, 8½in. Dixon patent top. £60

A small bag-shaped copper powder flask, 3¾in sprung common brass top. £25

A large 17th century European triangular musketeer's powder flask. £55

A bag-shaped copper pistol flask, 5¼in, top stamped: 'James Dixon and Sons, Sheffield'. £56

BEDS AND CRADLES

Solid satinwood poster bed, foot posts reeded and garlanded, swags and decorations carved from solid posts, circa 1850, 5ft. wide, 8ft. high.   £565

17th century tester bed with contemporary crewel work hangings.   £3,300

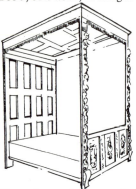

An 18th century oak canopy bedstead with moulded head and tailboards, 136cm. wide x 210cm. long.   £420

19th century Italian mahogany bedstead with a carved scroll cresting, 6ft. x 5ft.   £220

English 19th century four-poster bed.   £290

Chippendale design four-poster bed, with cornice carved in Chinese style, 5ft. wide.   £2,400

17th century oak four-poster bed, the
back carved, panelled and inlaid,
5ft. wide, 7ft. 3ins. long, 6ft. 7ins. high.
£3,500

The Wedgwood bed, an Elizabethan oak
four-poster, 244cm. high x 201cm. wide
x 163cm. long.   £1,400

17th century carved oak hooded cradle.
£380

Jacobean four-poster bed with hangings.
£1,200

Victorian four-poster bed decorated
with rococo carving.   £290

Hepplewhite mahogany four-poster bed
with a dentil cornice.   £477

BOOKCASES

Edwardian mahogany bookcase. £27

Mahogany dwarf cabinet bookcase, 5ft. wide. £50

19th century inlaid mahogany bookstand. £65

Victorian rosewood cabinet bookcase. £90

Mid 19th century satinwood bookcase, 8ft. £2,500

19th century mahogany cabinet bookcase. £180

Stained cabinet bookcase with domed pediment. £105

Late 19th century breakfront bookcase. £460

Heavily carved oak cabinet bookcase. £180

Victorian mahogany revolving bookcase. £50

Japanese lacquered Sho-Dana with silver mounts.£3,800

Bamboo revolving bookcase with lacquered top, circa 1890. £70

Oak cabinet bookcase, 6ft 4in wide. £250

19th century walnut cabinet bookcase, the upper part with four glazed doors, 2.65m. wide. £240

Victorian mahogany bookcase. £400

Mahogany cabinet bookcase, 7ft. high. £100

George III secretaire breakfront bookcase. £820

19th century mahogany cabinet bookcase. £200

18th century mahogany breakfront bookcase with astragal glazed doors.
£6,100

Edwardian inlaid mahogany three-tier magazine rack · with a cupboard in the base, 106cm. high.
£50

Early 19th century mahogany breakfront cabinet bookcase with glazed upper doors, 2.35m. wide.
£260

19th century breakfront rosewood bookcase with marble top and brass grilles, 44ins. wide.
£475

Chippendale mahogany library bookcase, circa 1770, 5ft. 3ins. wide.
£875

Victorian carved oak open shelves of three tiers, with spiral supports.
£80

19th century inlaid walnut bookcase with brass gallery.
£135

19th century mahogany bookcase with glazed doors.
£1,100

Late 19th century mahogany dwarf bookcase with glazed doors and bracket feet, 138cm. wide.
£105

Early 18th century walnut bureau decorated with cross and feather banding, 36ins. wide. £460

Queen Anne walnut bureau on bracket feet. £1,150

George III mahogany bureau with brass loop handles and ogee feet, 42ins. wide. £520

Late 18th century inlaid mahogany bureau with pierced brass handles and bracket feet. £370

Bureau a cylindre by Jean Henri Riesener, Louis XV period, 1.69m. wide. £20,000

Edwardian inlaid mahogany bureau on bracket feet. £130

20th century walnut bureau with three bow-fronted drawers, on cabriole legs, 67cm. wide. £60

Louis XV style kingwood and rosewood cylinder-fronted marquetry bureau de dame. £730

Chippendale style Georgian governess desk, circa 1820. £185

George I walnut
bureau on bracket
feet.   £500

Edwardian oak bureau
on turned legs, 2ft.
10ins. wide.   £65

Dutch marquetry bureau
richly inlaid all over in
floral sprays and urns.
£1,350

Late 18th century
Dutch marquetry
bureau on cabriole
legs.   £580

Continental walnut
and inlaid bureau,
ormolu mounted,
41ins. wide.   £2,700

Oak schoolmaster's
desk, circa 1780.
£250

19th century inlaid
mahogany bureau of
four long drawers,
3ft 2ins. wide.   £190

Mahogany bureau on
cabriole legs, 2ft. 6ins.
wide.   £50

Queen Anne walnut
and ebony inlaid
bureau, 76cm. wide.
£680

19th century Dutch colonial block-fronted bureau, 92cm. wide. £580

Edwardian inlaid mahogany bureau on splayed feet, 2ft. 6ins. wide. £75

Mid-18th century Italian bureau, walnut inlaid with ivory, 94cm. wide. £3,300

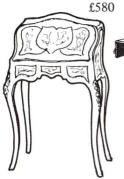

19th century kingwood and marquetry bureau. £400

18th century padouk-wood bureau with brass carrying handles and bracket feet, 105cm. wide. £695

Early 19th century French mahogany cylinder bureau, 37ins. wide. £440

18th century Dutch marquetry bombe bureau, 122cm. wide. £2,400

19th century mahogany bureau on bracket feet, 2ft. 6ins. wide. £85

George III mahogany bureau on shaped bracket feet. 3ft. wide. £180

BUREAUX

Good quality inlaid mahogany George III bureau with shell inlay, 91cm. wide. £420

Walnut office cabinet with numerous drawers and compartments. £440

Oak bureau with well and stepped interior, circa 1715, 3ft. wide. £350

Louis XVI tulipwood parquetry bureau a cylindre, by J. H. Riesener. £31,500

Queen Anne oak bureau with well, on bracket feet. £480

18th century Continental walnut bombe bureau with stepped interior, 3ft. 7½ins. wide. £1,000

Georgian mahogany bureau, interior fitments, 3ft 3in.£220

Edwardian inlaid mahogany and burr walnut banded bureau on square legs, 102cm. £170

Late 18th century mahogany bureau with an inlaid interior and bracket feet, 40in. wide. £300

Rare mid-18th century solid yew-wood bureau. £975

Louis XV design rosewood inlaid and parquetry bureau de dame, 72cm. wide.£290

George III mahogany and marquetry inlaid bureau, 3ft 10in wide.   £1,050

Louis XV period bureau de dame by I. Dubois, in japanned wood with gilt chinoiseries, 97cm.   £16,800

18th century Dutch walnut and marquetry bureau on bracket feet.   £1,300

18th century Georgian mahogany bureau on ogee feet.   £260

Marquetry bombe shaped bureau, on claw and ball feet. £1,800

19th century French mahogany cylinder bureau with ormolu cupids, scrolls and foliage.   £4,200

Mahogany bureau, 3ft 9in wide.   £190

BUREAU BOOKCASES

18th century Dutch marquetry cylinder front bureau bookcase, 1.34m. wide. £3,000

18th century mahogany bureau bookcase, adjustable shelves in top, fitted interior. £1,250

18th century Italian wainut bureau bookcase, 1.12m. wide. £3,500

An 18th century German bureau cabinet. £3,000

18th century North German walnut bureau cabinet. £820

An early 18th century walnut double dome bureau bookcase, 91.5cm. wide. £2,400

18th century Venetian marquetry bureau cabinet, 1.05m. wide. £2,900

19th century rosewood cylinder top bureau with pull-out writing board, a cupboard below and a bookcase above. £200

Mahogany bureau cabinet decorated overall with fine floral inlay. £3,000

Queen Anne oak bureau bookcase with brass drop handles. £680

Bureau bookcase with glazed doors. £1,550

18th century walnut bureau bookcase with mirrored doors. £1,900

Mid 18th century walnut and floral marquetry bureau-cabinet. £3,400

Victorian mahogany bureau bookcase painted with husk and floral chains, 2ft.8½ins. wide. £560

Edwardian mahogany bureau bookcase on cabriole legs, 92cm. wide. £200

Queen Anne walnut bureau cabinet decorated with crossbanding and feather-banding, 3ft. 3ins. wide. £1,950

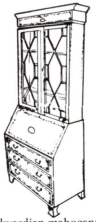

Edwardian mahogany inlaid bureau-bookcase, 3ft. wide. £250

Early 18th century walnut bureau-bookcase with damaged veneer, 2ft. 3ins. wide. £720

BUREAU BOOKCASES

Late 17th century walnut and marquetry bureau cabinet, 99cm. wide. £3,100

Superb walnut bureau bookcase by Stephen Wood of Southwark, with a double-domed top, 1m. wide £9,850

Small Queen Anne walnut bureau cabinet, 68.5cm. wide. £3,150

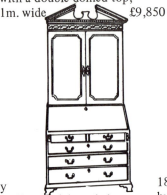

Late 19th century mahogany bureau bookcase decorated all over with inlaid leaves, scrolls and flowers. £1,450

Chippendale style bureau bookcase with broken arch pediment. £900

18th century mahogany bureau bookcase, decorated with bands of ivory and ebony, 39ins. wide. £2,000

Edwardian mahogany bureau bookcase with glazed doors and bracket feet, 100cm. wide. £230

Mid 18th century mahogany bureau bookcase with astragal glazed doors, 41ins. wide. £275

A superb early 19th century Dutch marquetry bureau cabinet, with a bombe front. £4,600

244

A fine quality Edwardian bureau bookcase with astragal doors and satinwood inlay, 33ins. wide £550

George I bureau cabinet, English, walnut veneer on oak, 76cm. wide. £4,800

19th century inlaid mahogany bureau bookcase with broken arch pediment, 3ft. wide. £900

19th century inlaid mahogany bureau bookcase, with astragal glazed doors and bracket feet, 93cm. wide. £440

Georgian mahogany bureau bookcase, 7ft. high, 3ft. 4ins. wide, 1ft. 10ins. deep. £650

Late 19th century mahogany bureau bookcase on cabriole legs. £110

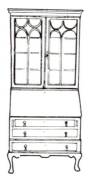

Hepplewhite satinwood bureau bookcase of elegant proportions. £4,800

Mahogany bureau bookcase on cabriole legs, with two glazed doors. £130

Early Georgian country-made bureau cabinet, with double-domed pediment, 40½ins. wide, 6ft. 9ins. high, 22ins. deep, in oak. £700

CABINETS

Small marquetry cabinet. £86

Ebonised wood cabinet attributed to P. Langlois, English, circa 1760. £6,500

One of a pair of French Empire style walnut, inlaid and kingwood banded pier cabinets.£1,000

Late 18th century cabinet on stand with Chinese decoration. £400

18th century Dutch marquetry display cabinet. £3,400

19th century Continental ebonised cabinet. £600

Early 18th century Flemish rosewood and red tortoiseshell cabinet, 1.35m. wide. £1,300

Mid 19th century French amboyna and tulipwood banded cabinet, 4ft. 4½in. wide. £1,000

Edwardian inlaid mahogany cabinet with astragal glazed doors. £310

Edwardian inlaid maho-
gany music cabinet of
six drawers, 3ft. 1in.
high: £50

Mid 19th century ebony
dwarf cabinet with lobed
white marble top, 120cm.
wide.   £400

19th century king-
wood and ormolu
mounted side cabi-
net.   £295

Oak cabinet by Moris
& Co., circa 1865.
                        £800

Mid 17th century Nether-
lands oak veneered cabi-
net on stand with silver,
ebony and tortoiseshell
decoration, 1.72m. wide.
                      £5,460

William and Mary
cabinet with ori-
ginal stand, circa
1690   £800

Dutch floral marquetry
and walnut glazed cabi-
net on matching bombe
chest, 6ft.4in.   £1,250

20th century mahogany
and marquetry display
cabinet by Moris of
Oxford Street.   £800

19th century Italian
walnut cabinet car-
ved with putti, 38½in.
wide.   £630

CABINETS

A Louis XV ebonised cabinet with burr walnut inlay and ormolu mounts. £1,750

Small 19th century Japanese lacquered cabinet of five drawers, 30cm. wide. £44

Edwardian inlaid mahogany music cabinet. £80

17th century vargueno in carved giltwood, from Equador. £300

Ebony and tortoiseshell-veneered 18th century Dutch cabinet, depicting bible scenes. £3,300

Wood and vellum cabinet by C. Bugatti, circa 1900. £267

Late 18th century cabinet of oyster pattern laburnum veneer on an oak stand.£550

Walnut and burr elm cabinet by Russell, circa 1928. £600

Georgian mahogany collector's cabinet, 63cm. wide. £170

One of a pair of French Louis XVI period cabinets, attributed to Adam Weisweiler, in oak veneered with ebony and inset with bronze and pietra dura plaques, 64cm. wide. £48,000

19th century ebonised and red boulle two-door side cabinet with ormolu mounts and marble top. £595

One of a pair of 19th century French cabinets. £850

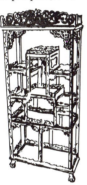

Chinese carved padoukwood etagere, 2ft. 6ins. wide. £210

William and Mary marquetry and walnut cabinet on stand. £700

Early 18th century Peruvian oratory cabinet in green painted wood. £800

Ornate Italian coromandel wood cabinet inlaid with variegated agates, 4ft. 10ins. wide. £2,900

William and Mary cabinet with elaborate marquetry decoration. £650

Small Chinese Chippendale-style cabinet. £260

CABINETS

German cabinet profusely inlaid with town scenes, musical trophies and flowers, 20½ins. wide, circa 1600. £820

A Ch'ien Lung black and gilt lacquered dwarf cabinet, 3ft. 8ins. wide. £340

Antique Spanish walnut-framed table top cabinet veneered with tortoise-shell panels with ivory borders, 16¼ins. wide. £220

Oak cabinet by Charles Rennie Mackintosh, circa 1905. £1,500

Victorian rosewood side cabinet inlaid with ivory and boxwood arabesques. £220

Continental oak cabinet, with moulded panels, on stand with baluster turned legs. £465

Victorian amboyna wood bonheur du jour mounted in ormolu with Sevres plaques, 44ins. wide. £900

18th century South European cabinet. £750

17th century Flemish oak armoire with original metalwork. £980

Unusual Sheraton
mahogany canter-
bury, circa 1780.
£500

Regency period
canterbury, with
drawer in the base.
£195

Victorian rosewood
music canterbury
with drawer. £100

Early 19th century
mahogany canterbury.
£145

George III mahogany
music canterbury.
£350

Hepplewhite style
mahogany canterbury,
circa 1785.   £365

Victorian burr walnut
canterbury with barley
twist divisions and a
drawer at the base. £75

Victorian burr walnut
music canterbury with
fretwork partitions.
£115

Early 19th century
mahogany music
canterbury.   £210

One of a set of six Victorian mahogany dining chairs. £140

One of a set of four 19th century mahogany dining chairs. £80

One of a set of five late 19th century mahogany chairs on turned legs. £50

Carved oak hall chair with hardwood seat. £22

One of a pair of George III mahogany spar back dining chairs. £37

One of a set of three 19th century marquetry dining chairs. £160

One of a pair of country made elm chairs with pierced splats. £14

One of two stained chairs of Cromwellian design with leather panel backs and seats. £26

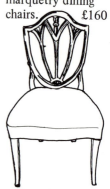

One of two Hepplewhite style mahogany shield back chairs. £40

One of a set of
six George III
mahogany dining
chairs.   £420

Part of a set of six
Victorian mahogany
dining chairs.   £160

One of a set of
eight 19th century
mahogany dining
chairs.   £340

One of a set of
four Victorian
mahogany chairs.
          £45

Victorian cast iron cir-
cular verandah chair
with acanthus leaf back.
               £18

Charles II walnut
high back chair with
velvet loose cushions.
               £130

One of a set of six
Victorian rosewood
dining chairs. £300

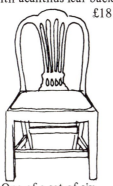

One of a set of six
Hepplewhite chairs.
               £800

One of a set of five
Victorian rosewood
dining chairs. £135

DINING CHAIRS

One of a set of six light mahogany chairs, circa 1870.   £245

One of a set of six George II red walnut dining chairs.   £780

One of a set of six mahogany Regency style dining chairs on sabre front legs.   £280

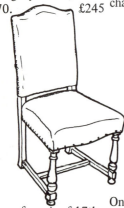

One of a pair of 17th century oak standard chairs.   £195

One of four Victorian salon chairs in mahogany with centre oval padded back panels, on delicate cabriole legs.   £310

One of a set of eight oak chairs, mid-19th century, leather seat.   £420

One of a set of six rosewood dining chairs, circa 1830.   £425

A small straight-back chair in ebonised wood, designed by Charles Rennie Mackintosh, 40ins. high.   £1,400

One of a set of four rosewood dining chairs with carved ball and turnball designs.   £80

Queen Anne single oak chair in original condition, 39ins. high, circa 1705. £58

One of a set of six Victorian walnut dining chairs. £180

A French provincial oak low seat. £60

One of a pair of 17th century oak standard chairs. £195

One of four mahogany dining chairs. £70

Set of four Adam style mahogany dining chairs. £460

One of a set of eight Hepplewhite style dining chairs. £600

One of a set of six Victorian mahogany dining chairs on cabriole legs. £300

One of a set of six George II fruitwood chairs with leather seats, circa 1740. £880

DINING CHAIRS

One of a set of four stained dining chairs on cabriole legs. £28

One of a set of six Chippendale style oak chairs, circa 1870. £275

One of a pair of Victorian carved oak hall chairs. £37

One of a pair of oak chairs, circa 1700. £110

One of three late 19th century ladder back chairs. £24

One of a set of six William and Mary style chairs, 19th century. £365

One of a set of four Victorian walnut chairs. £175

Mahogany chair with pierced ladder back. £24

One of a set of six oak chairs, circa 1800. £135

One of a set of six late 18th century Hepplewhite mahogany dining chairs.£290

One of a set of six carved oak 19th century Charles II style chairs with dished seats. £585

One of three George III mahogany dining chairs. £60

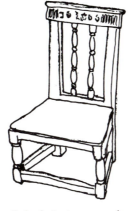

One of a set of six Dutch marquetry walnut chairs.£1,600

Oak chair, top carved and dated 1666. £48

Unusual laminated Regency period dining chair.   £155

One of a set of eight Sheraton style dining chairs.   £1,280

One of a set of six mahogany dining chairs.   £950

One of a set of eight draught back chairs, circa 1830.   £485

DINING CHAIRS

One of a set of ten ladder-back chairs in oak with rerushed loose seats, circa 1850. £685

One of a set of three Edwardian mahogany dining chairs with pierced splats. £38

One of a set of three Regency mahogany sabre leg chairs, circa 1810. £100

One of a set of six Victorian walnut cabriole leg chairs. £300

One of a set of six Yorkshire chairs with rush seats, 34ins. high, circa 1840. £175

One of a set of six Victorian mahogany dining chairs. £170

One of a set of five oak chairs of medium colour, circa 1800. £125

One of a set of six late 18th century Italian walnut chairs, heightened in gilt. £2,100

19th century child's chair in elm. £10

One of a set of four early 19th century French carved walnut chairs on cabriole legs. £130

One of a set of seven Regency period chairs in simulated rosewood, circa 1830. £245

One of a set of ten Regency mahogany dining chairs. £480

Queen Anne walnut side chair with pad feet, circa 1710. £85

One of a set of six Continental high-back chairs with cane seats and backs, 46ins. high, circa 1790. £495

Chippendale mahogany chair, carved top rail. £102

One of a set of twelve Regency period carved rosewood dining chairs with sabre legs. £2,100

One of a set of six Victorian walnut dining chairs on turned legs £115

Mahogany chair with solid splat and upholstered seat, on cabriole legs. £22

DINING CHAIRS

One of a set of ten Regency rosewood dining chairs. £660

One of a set of four Edwardian beech ladder back chairs. £28

One of a set of six spindle back rush seated chairs, circa 1770. £475

One of a pair of Charles II ash high back chairs. £290

One of a set of five Regency sabre-legged chairs in simulated rosewood, circa 1810. £270

One of a set of six 19th century mahogany sabre leg chairs. £230

One of a set of six Victorian walnut balloon back chairs. £300

One of a set of eight 19th century mahogany dining chairs. £270

One of a set of six Victorian rosewood boudoir chairs. £310

19th century mahogany dining chair with pierced vase shaped splat.   £10

18th century French oak bow seated chair.   £60

Queen Anne style walnut chair with ladder back. £115

One of a set of nine oak spoon back chairs on turned legs.   £95

One of a set of six Georgian period dark mahogany chairs, circa 1820.   £395

One of a set of six George III mahogany dining chairs.   £220

Victorian carved oak hall chair with hardwood seat.   £20

One of a set of twelve Regency rosewood dining chairs. £2,700

Victorian Gothic style carved oak hall chair.   £10

DINING CHAIRS

One of a pair of bamboo bedroom chairs.   £50

One of a set of eight mahogany bar back chairs on turned legs, circa 1835. £400

Edwardian inlaid mahogany dining chair.   £8

One of a set of six walnut side chairs with cabriole front legs, circa 1710.   £1,490

Walnut highback chair elaborately carved, circa 1675.   £150

One of a set of four 17th century carved walnut chairs. £600

Early 19th century Dutch marquetry chair with sabre legs.   £75

One of a set of six walnut chairs with fiddle back splats, circa 1740. £2,500

One of a pair of George III mahogany dining chairs with pierced splats.   £40

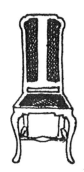

William and Mary period walnut single chair, splat with herringbone inlay. £110

19th century beechwood child's chair with caned seat. £11

Late 18th century oak dining chair. £20

Charles II walnut high back chair. £140

George III elm kitchen chair with a hard seat. £5

One of a set of six James II dining chairs with cane seats and splats, circa 1685. £2,950

Victorian oak hall chair on turned legs. £10

One of a set of four Victorian walnut chairs with cabriole legs. £185

One of a set of six spindle bobbin doll's chairs, circa 1800. £275

263

DINING CHAIRS

Two of a set of twelve 18th century Hepplewhite mahogany shield back chairs. £1,800

Two of a set of eight mahogany dining chairs with pierced splats and ball and claw feet. £420

Part of a set of six mahogany Chippendale style dining chairs with pierced splats and cabriole legs, one arm and five single. £360

Set of eight 19th century bar back chairs on turned legs. £320

Part of a set of two arm and two single 19th century elm ladder back chars.£45

Part of a set of six Regency rosewood sabre leg dining chairs. £500

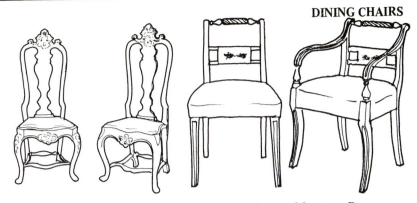

Pair of 18th century Portugese rosewood dining chairs.   £700

Two of a set of fourteen Regency
mahogany chairs, with sabre legs,
rope twist head rails and panel
backs inlaid with ebony. £2,500

Part of a set of nine, eight single
and one carver, Regency mahogany sabre leg chairs.   £520

Part of a set of six and two
Hepplewhite dining chairs
in mahogany.   £1,000

Part of a set of eight Chippendale
style chairs with pierced ladder
backs and square moulded legs.£380

Two of a set of twelve Chippendale
design mahogany chairs.   £1,500

DINING CHAIRS

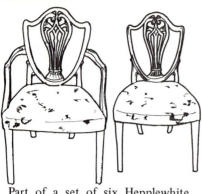

Part of a set of six Hepplewhite style mahogany dining chairs with carved shield shaped backs. £340

Part of a set of twelve, two arm and ten single, mahogany dining chairs with carved and pierced Gothic splats. £600

Part of a set of ten Hepplewhite carved mahogany dining chairs. £2,350

Part of a set of eight Chippendale style mahogany dining chairs. £500

Part of a set of twelve Chippendale style dining chairs (two arm and ten single). £425

Part of a set of one arm and three single Regency sabre leg mahogany dining chairs. £85

Two of a set of six 19th century mahogany dining chairs with spar backs and square tapered legs. £160

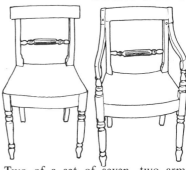

Two of a set of seven, two arm and five single, Victorian mahogany dining chairs. £120

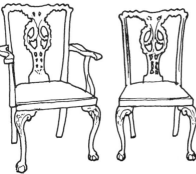

Two of a set of eight Chippendale style mahogany dining chairs with shaped top rails.£480

Two of a set of five Hepplewhite style chairs, three dining and two elbow. £110

Two of a set of eight mahogany inlaid dining chairs, two arm and six single. £380

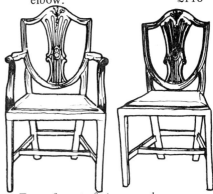

Two of a set of eleven mahogany dining chairs, backs of Hepplewhite design, (two arm and nine single). £480

DINING CHAIRS

Two of a set of six mahogany dining chairs with serpentine fronted seats. £550

Two Charles II chairs, different. £270 pair

Two of a set of fourteen Victorian oak chairs in the 'Jacobean' style. £700

Two of a set of twelve single and two arm Victorian oak dining chairs with heavily carved backs, turned legs and stretchers. £650

Two of a set of twelve Chippendale period dining chairs with claw and ball feet. £1,800

Two of a set of six mahogany chairs with 'Prince of Wales' carved backs, circa 1860. £445

Elm rocking chair with rush seat, circa 1800. £65

One of a set of five late 18th century yew wood Windsor chairs.   £530

One of a set of four pine chairs, circa 1900. £100

One of a set of four Gothic Revival chairs. £6,000

Child's Chinese bamboo chair, circa 1880.   £28

East Anglican oak wainscot chair, circa 1700. £232

Early elm country armchair on turned legs with stretchers. £65

George I oak wainscot chair.   £90

Yew wood Windsor chair with straight legs and crinoline stretcher.   £165

ELBOW CHAIRS

Edwardian inlaid tub chair on turned legs. £24

Louis XV beech-wood chair on cabriole legs, circa 1750. £180

Yew wood backed wheel chair, circa 1780. £95

One of a pair of oak thrown-chairs, original condition. £225

One of a pair of Spanish walnut armchairs, circa 1700. £420

Mid 17th century upholstered 'X' frame chair. £250

One of a set of eight oak dining chairs, 17th century. £840

One of a set of six reproduction oak dining chairs. £370

One of two Edwardian mahogany inlaid tub chairs on cabriole legs. £70

Stained corner chair
with cane back and
seat.   £18

One of a pair of
Sheraton style
elbow chairs, in
mahogany, circa
1810.   £155

One of a pair of country-
made rocking chairs with
bobbin turned splats,
circa 1830.   £160

Edwardian mahogany
tub chair on turned
legs.   £24

One of a pair of
Chinese padouk-
wood elbow chairs.
                  £200

17th century oak
armchair with
scroll carving.£750

Charles II carved
walnut armchair.
            £150

One of a set of six
Chippendale ribbon
back chairs, circa
1850.   £395

Edwardian mahogany
and marquetry inlaid
armchair.   £52

ELBOW CHAIRS

One of a pair of Victorian scroll armchairs on turned legs. £67

Elm high ladder-back armchair with rush seat. £20

Mahogany bergere armchair on square tapered legs with Adam designs. £22

Georgian mahogany desk chair, circa 1820. £115

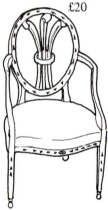

An Adam style cream and green enamelled armchair with oval back. £100

Indian carved teak armchair on turned legs and stretchers. £80

One of a set of eight oak chairs, circa 1800. £295

William IV marquetry carver chair with scroll arms. £175

One of a set of 12 Chippendale mahogany dining chairs. £1,600

George III walnut
Captain's chair with
solid walnut seat,
circa 1760.   £78

18th century elm
splat back chair.
£32

Mahogany elbow chair
in mid 18th century
style with tapestry
work seat.   £65

Mahogany armchair
on cabriole legs. £30

Decorated Sheraton
armchair, cane seat,
circa 1790.   ·£140

Late 18th century
Chippendale maho-
gany scroll arm
elbow chair. £370

Yew-wood Windsor
chair with straight
legs and crinoline
stretcher.   £145

A giltwood bergere
chair, circa 1830.
£180

Regency period
ebonised elbow
chair.   £75

EASY CHAIRS

Victorian carved oak
open armchair. £30

George III mahogany wing
chair with carved paw feet
and cabriole legs. £3,500

Victorian carved
walnut high back
armchair. £52

Queen Anne faded
walnut wing chair,
circa 1712. £1,160

George I elm wing
armchair, circa
1725. £850

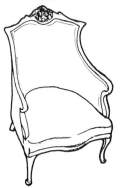

Mahogany framed
circle back easy chair.
£50

George I mahogany
wing armchair. £2,550

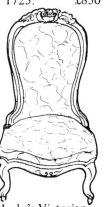

Lady's Victorian
carved walnut easy
chair. £145

Oak armchair. £14

Hepplewhite elbow chair with cabriole legs. £320

A Victorian stained and carved armchair on spiral legs and stretchers. £44

One of a set of four Louis XVI design gilt fauteuils. £1,900

Victorian rosewood circle back armchair covered in green velvet on turned legs. £30

Queen Anne wing chair with 'C' scroll arms, circa 1705. £1,500

Beech-framed caned campaign chair. £18

Mahogany open armchair with hoop panel back. £30

Wicker beach chair with hood. £48

One of a pair of Sheraton painted elbow chairs. £700

EASY CHAIRS

Lady's Victorian walnut chair on turned legs. £32

One of a suite of four Louis XV fauteuils by Nogaret of Lyon. £2,780

Victorian lady's carved mahogany easy chair. £90

Tub-shaped wing chair in Hepplewhite manner, circa 1790. £775

James II wing chair with elaborately carved scroll-work, circa 1685. £1,750

George I walnut wing chair with scroll arms. £1,650

Victorian carved mahogany easy chair on cabriole legs. £220

George I walnut wing chair, circa 1720. £1,800

Late 19th century carved mahogany arm chair. £30

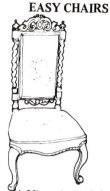

Victorian rocking chair, the panel back and seat in uncut moquette. £34

Gentleman's Victorian mahogany easy chair on turned legs. £105

A Victorian lady's chair covered in sewedwork, on cabriole legs. £70

Lug easy chair on cabriole legs. £95

Victorian walnut devotional chair on cabriole legs. £80

Regency tub shaped wing chair with mahogany legs, circa 1820 £205

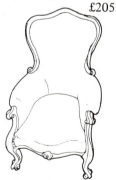

Victorian carved mahogany easy chair on turned legs. £75

Queen Anne walnut wing chair with scroll arms and diamond shaped feet. £2,550

Gentleman's Victorian mahogany easy chair. £155

EASY CHAIRS

One of a set of six William and Mary walnut chairs.
£440

Victorian steel-framed rocking chair with leather upholstery.
£130

19th century Italian style black painted open arm chair with scroll legs and stretchers.
£57

Shell-shaped Victorian button-back bedroom chair.
£60

Georgian mahogany library chair on shaped legs.
£210

Lady's Victorian carved easy chair in mahogany.
£70

One of a rare pair of Louis XV large fauteuils stamped J. Blanchard. £9,445

French 19th century sedan chair lacquered cabinet embellished with ormolu mounts in the style of Vernis Martin, 51½ins. high, 22½ins. wide, 18½ins. deep. £795

One of a pair of French style walnut open arm chairs on cabriole legs.
£380

William and Mary marquetry chest with intricate foliate designs, 97cm. wide.   £2,100

Georgian mahogany serpentine-front chest on splay feet, 3ft. 6ins. wide. £800

A mahogany chest of drawers, circa 1840, 40ins. wide.   £215

A small Queen Anne walnut chest of four long graduated drawers, with fitted slide to the frieze, 24in. wide.   £2,000

Mid-19th century mahogany chest of three long and two short graduated drawers, on splay feet.   £45

Jacobean style oak chest of drawers on bracket feet.   £105

Good quality Victorian rosewood Wellington chest of seven drawers, 2ft. wide.   £110

Victorian mahogany chest of drawers.   £60

Tall mahogany secretaire chest with fitted interior.   £1,800

Queen Anne walnut chest of four graduated drawers with a fitted brushing slide, 32in. wide.   £700

Georgian mahogany bonnet chest with brushing slide and original handles, about 1760.   £265

Queen Anne walnut bachelor's chest, early 18th century.   £5,750

Mahogany chest commode, circa 1798.   £65

Rare captain's secretaire chest from China, ivory inlays, circa 1850, rich walnut colour.   £385

Late 18th century bow fronted chest with brushing slide, 3ft.2in. wide.   £260

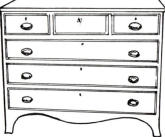

Small mahogany chest of drawers, 2ft. 9in. wide, circa 1810. £155

Early 19th century mahogany straight front chest with shaped apron and splayed feet, 3ft.3in. wide.   £85

An Edwardian walnut chest of drawers with pierced brass handles.   £15

19th century mahogany chest of four long drawers, on bracket feet, 84cm. wide. £85

William and Mary oak bonnet chest with moulded front drawers, about 1690, 3ft.3in. high x 3ft.5in. wide x 1ft.8in. deep. £750

George III mahogany chest with brass drop handles, 89cm. wide. £190

Mahogany chest of drawers with brushing slide, good colour, circa 1770. £335

Charles II cedarwood chest of drawers inlaid with walnut and ebony, about 1670. £590

Small late 18th century mahogany chest of drawers, 32½in. wide. £825

17th century Bergamo marquetry chest with shaped front. £700

Faded mahogany and satinwood serpentine fronted chest of drawers, about 1820. £350

Queen Anne walnut chest with marquetry panels and bracket feet, 95cm. wide.£300

CHESTS

19th century inlaid mahogany chest, 3ft. 6ins. wide. £55

Arts and Crafts Movement amboyna and satinwood chest of drawers, 2ft. 9ins. high x 2ft. 7½ins. wide x 1ft. 10ins. deep. £325

Early 19th century oak mahogany and inlaid chest of five drawers, 121 cm. wide. £95

Mahogany French chest of drawers of unusual design, ormolu mounts, 36ins. wide, 33ins. high, circa 1850. £215

Late 18th century oak Yorkshire chest of drawers with crossbanding round the edge of the drawers, 3ft. 11ins. high x 3ft. 4 ins. wide x 1ft. 9ins. deep. £170

Georgian pine chest of drawers with splayed feet, 3ft.6in. high x 3ft.6in. wide x 1ft. 8½in. deep. £68

Oak chest of three long and two short drawers, 3ft. 6ins. wide. £50

Late 18th century mahogany serpentine fronted chest of drawers. £600

Late 17th century oak chest of four long drawers. £600

Early 19th century inlaid mahogany chest of five drawers on bracket feet, 104cm. wide.   £65

Walnut chest of drawers, 19ins. x 38ins. x 42ins. high, circa 1720.   £366

Small faded mahogany chest of drawers on bracket feet, about 1770-80, 2ft. 8ins. high x 3ft. wide x 1ft. 6ins. deep.   £485

Queen Anne walnut bachelor's chest, 81cm. wide. £2,300

Quaint poker work chest of drawers, signed by Laura Allsop, 35ins. wide x 32ins. high, circa 1845.   £165

Elegant Georgian mahogany chest of drawers, circa 1775, 3ft. wide, 20in. deep, 2ft. 11in. high.   £245

Early 19th century inlaid chest of three long and two short drawers, 3ft. 8ins. wide.   £105

18th century walnut veneered chest, 82cm. wide.   £300

Two-part military chest, fully brass-bound with iron carrying handles, circa 1850, 42ins. long x 18ins. deep x 42ins. high. £215

283

CHESTS

Early 19th century oak chest of two long and two short drawers, 2ft. 10in. wide. £52

19th century mahogany mule chest with hinged lid, having four actual and four dummy drawers below, 178cm. wide. £115

French Provincial walnut veneered chest of drawers, Charles X period, circa 1820. £250

Regency mahogany bow fronted chest of drawers with ebony crossbanding, about 1810, 3ft.5in. high x 3ft.4in. wide x 1ft.10in. deep. £345

Mid 17th century oak chest of drawers with moulded fronts. £600

William and Mary period inlaid burr walnut chest on bun feet. £720

Small George IV mahogany chest of three long and two short drawers, 67cm. wide. £130

A marquetry Wellington chest stamped by Edward & Roberts, 24in. high. £420

Late 19th century walnut chest of three long and two short drawers on a plinth base. £20

George I walnut and yew wood parquetry chest inlaid with satinwood, 39in. wide.   £500

William and Mary period oak cushion moulded chest, circa 1695, 2ft. 10in. wide.   £335

Small early 19th century mahogany chest of four long drawers.   £110

Queen Anne walnut bachelor's chest, with crossbanding and featherbanding, 26in. wide.   £1,050

Oak chest of drawers with moulded fronts, 41in. wide, circa 1760.   £345

George III mahogany bow fronted chest, 35in. wide.   £90

George III mahogany chest of three long and three short drawers, 110cm. wide.   £110

Small bow fronted mahogany chest of drawers, 2ft. 9½in. wide.   £102

William and Mary walnut and crossbanded chest on bun feet, 94cm. wide.   £230

CHEST ON CHEST

George III mahogany tallboy with original handles, 47½ins. wide. £325

18th century ebonised tallboy decorated in the Chinese manner, 128 cm. wide, as found . £290

18th century oak tallboy of four long and four short drawers, on bracket feet £170

Attractive Chippendale mahogany tallboy. £355

George I walnut tallboy on bracket feet. £1.100

Queen Anne period walnut tallboy chest with sunburst. £1,400

An early George I walnut tallboy chest of six long and three short drawers, 97cm. wide. £820

George III inlaid mahogany tallboy with carved fretwork canted corners, 104cm. wide. £270

Mid-18th century mahogany chest on chest, 44ins. wide. £170

18th century oak chest on stand of rich brown colour, 38ins. wide. £400

18th century oak chest on stand, with drop handles. £260

William IV walnut chest on stand with barley twist supports. £545

18th century cross-banded and oyster veneered chest on stand. £700

Walnut chest on stand with original handles, circa 1700, 44ins. wide, 64ins. high. £725

Early 18th century walnut chest on stand. £310

Early 18th century walnut veneered and boxwood strung chest on stand. £380

Charles II period walnut veneered chest on stand, with marquetry decoration, 5ft. 3ins. high, 48½ins. wide, 1ft. 8ins. deep, circa 1685. £5,000

Chest on stand with crossbanded drawers, circa 1800, 37½ins. wide. £385

CHIFFONIERS

Regency mahogany chiffonier with scroll supports. £330

Early 19th century rosewood chiffonier with unusual fretted door panels, 15½ins. deep, 54ins. wide, 49ins. tall. £225

Regency rosewood and inlaid bookcase, 31in. wide. £1,120

Regency chiffonier on turned legs, with brass grilles to the doors. £625

Finely figured mahogany Regency chiffonier with high patina medium faded colour, 3ft. 1in. wide, 1ft. 4ins. deep, 4ft. high. £295

Rare rosewood secretaire in original condition, cedarwood lined drawers and ormolu mounts, 3ft. 8ins. wide, 1ft. 8ins. deep, 4ft. 10ins. high. £748

Victorian mahogany chiffonier, with arched panel doors. £18

Marble-topped Regency rosewood chiffonier in breakfront style, 4ft. 8½ins. wide, 1ft. 9ins. deep, 3ft. high. £295

Regency rosewood writing desk, 37ins. wide. £580

Fine quality Edwardian satinwood display cabinet in the Hepplewhite style, inset with Wedgwood medallions, 4ft. wide. £1,000

Edwardian mahogany oblong curio table on cabriole legs with under-shelf, 64cm. wide. £55

19th century mahogany china cabinet with astragal glazed doors, 1.22m. wide. £150

Unusual Oriental bamboo china cabinet, circa 1900. £100

Breakfront walnut cabinet, raised on dwarf cabriole legs, carved and lightly gilded, circa 1850, 5ft. wide, 1ft. 9ins. deep, 4ft. 6ins. high. £325

19th century mahogany cabinet with sphinx monopodia to columns, 86ins. high. £195

Mahogany, collector's cabinet in form of miniature chest of drawers, with china cabinet above, 35ins. high, 25½ins. wide, 7½ins. deep, circa 1830. £285

Mahogany, serpentine display cabinet veneered with ebony, and with white marble top, 45ins. wide, 34ins. high. £300

19th century satinwood collector's cabinet. £550

CHINA CABINETS

One of a pair of Georgian mahogany glazed front display cabinets, 43in. wide. £135

19th century marquetry bijouterie table with glazed top and sides, 62cm. wide. £120

Mahogany inlaid bow front china cabinet, 3ft. 4ins. high. £32

19th century satinwood display cabinet decorated in the Sheraton manner, 48ins. wide. £720

18th century Dutch walnut marquetry display cabinet, 60ins. wide. £1,400

Oak china cabinet of Flemish design with scroll pediment, on cabriole legs. £320

19th century French vitrine in rosewood with inlaid flowers, 3ft. wide x 6ft. high. £495

Walnut Dutch marquetry display cabinet. £1,400

French kingwood vitrine of Louis XV design, 57ins. wide. £1,050

Edwardian mahogany china cabinet enclosed by three glazed doors, 4ft. 6in. wide. £70

Ebonised oblong display table on cabriole legs. £58

Mid 18th century pine buffet, about 1760. £550

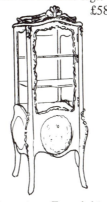

Edwardian inlaid mahogany china cabinet with bow centre and glazed gables, 3ft 6in wide. £80

19th century French kingwood vitrine with serpentine front and sides and chased ormolu mounts, 31in. x 69in. £1,495

French kingwood and mahogany vitrine, enclosed by two glazed doors, on cabriole legs, 3ft. 6in. wide. £200

18th century French provincial pine buffet, 55 in. wide. £575

Victorian walnut and ebony banded china cabinet, 183 cm wide. £200

French Empire style display cabinet with mirror back, 30in by 72in. £610

COMMODE AND POT CUPBOARDS

Victorian mahogany pot stand, with fluted sides and marble top. £35

Mahogany arm seat with hinged panel back and box seat. £38

Mahogany circular bedside cupboard, 2ft. 6ins. high. £30

19th century satinwood inlaid mahogany bedside stand with tambour front. £48

Georgian style mahogany bedside cupboard with tray top and drawer below. £65

Edwardian mahogany bedside cupboard. £8

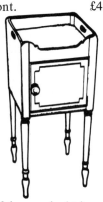

Mahogany bedside cupboard with tray top. £35

Georgian mahogany commode cupboard (converted to a cocktail cabinet) 22in. wide.£80

19th century square tray-topped bedside cupboard. £42

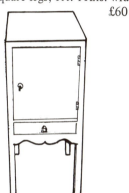

Georgian style mahogany oblong tray top bedside cupboard with drawer, on square legs, 1ft. 11ins. wide. £60

Mahogany inlaid square bedside stand with under-shelf and a drawer.   £36

George III mahogany tray top commode with drawer and cupboard.   £75

Mahogany and rosewood banded square bedside cupboard with a drawer.   £28

Early 19th century mahogany tray top commode.   £100

A mahogany square bedside cupboard, with tray top and standing on turned legs.   £30

A mahogany inlaid bow front commode with hinged top and front of simulated drawers, 2ft. 1in. wide.   £45

Victorian mahogany one step commode on short turned legs.   £10

18th century mahogany pot cupboard with a fretted frieze.   £75

COMMODE CHESTS

19th century French commode chest in kingwood with marquetry inlay £495

18th century kingwood commode chest, 47 ins. wide £1,250

Fine transitional commode by P. A. Foullet. £21,000

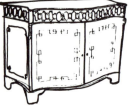

18th century English commode in yew wood and sycamore veneers. £1,850

Louis XV kingwood commode stamped N.A. Lapie. £2,200

Fine Louis XV commode in oak with serpentine front, 35 ins. high x 51 ins. wide x 25 ins. deep £1,250

18th century Scandinavian walnut commode £1,500

19th century French purplewood and harewood commode. £550

One of a pair of French 19th
century commode cabinets.£7,000

French provincial oak serpentine
commode, about 1750. £1,850

18th century Genoese cream painted and decorated bombe commode £2,300

17th century Italian walnut and
inlaid serpentine commode.£1,550

19th century Continental inlaid
walnut shaped front commode,
64in. wide.   £360

18th century French provincial
walnut serpentine bombe commode,
51 ins. wide   £1,250

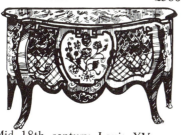

Mid 18th century Louis XV
style marquetry commode
with a Breccia marble top. £6,300

French rosewood and marquetry
inlaid serpentine front commode
                              £520

COMMODE CHESTS

18th century Dutch marquetry commode on paw feet. £560

Louis XV walnut commode, 50ins. wide. £850

Small marble topped commode. £1,770

Miniature commode in honey coloured walnut, 24ins. wide, circa 1790. £475

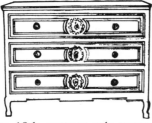

Late 18th century oak commode with leaf decoration, 50ins. wide, circa 1780. £1,400

18th century German commode chest with parquetry decoration. £1,000

French ormolu mounted rosewood commode with a white veined marble top after Guillaume Benneman, 7ft. wide x 3ft. 3ins. high. £1,700

One of a pair of late George III ivory painted bedroom commodes, 97cm. wide. £869

Faded mahogany corner cupboard, circa 1820, on a later stand, 38ins. wide. £245

George III mahogany bow-fronted cupboard with two doors, 105cm. high. £145

Attractive inlaid mahogany bow-fronted corner cabinet, 36ins. wide, circa 1840. £285

Walnut bow-fronted corner cupboard, circa 1730. £155

Victorian mahogany wall medicine cabinet with a glazed door, 58cm. wide. £22

18th century oak carved display cabinet with astragal glazed door. £84

19th century oak corner cupboard enclosed by panelled doors, 2.30 m high £140

Late 18th century oak corner cupboard with panelled doors. £160

19th century white painted pine corner cupboard, 2.11m. high. £50

CORNER CUPBOARDS

Continental rosewood corner cupboard with scroll shaped pediment, 7ft. high. £180

Late 19th century satinwood standing corner display cabinet, 42in. wide. £270

19th century pine corner cupboard with panel door above and below. £90

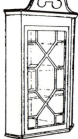

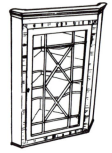

19th century mahogany corner cupboard with an astragal glazed door. £70

Mahogany bow-fronted corner cupboard, circa 1750. £145

19th century mahogany corner cupboard with glazed door. £60

Late 18th century Dutch marquetry standing corner cupboard, 50 in. wide. £880

Mahogany inlaid corner cupboard, 5ft 8in. high. £205

Dutch marquetry cupboard. £1,400

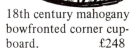

19th century inlaid mahogany and satinwood banded corner cupboard.£360

George III mahogany bowfronted corner cupboard with panelled doors. £165

Georgian mahogany corner cupboard with glazed door.   £240

18th century oak corner cupboard, 3ft 6in.   £65

A carved oak corner cupboard the panel door with inlaid motifs of shell and print.   £85

18th century mahogany bowfronted corner cupboard.   £248

One of a pair of Edwardian corner cupboards.   £380

George III pinewood corner cupboard.£120

Oak corner cupboard with glazed door.   £155

COURT CUPBOARDS

A late 17th century oak tridarn, 53ins. wide. £760

17th century oak court cupboard, bearing the date 1675. £350

17th century oak court cupboard with carved cornice, 64½ins. wide. £640

18th century oak tridarn with fielded decoration. £820

Carved oak hall court cupboard, 3ft. 6ins. wide. £70

A 17th century oak tridarn, the frieze and central cupboards carved with rosettes and geometric design, 66ins. wide. £560

Oak duodarn with carved borders and pilasters, 1.75m. high. £420

A 17th century oak court cupboard, 61 ins wide. £700

Jacobean oak court cupboard of good colour, 82ins. high. £410

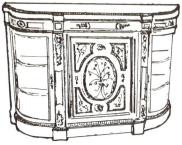

French ebonised Pietra Dura credenza, 6ft. wide. £560

Victorian walnut and marquetry credenza with velvet-lined shelves and ormolu mounts, 67ins. wide. £820

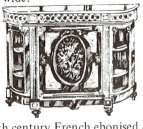

19th century French ebonised cabinet inlaid with hardstone and boullework. £650

19th century boulle credenza with ormolu mounts. £290

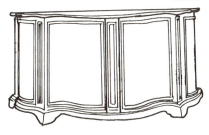

18th century Venetian buffet, 2.54m. wide. £2,500

One of a pair of walnut and satinwood serpentine-front cabinets. £1,050

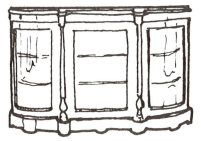

A Victorian walnut credenza with bowed glass ends, 1.75m. long. £540

Victorian walnut inlaid, banded and marquetry serpentine-fronted cabinet of French design, 5ft. 3ins. wide. £500

CUPBOARDS

Late 18th century marquetry buffet with rising top, 39½ins. wide. £400

Queen Anne oak cupboard. £260

Early oak food hutch. £650

17th century oak hall cupboard, 59ins. wide. £480

18th century Flemish oak cupboard. £325

Massive oak cupboard, 16th century, 49½ins. wide, 66ins. high. £650

A fine 18th century oak livery cupboard, handles not original, 72ins. high. £300

Fine 17th century carved oak Flemish cupboard. £3,600

Early 18th century oak Continental cupboard with painted decoration, 1.29cm. wide. £1,650

Late 17th century Dutch carved and ebonised Kas, 1.65m. wide.   £2,500

French 18th century walnut bread hutch, 32ins. wide.   £450

Oak cupboard by Heal and Sons, circa 1905. £100

17th century oak cupboard, 5ft. 2ins. tall.   £340

18th century French oak double cupboard.   £740

19th century faience store on claw feet with a black marble top.   £330

George III oak cupboard, 53½in. wide.   £260

18th century oak cupboard, 60ins. wide, 78ins. high.   £175

17th century side cupboard, inlaid with ivory and mother-of-pearl.   £650

Regency mahogany davenport, 20ins. wide. £400

Victorian, inlaid burr walnut davenport with four drawers to the side, 55cm. wide. £150

Fine quality Regency rosewood davenport, the top of which slides forward for writing. £365

Regency period rosewood davenport. £395

Victorian, walnut davenport writing desk, 2ft. 1in. wide, with four drawers to side enclosed by a door. £250

Unusual rosewood davenport with carved corners, the slide forward top with fitted interior, 19ins. x 23ins. x 34ins. high, circa 1830. £445

Victorian burr walnut davenport inlaid with boxwood. £440

Victorian, satin birch veneered and inlaid davenport, 58cm. wide. £180

Victorian burr walnut davenport. £260

Small Victorian walnut davenport. £130

Victorian walnut davenport. £220

Oak davenport with sliding top, pen drawer, and two slides, 22ins. x 20ins. x 37ins. high, circa 1820. £268

Fine Regency davenport in mahogany, the side cupboard with four drawers and rare spring-operated secret compartment, circa 1820, 21½ins. wide x 21½ins. deep. £550

Attractive Regency rosewood davenport, with shelf over and fitted maple interior, 27ins. wide. £390

Pale chestnut-coloured rosewood Regency davenport, 19½ins. wide, 21ins. deep, 37ins. high. £385

Early 19th century mahogany sliding top davenport. £255

George IV rosewood davenport with sliding top, 19ins. wide. £270

Mahogany davenport desk with leather covered writing slides, circa 1830. £400

DRESSERS

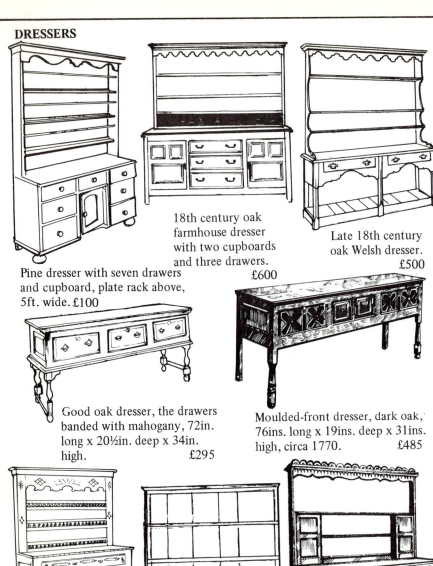

18th century oak
farmhouse dresser
with two cupboards
and three drawers.
£600

Late 18th century
oak Welsh dresser.
£500

Pine dresser with seven drawers
and cupboard, plate rack above,
5ft. wide. £100

Good oak dresser, the drawers
banded with mahogany, 72in.
long x 20½in. deep x 34in.
high.   £295

Moulded-front dresser, dark oak,
76ins. long x 19ins. deep x 31ins.
high, circa 1770.   £485

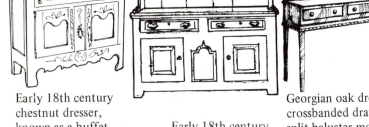

Early 18th century
chestnut dresser,
known as a buffet-
vaisselier, 55ins. wide. £945

Early 18th century
oak dresser.   £500

Georgian oak dresser with
crossbanded drawers and
split baluster moulding,
72in. long.   £575

Early Georgian country-made farmhouse dresser, 7ft. wide x 6ft. 8in. high x 20½in. deep. £925

Georgian oak dresser with cabriole legs and three drawers. £620

18th century Welsh oak tridarn. £800

An 18th century oak dresser base. £395

Charles II oak dresser of three drawers, 7ft. wide. £780

19th century pine potboard dresser. £225

Late Georgian Welsh oak dresser, 72 ins. wide. £900

Oak potboard dresser with rack, circa 1800, 5ft. 3ins. wide. £525

Charles II oak dresser with geometric
moulding on the three drawers, 6ft.
wide.   £1,000

Welsh oak dresser with five drawers,
74ins. long, 20ins. deep, 34ins. high,
circa 1840.   £450

Attractive oak Delft
rack, circa 1740,
46ins. wide x 45½ins.
high.   £125

Small oak and fruitwood
dresser, 4ft. 6ins. wide,
circa 1800.   £575

Victorian carved oak
open plate rack,
107cm. wide.   £20

A fine early Georgian yew wood dresser
of four drawers, supported on cabriole
legs.   £1,100

17th century oak dresser base, 7ft. 9ins.
wide.   £1,000

18th century oak dresser, 37½ins. tall, 19ins. deep, 6ft. 6ins. long.   £550

18th century oak dresser on cabriole front supports.   £570

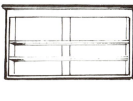

Large, late 18th century, North Country oak dresser.   £700

Oak Delft rack, circa 1740, 72ins. wide x 41ins. high.   £125

18th century oak crossbanded dresser on cabriole legs.   £760

18th century serving dresser, circa 1780.   £250

Jacobean oak dresser base, with three short drawers to the frieze, 81½ins. long.   £520

DRESSING TABLES

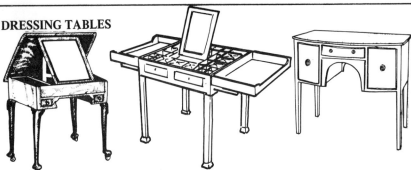

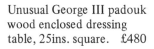

Georgian red walnut dressing table with rising top, 2ft. 7ins. wide.   £350

Unusual George III padouk wood enclosed dressing table, 25ins. square.   £480

Small late 18th century bow-fronted mahogany dressing table.   £200

Inlaid mahogany dressing table, on tapered legs, circa 1780.   £450

Gentleman's mahogany dressing table, circa 1800, with top opening to show mirror.   £165

Fully fitted mahogany campaign chest, circa 1810.   £675

Late 18th century gentleman's bow-fronted mahogany chest of drawers, 42ins. wide.   £430

George III kneehole dressing table, 41ins. wide.   £95

A superb George III mahogany serpentine-front chest, with a fitted interior containing an adjustable mirror.
                                £1,600

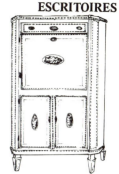

Dutch marquetry upright escritoire. £650

A superb 18th century cross-banded walnut escritoire-on-stand, the interior fitted with eight pigeon-holes concealing other drawers. £940

Sheraton period escritoire in mahogany inlaid with harewood and satinwood 2ft. 10ins. wide. £490

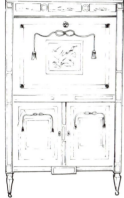

19th century French secretaire a abattant. £1,000

Queen Anne style escritoire on cabriole legs. £1,100

18th century walnut and marquetry scriptoire, 43½ins. wide. £920

Late 18th century Dutch marquetry escritoire. £880

Queen Anne walnut escritoire, the upper section with cushion drawer, the fall flap enclosing a fitted interior, and with two short and two long drawers below. £800

Mid-19th century French ebonised bonheur du jour. £100

LOWBOYS

18th century oak table, narrow mahogany mouldings, 33ins. x 18ins. £200

Mahogany lowboy on square legs, circa 1780. £225

Honey-coloured George I oak lowboy crossbanded with walnut, circa 1720. £195

Queen Anne style mahogany lowboy with broken apron and three drawers, 80cm. wide. £110

George I red walnut lowboy on shaped legs. £195

George I lowboy, on cabriole legs, 32ins. wide, 19½ins. deep, 19ins. high, circa 1720. £425

George I mahogany lowboy, cross-banded top, 30ins. x 18ins. x 28½ins. high. £400

18th century oak side table with cross stretchers. £135

George III satinwood partners' desk with green gilt tooled leather top, 5ft. 3ins. wide x 3ft. 1in. deep. £1,800

Late 19th century Chippendale style director's desk with ogee feet, canted corners, leather top and mahogany linings, 4ft. 9 ins. wide, 2ft. 9 ins. deep, 2ft. 11 ins. high. £245

Mahogany kneehole desk with green hide top, 46ins. wide, circa 1840. £375

Oak breakfronted pedestal writing table, 5ft. 1in. wide. £210

Victorian mahogany pedestal writing table of nine drawers, 138cm. wide. £85

Victorian mahogany pedestal desk with brass handles. £105

Executive's mahogany double pedestal writing table, 6ft. 6ins. long x 3ft. 6ins. £230

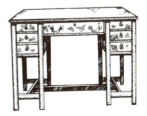

Walnut desk inlaid with various woods by Daneway, circa 1910. £300

An early 18th century walnut kneehole desk, the top moulded and inlaid with feather stringing, on bracket feet. £850

19th century carved mahogany kneehole desk of breakfront outline. £620

One piece mahogany pedestal writing desk, circa 1760, 81cm. wide. £1,270

19th century walnut and kingwood, kidney-shaped kneehole desk, the top lined with tooled leather. £1,300

19th century inlaid and satinwood banded pedestal writing table on bracket feet, 80cm. wide. £210

18th century walnut desk with crossbanded top. £800

Late 19th century oak desk with tambour top, 4ft. wide. £135

George II mahogany kneehole desk with brushing slide, 30ins. wide. £740

Early 18th century walnut kneehole desk. £750

18th century kneehole desk on a plinth base, 75cm. wide.   £380

Victorian mahogany pedestal desk of nine drawers with turned wood knobs.   £100

An 18th century country-made desk.   £350

Victorian mahogany cylinder desk with turned wood handles.   £150

19th century secretaire kneehole desk in mahogany, 3ft. 1in. wide.   £285

Mid 19th century Anglo-Indian ivory inlaid kneehole desk, 105cm. wide.   £2,400

Walnut kneehole writing desk with a recessed cupboard and pierced brass handles.   £2,000

William and Mary style seaweed marquetry secretaire kneehole desk.   £840

George II mahogany kneehole desk on ogee feet.   £600

SCREENS

19th century mahogany cheval firescreen with crimson cloth panels. £14

18th century black lacquer eight-fold screen, 2.13m. wide. £1,300

20th century firescreen with tapestry decoration. £9

19th century mahogany-framed three-leaf screen with glazed and cloth panels. £30

George III rosewood pole screen with a tapestry inset. £50

19th century mahogany-framed two-leaf draught screen with silk panels. £34

Two-fold Shibayama table screen, richly encrusted with mother-of-pearl, each leaf measuring 8¼ins. x 3¼ins. £360

Japanese carved and ebonised four-leaf draught screen, 6ft. 3ins. high. £170

Two-fold bamboo firescreen with painted glass panels. £25

Victorian mahogany secretaire chest with inlaid interior and bracket feet, 125cm. wide. £85

Mahogany secretaire with satinwood interior, circa 1800. £295

18th century mahogany secretaire with satinwood interior. £375

Georgian period mahogany secretaire with fully fitted interior, circa 1810. £195

Late 18th century marquetry fall front secretaire. £720

Late George III mahogany upright secretaire chest on bracket feet, 64cm. wide. £1,800

Dutch marquetry upright secretaire. £650

Georgian mahogany fall-front secretaire, circa 1835. £320

Louis XVI brass-mounted satinwood and purpleheart secretaire a abattant, signed A. Weisweiler. £4,200

SECRETAIRE BOOKCASES

Sheraton style mahogany secretaire bookcase on bracket feet, decorated with satinwood inlay. £425

Sheraton period secretaire cabinet, veneered in mahogany and banded with rosewood. £3,700

Mahogany secretaire chest, with four long drawers below and a bookcase with two glazed doors above, 4ft. 4in. wide. £260

Small mahogany secretaire bookcase, 3ft. wide x 6ft. 6ins. high, original brasses. £480

Early 19th century mahogany Sheraton style secretaire bookcase cabinet, 46ins. wide, 7ft. 8½ins. high, 23ins. deep. £575

Late Georgian mahogany secretaire bookcase on bun feet. £200

Late 17th century green lacquered double-domed secretaire cabinet, 1.04m. wide. £3,100

George III mahogany breakfront secretaire library bookcase. £1,500

George III mahogany secretaire open book-case, 81cm. wide. £1,900

Victorian mahogany secretaire bookcase with glazed doors, 3ft. 6ins. wide. £125

Late Georgian mahogany secretaire bookcase with fret carved broken pediment 3ft. 6½ ins, wide £1,400

19th century mahogany inlaid and rosewood banded secretaire, 4ft. 4ins. wide. £170

Georgian mahogany secretaire bookcase with finely figured interior, 2ft. 9in. wide. £895

Regency secretaire military cabinet in burr elm, circa 1820. £1,550

Antique Chippendale carved mahogany secretaire bookcase in two sections, 2.51m. wide. £600

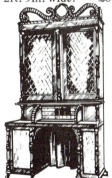

Rare mahogany secretaire bookcase with gilt enrichments, possibly Irish, circa 1835, 258cm. high. £1,200

Georgian faded mahogany secretaire with glazed top. £4,700

George III mahogany breakfront secretaire cabinet bookcase £2,200

SETTEES AND COUCHES

Regency rosewood and brass inlaid settee, 8ft. 3in. wide. £210

Late 17th century highly decorated Northern English oak settle. £610

17th century oak table settle of good colour. £600

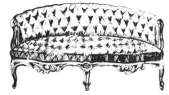

19th century upholstered and gilt-wood sofa in the Louis XV style. £165

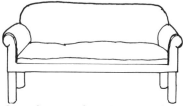

One of a pair of Art Deco maple settees, circa 1830, 163cm. long. £80

Oak settle with fielded panels, 22in. x 71in. x 43in. high, circa 1710. £160

Satinwood sofa with painted decorations, 59in. x 21in. x 33in. high, circa 1800. £350

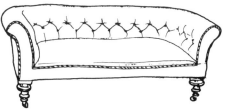

Victorian settee with circle back on turned legs. £75

Ebonised Empire-style chaise longue with painted decoration. £250

Oak settle, the shaped back panels banded with walnut, circa 1830. £165

Satinwood inlaid arm settee with pierced splat and panel back. £70

One of a pair of Victorian square backed settees with lion mask arm terminals. £290

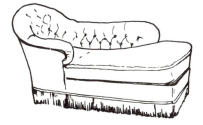

Upholstered day bed with circle end and half back, 156cm. long. £110

An elaborately carved Continental locker seat. £200

Late 17th century oak settle with a fall-down table. £710

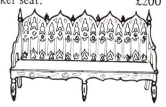

Settee from a set of English oak hall furniture, mid 19th century. £480

SETTEES AND COUCHES

Victorian carved walnut frame chaise longue on cabriole legs. £210

A square back arm settee on mahogany square tapered legs, 189cm.
£150

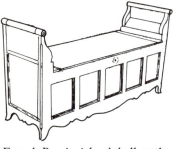

French Provincial oak hall settle with box seat and scroll arms. £260

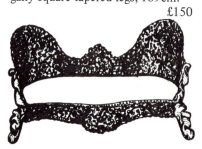

Burmese settee of serpentine shape extensively carved and pierced.
£300

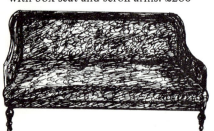

Late 19th century upholstered settee on turned legs. £30

17th century oak monk's bench.
£220

Victorian mahogany double scroll end sofa in gold dralon. £150

Caned mahogany couch, circa 1810, 72in. wide. £490

Carved oak arm settle with box seat, 3ft.6in.   £70

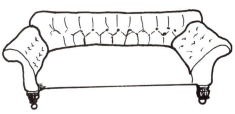

Victorian arm settee buttoned in green velvet, 2.23m. wide.   £90

English wrought-iron seat in Chippendale style, about 1760.   £375

Late 18th century Welsh oak settle with a box seat. £170

Early 19th century Welsh bacon settle in elm.   £200

Victorian scroll back chaise longue on turned legs.   £85

Edwardian inlaid mahogany couch on cabriole legs. £100

French carved walnut arm settee on cabriole legs, 175cm. wide. £145

SIDEBOARDS

Edwardian carved oak shaped front sideboard on bulbous legs, 210cm.£45

George III mahogany bow-fronted sideboard, 1.42m high.£960

19th century inlaid mahogany stage sideboard, with rounded ended and square tapering legs, 216cm. wide.   £180

Victorian mahogany breakfront pedestal sideboard, 7ft.1in. wide.   £72

Edwardian mahogany shaped fronted sideboard , 214cm. wide.£35

Ebonised sideboard with silver-plated mounts, about 1875. £6,200

Georgian mahogany serpentine fronted sideboard, 3ft.5in. wide.£390

Mahogany inlaid serpentine fronted sideboard of Sheraton design. £170

19th century carved oak breakfronted sideboard, 200 cm. wide.   £120

Edwardian mahogany sideboard of three drawers, 168cm. wide.   £15

Late 19th century mahogany sideboard with a mirrored back.   £42

Sheraton mahogany bow fronted sideboard, 56in. wide.   £650

Early 19th century inlaid mahogany shape fronted stage sideboard. £240

Edwardian mahogany sideboard with two drawers, 168cm. wide.£40

Mahogany breakfronted sideboard, 5ft. wide.   £10

Mahogany serpentine fronted sideboard, 4ft. 10in. wide.   £80

SIDEBOARDS

Neat mahogany inlaid sideboard with five drawers, on square tapering legs, 3ft. 6ins. wide. £150

Small George III mahogany bowfront sideboard, 48ins. wide. £110

Late 18th century padoukwood sideboard. £295

19th century German carved oak sideboard. £500

19th century mahogany sideboard with concave centre and cellaret drawer, 65ins. long. £375

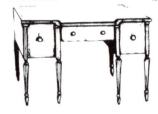

Regency mahogany breakfront sideboard, 5ft. 6ins. long. £380

Normandy oak sideboard with two carved and moulded doors, 148cm. wide. £100

Late Georgian mahogany bowfronted sideboard. £300

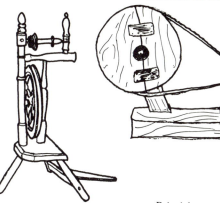

Oak bobbin
winder.
£16.50

18th century oak
spinning wheel.
£40

Primitive wooden
bobbin winder,
about 1850.
£10

Oak and elm
spinning wheel.
£55

Late 18th century
Dutch walnut and
fruitwood spinning
wheel.
£85

Stained wood
spinning wheel.
£26

STANDS

Chinese carved padoukwood jardiniere stand, 2ft. high. £60

19th century Chinese carved ironwood circular jardiniere stand with inset marble top. £77

Oval rosewood ormolu mounted plant pedestal with kingwood frieze. £90

Jardiniere with four scroll handles, on round column stand, 60 in. high. £340

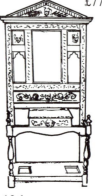

Late 19th century carved oak hallstand with mirror and glove box, 3ft. wide. £34

Oval rosewood jardiniere stand with brass gallery and ormolu mounted feet. £50

One of a pair of 19th century figured walnut pedestals. £420

Carved, marble topped plant stand with carved frieze and cabriole legs. 36in. high. £50

Victorian mahogany lamp stand on tripod feet, 3ft 11in. £18

Round gueridon with mosaic marble top, standing on four fluted, tapered legs. £270

Round cistern stand with marble top, carved legs, frieze and undershelf.
£100

Ebony jardiniere, with carved circular top and trunk patterned stem, 3ft 3in. high. £150

18th century mahogany wine/lectern table with adjustable height. £225

Regency folio stand.
£1,200

Victorian carved padoukwood jardinere stand with an inset marble top, 93cm high. £50

Heavily carved black wood marble topped plant stand, 28in. £70

19th century pair of Japanese red lacquer fan shaped trays on a bamboo stand, 54 cm. wide. £26

One of a pair of George III mahogany dining-room urns and pedestals.
£682

STANDS

Victorian mahogany lamp stand with spiral pillar, 122cm. high.   £18

18th century mahogany easel table on pad feet.
£275

Continental carved wood cherub plant holder.   £310

Bamboo plant stand with tiled top, circa 1900.
£40

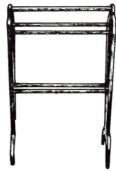

Victorian mahogany triple towel rail.
£16

Edwardian inlaid three-tier cake-stand.   £22

Early 19th century rosewood inlaid escritoire fire screen, 3ft. 9ins. high. £295

Regency rosewood music stand with reeded legs.   £350

18th century mahogany music stand.   £375

An Elizabethan oak joint stool, maker's mark I.A., 1ft. 6½ins. wide. £280

Early 19th century window seat in the manner of Duncan Phyfe. £1,200

Bamboo piano stool, dated 1890. £36

Victorian mahogany revolving piano stool. £25

Victorian, adjustable, rosewood music seat with lyre-shaped splat. £125

Early 18th century Italian prie dieu inlaid with ivory. £800

Sheraton style mahogany box strung and upholstered lyre-shaped window seat. £65

Hepplewhite stool. £125

Edwardian manogany piano stool with a lift-up seat and two drawers with drop fronts. £20

STOOLS

Late 19th century circular mahogany revolving piano stool on square tapering legs. £20

Oriental carved wood stool. £15

Edwardian mahogany dressing stool with trellis and scroll arms, £26

Revolving piano stool on turned legs with brass dolphin toes. £20

Cameroons Bekon chiefs' circular stool the top supported by four natives and two animal figures. £95

19th century reproduction oak joint stool. £45

Charles I joint stool with moulded top, the frieze carved with lunettes and foliage. £53

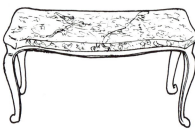

French style walnut duet stool on cabriole legs, seat covered in printed cretonne. £34

Child's beechwood stool on turned legs. £10

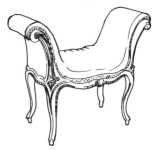

One of a set of four
Regency ebonised
stools attributed to
Gillows, 56cm. wide.
£525

One of a pair of
Louis XV cream
painted and gilt
decorated win-
dow seats.
£1,150

Jacobean carved
oak oblong joint
stool on turned
legs with stretchers,
45cm. wide.   £75

17th century oak
joint stool. £260

African hardwood Chieftain's
stool of Yoruba origin, single
plank top adzed underneath,
23½in. long, 15½in. high.
£475

African carved
teak circular
stool with ten
legs, 16½in.
diameter. £22

Carved walnut French
style oval footstool,
covered in green velvet.
£28

Victorian circular,
mahogany, revolving
piano stool.   £28

Mahogany scroll
shaped footstool.
£12

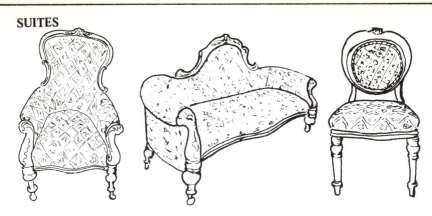

Victorian carved mahogany parlour suite comprising a settee, an easy chair and six single chairs.   £520

English cast iron seat with two chairs decorated in the fern pattern, about 1870-80, seat 4ft.6in. wide, chair 2ft. wide.   £200

An Adam style drawingroom suite comprising circle back settee, four dining chairs and two armchairs, with the frames painted, carved and fluted.   £1,600

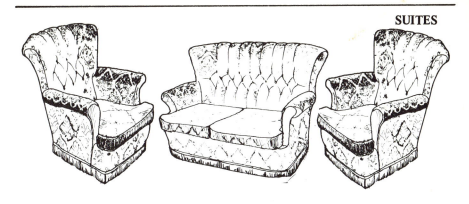

Three piece lounge suite in gold velvet.   £150

Edwardian seven piece satinwood salon suite comprising
a settee, two carvers and four dining chairs.   £320

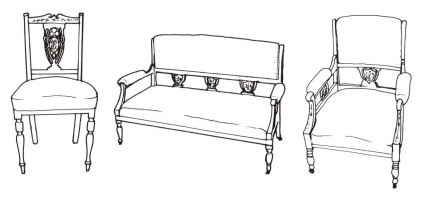

Edwardian rosewood inlaid drawingroom suite of armed settee
and two easy chairs and four inlaid single chairs (seven pieces
in all).   £270

Edwardian carved mahogany drawingroom suite comprising an arm settee, two easy chairs and four single chairs.   £380

Lounge suite of lug settee and two lug easy chairs. £170

Part of a French giltwood chateau suite of Louis XV design, comprising a canape, four fauteuils, banquette stool, firescreen and three-fold screen.   £6,600

Mahogany framed bergere suite with cane backs and
sides and flowered silk damask cushions.   £370

Edwardian mahogany inlaid drawingroom suite of
settee and two easy chairs.   £170

Part of a Victorian nine piece suite comprising a
set of six, chaise longue, and two easy chairs.
                                              £1,150

CARD AND TEA TABLES

One of a pair of Regency bird's eye maple 'D' shaped card tables, 37in. wide.
£1,550

James I oak credence table with fold-over top, English about 1620.
£950

Small inlaid folding-top card table in Dutch marquetry.
£390

Victorian carved walnut fold-over card table.
£130

Late 18th century Dutch marquetry inlaid card table.
£390

A fine George II games and tea table in Spanish mahogany, circa 1740.
£690

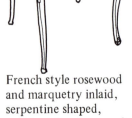

Hepplewhite mahogany serpentine fronted fold-over top card table, with Tunbridgeware stringing.
£980

Victorian walnut serpentine shaped folding-over card table, 3ft. wide.
£180

French style rosewood and marquetry inlaid, serpentine shaped, envelope flap-over card table.
£290

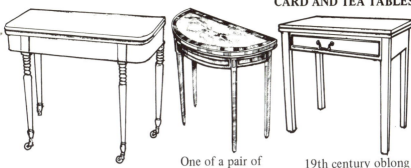

Victorian rosewood folding over card table, 3ft. wide. £60

One of a pair of Sheraton style card tables in bird's eye maple. £2,500

19th century oblong, mahogany folding top tea table on square legs, 2ft. 6in. wide. £100

A Sheraton period 'D' shaped satinwood card table, 36in. wide. £380

Late 18th century Dutch walnut and marquetry inlaid triangular shaped folding table, 95cm. wide. £340

19th century inlaid mahogany folding card table on square tapered legs. £75

Mahogany serpentine card table with folding-over top, circa 1760. £575

One of a pair of Victorian burr walnut and marquetry inlaid card tables, 36in. wide. £380

Early 19th century inlaid mahogany half-round card table, 82cm. wide. £190

CARD AND TEA TABLES

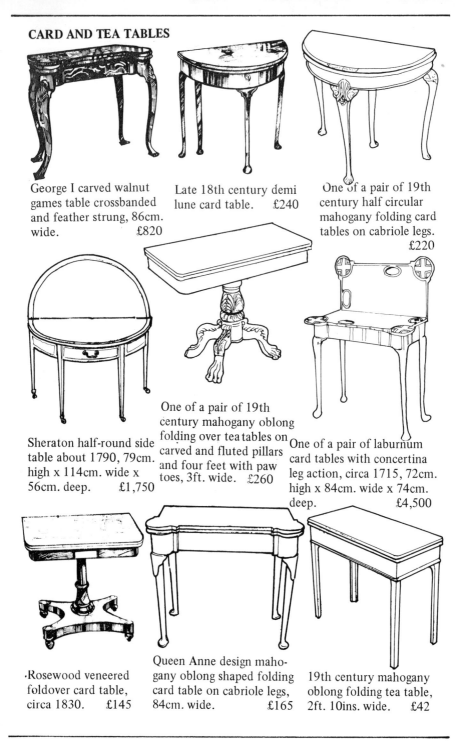

George I carved walnut games table crossbanded and feather strung, 86cm. wide. £820

Late 18th century demi lune card table. £240

One of a pair of 19th century half circular mahogany folding card tables on cabriole legs. £220

Sheraton half-round side table about 1790, 79cm. high x 114cm. wide x 56cm. deep. £1,750

One of a pair of 19th century mahogany oblong folding over tea tables on carved and fluted pillars and four feet with paw toes, 3ft. wide. £260

One of a pair of laburnum card tables with concertina leg action, circa 1715, 72cm. high x 84cm. wide x 74cm. deep. £4,500

·Rosewood veneered foldover card table, circa 1830. £145

Queen Anne design mahogany oblong shaped folding card table on cabriole legs, 84cm. wide. £165

19th century mahogany oblong folding tea table, 2ft. 10ins. wide. £42

Victorian mahogany foldover tea table with boxwood string inlay, on turned legs.   £45

George II mahogany card table with con- certina leg action, circa 1730.   £585

Edwardian satinwood and mahogany patience table with swivel top, 73cm. high x 53½cm. wide x 38cm. deep (closed) 75½cm. (open) £130

Early 19th century inlaid tea table. £250

Oak card table on carved cabriole stand about 1860, 74cm. high x 87cm. wide x 47cm. deep (closed) 92cm. deep (open). £125

An attractive 18th century folding-top table with floral marquetry and ormolu mounts.   £880

Chippendale style mahogany oblong foldover tea table with carved claw and ball feet, 2ft. 8ins. wide.   £160

Sheraton inlaid card table on square tapered legs, 3ft. wide.   £245

Late 19th century oak oblong foldover card table on turned legs with stretcher, 3ft. wide. £42

CARD AND TEA TABLES

French boulle card table, on cabriole legs with fine ormolu mounts, circa 1860, 36ins. wide.   £525

Mahogany tea table of serpentine shape with boxwood stringing, circa 1830.   £165

One of a pair of 19th century rosewood side tables, 42ins. wide.   £275

A Victorian rosewood folding-over card table with rounded corners, on a turned and partly fluted pillar, and shaped base with scroll feet, 3ft. wide.   £145

Important mid-19th century kingwood and tulipwood card table with ormolu decoration, 2ft. 9ins. wide.   £1,500

Bamboo card table with fold-over lacquered top, circa 1905.   £70

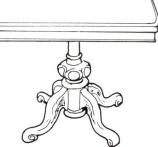

Edwardian folding top card table in walnut.   £40

Victorian walnut folding-over tea table on pillar and claw, 3ft. 1in. £100

19th century French inlaid rosewood and marquetry games table, 25ins. wide. £340

English mahogany card table with semi-circular swivelling top, circa 1845.   £140

Triple-leaf, George II mahogany card table with guinea wells, 69cm. high, 81cm. wide   £360

Sheraton period card table with satinwood crossbanding, and standing on tapered legs, circa 1790. £425

Victorian walnut card table.   £310

Antique mahogany games table with shaped triple-fold top, 2ft. 9ins. wide.   £560

Edwardian mahogany envelope card table on cabriole legs.   £75

Victorian inlaid burr walnut folding-top card table on a stretcher base.   £125

Mahogany inlaid oblong folding-over tea table, 3ft. wide.   £90

An Adam period semi-circular fold-over card table in satinwood with kingwood crossbanding, 3ft. 3ins. wide.   £540

SUTHERLAND TABLES

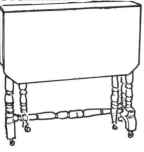

Walnut Sutherland tea table with two drop leafs, on turned legs, 2ft. 5½ins. wide. £26

Mahogany Sutherland tea table with two drop leafs, 2ft. 3ins. wide. £38

Victorian walnut Sutherland table on turned legs, 76cm. wide. £50

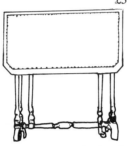

Victorian ebonised Sutherland table, 1ft. 9ins. wide. £22

Mahogany, inlaid and satinwood banded, Sutherland tea table on turned legs, 2ft. wide. £65

Mid-19th century burr walnut Sutherland table. £90

CONSOL TABLES

Victorian mahogany consol table, with a figured marble top and cabriole leg front support. £14

Louis XV carved giltwood consol table, 95cm. wide. £700

Large French Regency giltwood consol table, 6ft. 5ins. wide. £2,400

Early 19th century rosewood dining table with gilt paw feet.   £350

Sheraton period satinwood centre table, 40ins. wide.   £2,000

Regency mahogany and rosewood cross-banded circular breakfast table on reeded legs.   £220

19th century Sevres porcelain and ormolu mounted centre table.   £3,400

Regency zebra wood breakfast table with mahogany crossbanding, 4ft. 8ins. x 3ft. 6ins.   £1,200

Plum pudding mahogany pedestal dining table, circa 1840, 48ins. diam.   £205

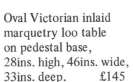

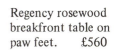

Georgian mahogany rent table with cupboard base and leather top.   £1,000

Oval Victorian inlaid marquetry loo table on pedestal base, 28ins. high, 46ins. wide, 33ins. deep.   £145

Regency rosewood breakfront table on paw feet.   £560

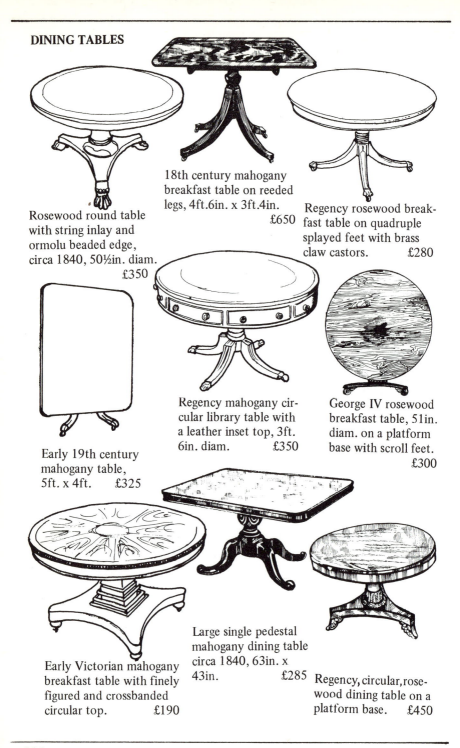

Rosewood round table with string inlay and ormolu beaded edge, circa 1840, 50½in. diam. £350

18th century mahogany breakfast table on reeded legs, 4ft.6in. x 3ft.4in. £650

Regency rosewood breakfast table on quadruple splayed feet with brass claw castors. £280

Early 19th century mahogany table, 5ft. x 4ft. £325

Regency mahogany circular library table with a leather inset top, 3ft. 6in. diam. £350

George IV rosewood breakfast table, 51in. diam. on a platform base with scroll feet. £300

Early Victorian mahogany breakfast table with finely figured and crossbanded circular top. £190

Large single pedestal mahogany dining table circa 1840, 63in. x 43in. £285

Regency, circular, rosewood dining table on a platform base. £450

Georgian oval mahogany breakfast table with rosewood crossbanding, 54in. x 41in. £600

Victorian mahogany oval breakfast table on a quadruple base with centre pillar, 148cm. wide. £100

Well figured and original mid 19th century walnut tilt-top table, 4ft.6in. wide. £265

George III inlaid mahogany drum top rent table, 96cm. diam. £920

Victorian mahogany oval breakfast table on pillar and claw base, 4ft. 6in. diam. £85

Fine Regency mahogany breakfast table, circa 1810, figured top with crossbanding and beaded edge, 45½ in. x 55½in. x 27½in. £485

Circular well figured mahogany dining table with stringwood crossbanding and a reeded edge, circa 1810. £525

Early 19th century mahogany breakfast table with boxwood string inlay. £150

Regency rosewood circular table with brass inlay and mountings, 46in. diam. £800

DROP LEAF TABLES

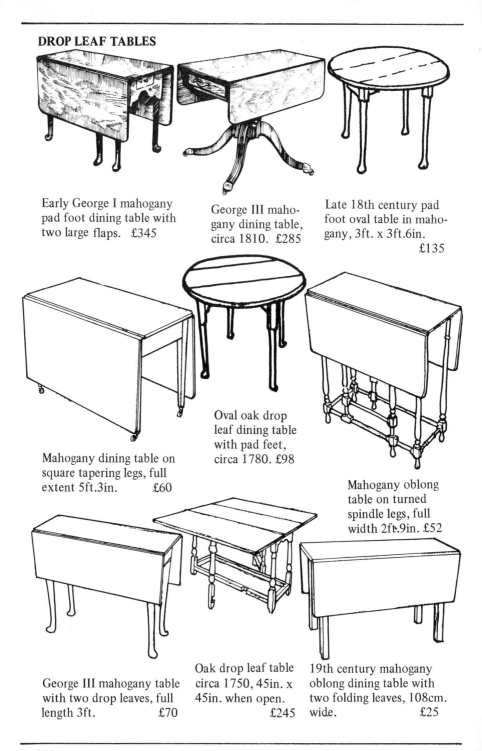

Early George I mahogany pad foot dining table with two large flaps.   £345

George III mahogany dining table, circa 1810. £285

Late 18th century pad foot oval table in mahogany, 3ft. x 3ft.6in.
£135

Mahogany dining table on square tapering legs, full extent 5ft.3in.   £60

Oval oak drop leaf dining table with pad feet, circa 1780. £98

Mahogany oblong table on turned spindle legs, full width 2ft.9in. £52

George III mahogany table with two drop leaves, full length 3ft.   £70

Oak drop leaf table circa 1750, 45in. x 45in. when open.   £245

19th century mahogany oblong dining table with two folding leaves, 108cm. wide.   £25

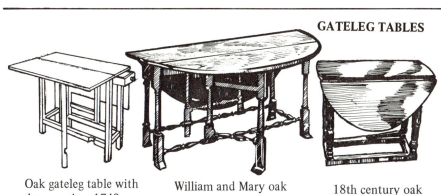

Oak gateleg table with drawer, circa 1740, 33in. x 38in. when open.   £125

William and Mary oak gateleg table, circa 1690, 59½in. diam.   £950

18th century oak oval gateleg table with ground level stretchers, 80cm. wide.   £120

Oak gateleg table, 52in wide, circa 1700. £475

Late 17th century yew wood gateleg oval table, extending to 58in. £670

Early English oak gateleg with barley sugar legs, circa 1780.   £2,750

Small oval gateleg table on turned legs with rare feature of shaped apron on top of hinged gates as well as ends, circa 1690, 45in. across.   £225

18th century Cuban mahogany double gateleg table.   £3,000

Victorian oak gateleg dining table with a carved border and spiral legs.   £50

LARGE TABLES

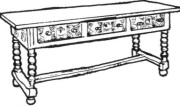

17th century Spanish walnut centre table, 78in.   £650

Oak refectory table with ground level stretchers, circa 1700.   £495

Elizabethan oak refectory table on six carved bulbous legs.   £2,200

Oak Dutch draw leaf table.   £1,450

19th century Italian carved giltwood table with inlaid marble top.   £2,000

George III mahogany twin-pedestal dining table.   £1,000

Mahogany two pedestal dining table with a central leaf, circa 1810.   £800

Superb four pedestal mahogany dining table, overall length 3m.58cm.   £6,500

17th century Dutch draw leaf table, full extension 9ft. £1,400

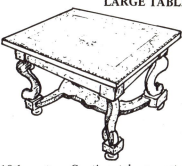

18th century Continental marquetry inlaid walnut table 3ft. 7½in. by 2ft. 8½in. £300

Mahogany two flap dining table on six square tapered legs, circa 1820. £235

Late 17th century Welsh farmhouse table with an ash top and oak underframe. £800

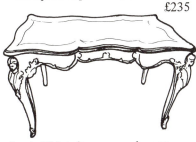

Louis XV style rosewood crossbanded and marquetry inlaid table with chased brass mounts.£600

George II oak refectory table, 7ft.3in. long, circa 1760. £610

Georgian mahogany three part 'D' end dining table, 90in. long, circa 1770. £430

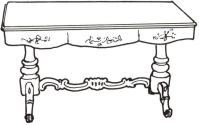

Victorian walnut inlaid table with floral marquetry border and centre, 4ft.6in. wide. £420

LARGE TABLES

Set of mahogany inlaid dining tables with banded borders D ends, on square tapering legs, full extent 9ft 6in.   £540

17th century type oak refectory dining table on turned baluster legs and square stretchers, 7ft 3in wide x 2ft 6in.   £190

Late 19th century oak refectory table bearing trade lable of W. Walker & Son, London.   £85

Victorian mahogany dining table in two parts on turned legs, 172cm long.   £150

Six-legged oak refectory table.   £1,450

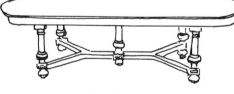

Oak boardroom table with rounded ends, the top inset with rexine, on turned legs with flat stretchers, 9ft long. £20

A 19th century mahogany set of three dining tables on square tapered legs.   £300

Reproduction oak refectory table.   £395

Farmhouse oak refectory table with honey-coloured patination, circa 1730, 56in long x 26½in wide x 29½in high.
£280

Reproduction mahogany dining table on two pillars with claw feet, 6ft 6in long.
£95

George III three pedestal mahogany dining table 137cm x 356cm. £850

Oak telescopic dining table on six carved bulbous legs, (two folded up), 14ft 6in.
£120

Victorian mahogany telescopic dining table with circle ends and one loose leaf, 130 cm long. £140

Large mahogany boardroom table with a horse shoe pattern end, 21ft 6in long.
£320

Oak refectory table in original condition, 7ft 1in long, 29in wide, circa 1750.
£300

18th century Continental walnut drawleaf table, 41in x 9ft 6in. maximum.
£920

Indo-Portugese hardwood table inlaid with ivory and mother-of-pearl.   £78

Georgian mahogany tripod table, circa 1780.   £110

19th century French inlaid rosewood boudoir table. £330

Mahogany circular snap over top table on pillar and claw, 1ft. 11in. diam.   £40

Nest of three gilt lacquered tables on spindle legs.   £38

Victorian rosewood table with drawer, 18in. square.   £30

French fruitwood and marquetry inlaid kidney shaped table, 19th century.   £190

Mahogany oblong table on octagonal pillar and block, 2ft. 4in. wide.£22

19th century Burmese carved teak circular table, 67cm.£50

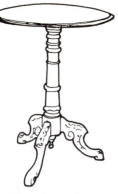

Mid 19th century French kingwood table inlaid with ebonised flowers. £550

Victorian walnut circular table on tripod base. £32

Louis XV style kingwood and rosewood banded serpentine shaped table, 19th century. £230

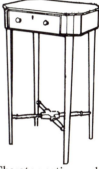

Mahogany urn table with serpentine carved gallery, on cabriole legs, circa 1770. £1,500

English papier mache occasional tea table with tip-up top. £70

Sheraton satinwood occasional table, circa 1790. £650

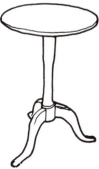

18th century oak and elm tripod table. £42

A marquetry centre table on barley twist legs with cross stretchers. £500

A late 18th century black and gilt lacquered tripod table £85

OCCASIONAL TABLES

19th century Burmese carved teak wood table with pierced apron, 68cms. diam. £42

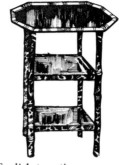

English two-tier occasional table with Japanese lacquer panels, circa 1880-1905. £32

Edwardian inlaid mahogany oval serpentine shaped table on cabriole legs. £60

French marquetry table with gilt-bronze scroll feet, mid 19th century, 81.5cm. high. £420

Amboyna wood table of Louis XVI design. £580

Chippendale mahogany serpentine shaped table on fluted turned pillar, 2ft wide x 1ft 6in.£260

Georgian mahogany birdcage tilt top table, 23½in. diam. £50

Circular Victorian table in prime condition. £70

Set of early 19th century mahogany and rosewood banded quartette tables, 53cm. wide. £680

18th century mahogany shaped top table, 81cm. diam. £85

English bamboo flap tea table with Japanese lacquer panels, circa 1880-1905. £38

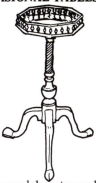

Chippendale octagonal top tripod kettle stand, 1ft 10in high x 10in wide, table top. £1,800

Late 18th century walnut cricket table. £185

Regency mahogany dumb waiter on tripod stand. £470

Mid 19th century French gilt metal gueridon table, inset with Sevres plaques, signed S. Simonnen, 3lin. diam. £4,500

Victorian papier mache table with inlaid mother-of-pearl chess board, 68 cm high. £48

Late 19th century pub table with wooden top, 2ft 3in high x 2ft diam. £43

Art furniture design two-tier table in ebony and specimen wood, circa 1880. £120

OCCASIONAL TABLES

Unusual Sheraton mahogany, corner table with platform. £375

One of a pair of Regency rosewood occasional tables with brass feet.£650

Late 19th century inlaid mahogany occasional table with undershelf, 3ft 1in wide. £40

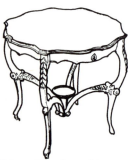

Edwardian shaped top mahogany centre table, on carved cabriole legs, 2ft 6in diam. £25

Victorian walnut and marquetry and parquetry inlaid circular games table, 1ft. 8½ins. diam. £55

Edwardian inlaid mahogany shaped top table, 2ft. 4in. diam. £26

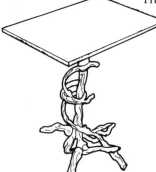

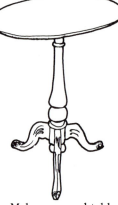

Lacquered oblong table on tree trunk stem. £22

Faded mahogany tripod tea table, circa 1750, 2ft 2in high. £650

Mahogany oval table on pillar and claw base, 2ft. wide. £12

Mid 19th century mahogany tilt-top tripod table, 2ft. 1in. x 1ft. 5ins. £45

19th century Japanese table with lacquered top. £38

George III mahogany bird cage table with moulded pie crust border, 78cm. diam. £140

Mahogany inlaid octagonal table, 1ft. 6ins. £28

Late 19th century inlaid mahogany table with drawer, on a tripod base, 1ft. 8ins. wide. £38

A nest of three onyx top tables. £62

Satinwood occasional table with rosewood inlay, circa 1790, 2ft. 4ins. high x 1ft. 9ins. wide x 1ft. 4ins. deep. £1,600

Late 18th century Cuban mahogany tambour corner cabinet with tripod support, 1ft. 6ins. wide. £685

Lady's tulipwood work table in the Sheraton style with purplewood marquetry, 1ft. 10¼ins. wide. £1,150

OCCASIONAL TABLES

Victorian pub table with 21in. diam. copper top, circa 1860.   £78

Good quality Chinese padouk wood table profusely inlaid with mother-of-pearl.   £1,500

Unusual oak circular table with inlaid top, the central band carved 'Rowland Naylor, 1862', 22in. diam.   £225

19th century Louis XV style kingwood occasional table inset with a porcelain plaque, 58.5 cm. wide.   £750

19th century mahogany circular tip-up table, 2ft.8in. diam.   £28

Bamboo tea table with lacquered top, circa 1900.   £20

George III mahogany tripod table.   £35

Early 19th century rosewood stretcher table.   £75

Victorian papier mache tripod table inlaid with mother-of-pearl. £50

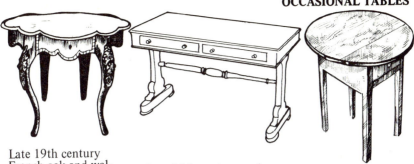

Late 19th century French oak and walnut centre table with ormolu embellishments, 53in. wide.   £280

Late 19th century mahogany oblong toilet table, 4ft. wide.   £42

17th century oak centre table, 27in. wide.   £80

Sheraton style satinwood occasional table.   £150

Oriental carved blackwood and inlaid circular coffee table on a folding stand, 61cm. diam.   £18

17th century laburnum wood Carolean centre table.   £80

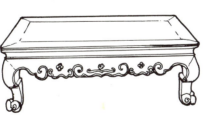

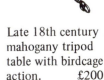

Early Victorian cast iron pedestal table painted with a view of shipping in the Clyde.   £150

Late 18th century Chinese Hua-li low table, 11ins. high x 2ft. 7½ins. wide x 1ft. 5½ins deep.   £355

Late 18th century mahogany tripod table with birdcage action.   £200

PEMBROKE TABLES

Sheraton style inlaid mahogany and satinwood banded oval Pembroke table, 76cm. wide.   £120

Late 19th century mahogany oval Pembroke table on square tapered legs, 92cm. wide.   £40

Victorian mahogany Pembroke table on octagonal legs, 103cm. wide.   £32

Late 18th century Sheraton style inlaid and satinwood banded mahogany Pembroke table painted with flowers, husks and scrolls, 81cm. wide.   £180

Mahogany pedestal Pembroke table, 42ins. x 46ins. x 29ins. high, circa 1800.   £360

Georgian partridge wood Pembroke table on finely turned legs.   £345

19th century mahogany Pembroke table with two drop leaves, 3ft. 9ins.   £125

Mahogany Pembroke table crossbanded in tulipwood.   £120

An elegant George III mahogany Pembroke table in the French Hepplewhite style.   1,800 gns.

19th century mahogany oblong Pembroke table with folding leaves, 81cm. wide. £44

Sheraton period mahogany Pembroke table with crossbanded top and brass toe castors, 33ins. wide. £150

Late 18th century Adam design inlaid mahogany and kingwood banded Pembroke table. £180

Georgian inlaid mahogany Pembroke table. £300

Hepplewhite mahogany Pembroke table, 29ins. wide. £100

George III satinwood and rosewood banded drop leaf table. £340

A Georgian mahogany Pembroke table with two 'D' shaped leaves and a drawer, on square tapering legs, 2ft. 8ins. wide. £40

George III yew wood, mahogany and marquetry Pembroke table, 97cm. wide. £735

George III mahogany and tulip banded Pembroke table. £140

SIDE TABLES

George III mahogany two-drawer side table with original ring handles, circa 1780. £105

Chippendale style mahogany oblong side table on cabriole legs and paw feet, 3ft. wide. £210

George I walnut pad foot centre table with original brass handles, circa 1720, 34in. wide. £385

North Italian giltwood side table with rectangular veined white marble top, 1.30m. wide. £441

Marquetry curved side table designed by Chippendale. £8,000

A carved oak hall table with drawer and panel back, 3ft.6in. wide. £42

Mid 17th century North Italian gilt-wood side table. £525

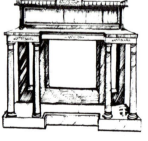

Rosewood side table with mirrored panels, 63in. wide, circa 1825. £375

An 18th century oak side table with cross stretchers, 30½in. wide.   £120

Oak side table with bobbin turned legs and flat cross stretchers, circa 1680.   £340

Late 19th century carved oak oblong hall table of Italian design, 105cm.£30

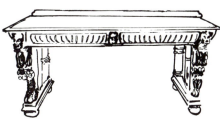

Victorian oak side table with two frieze drawers and carved scroll end supports, 215cm. wide.   £45

Louis Phillipe kingwood centre table, the parquetry top cross-banded and rimmed with gilt brass, 3ft.8in. wide.   £3,200

An early 18th century yew wood side table, 30in. wide.   £310

18th century marble topped Louis XVI marquetry table. £5,800

Mahogany oblong table with two pull-out slides, carved apron and cabriole legs with flower motifs, 3ft. wide.   £210

SOFA TABLES

Mahogany and satinwood banded sofa table, 1.60m. x 64cm. extended. £270

Fine Sheraton mahogany sofa table, crossbanded with yew wood, 34ins. x 29ins. (closed), 54ins. x 29ins. (open). £850

Mahogany Sheraton style sofa table with rosewood crossbanding and boxwood inlay. £385

Regency rosewood sofa table on a platform base with reeded legs. £400

Regency mahogany sofa table with crossbanded top, 38ins. wide. £490

Regency style rosewood sofa table with kingwood crossbanding and brass claw feet, full extent 5ft. £300

Early 19th century rosewood sofa table on end supports with brass paw feet. £200

Regency rosewood sofa table, 91cm. wide. £520

George III mahogany sofa table on reeded legs, 36ins. wide. £510

Early 19th century rosewood and brass inlaid sofa table, 1.38m. x 39cm. £540

Regency rosewood sofa table banded with satinwood, 1.37m. extended. £2,500

Regency period mahogany crossbanded sofa table. £450

TRUNKS AND COFFERS

Oak mule chest crossbanded in mahogany, 55 in. long, circa 1780.   £185

17th century oak panelled coffer, the front carved with lozenges   £105

Old English carved and panelled oak coffer, rising top, 4ft.   £130

Early oak coffer, circa 1740, 38in. wide x 18½in. deep x 19in. high.£165

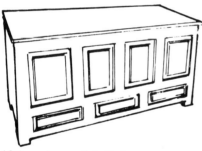

18th century oak hall chest with a moulded panel front, 156 cm. £85

17th century oak coffer.   £160

Late 16th century French Gothic oak coffer, 71 in. wide.   £1,800

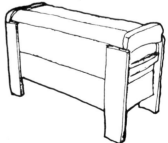

15th century oak chest, 67cm. high x 112cm. wide x 51cm. deep. £560

17th century carved oak rug chest.
£280

Oak hall chest with two drawers in base, 5ft. 6in. wide. £155

Large French oak chest, 16th century, 72½ in. £580

Early oak coffer with panelled front and sides, 62in. long, circa 1730.£125

17th century German iron strongbox, the lid and sides overlaid with trellis-work and painted with roses. £380

16th century iron bound oak coffer, with running plank top, 5 ft. wide.
£1,650

14th century walnut coffer with plank top. £420

17th century carved oak coffer, circa 1680, 49in. wide, 22in. deep, 28in. high. £285

TRUNKS AND COFFERS

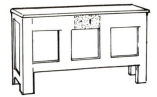

17th century oak linen chest,
3ft.2in. wide.　　　£143

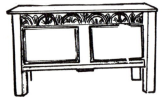

Late 17th century oak chest,
42½in. wide.　　　£178

Brass mounted kingwood coffer,
17in. on teak stand of Chippendale design.　　　£350

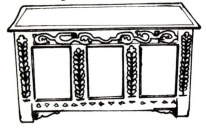

19th century oak hall chest
with carved panels to the front,
188cm. wide.　　　£40

17th century oak Welsh love chest,
with iron lock, 25in. wide.　£85

Late 18th century elm
dower chest .　　　£48

Good oak chest with original
carving, 55in. long, circa 1730.
　　　£245

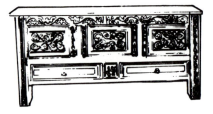

18th century carved oak
marriage chest.　　£240

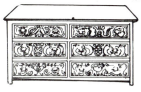

17th century oak dower chest, extensively carved with rosettes, 57in. wide.   £270

Oak coffer with panelled top and linenfold front, 89cm. wide. £720

French Provincial oak chest, 5ft.3in. wide.   £105

17th century oak coffer, 48in. wide.   £75

Small oak mule chest, 44in. wide, circa 1780.   £150

16th century Continental coffer with hinged lid, 57½in. long.£180

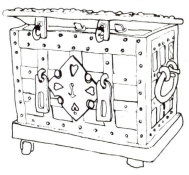

19th century oak hall chest with carved panel front, 3ft.11in. wide.   £65

17th century iron strong chest.   £450

WARDROBES

Victorian mahogany break-front wardrobe enclosed by four doors, 216cm. wide.
£65

19th century gentleman's mahogany wardrobe with panel doors, 128cm. wide. £45

Victorian mahogany wardrobe with two mirror doors, 1.86m. wide £35

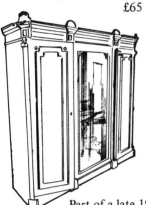

Part of a late 19th century three-piece bedroom suite of wardrobe, dressing table and double bed. £195

Louis XV walnut armoire with rococo panels, circa 1740. £1,200

A 17th century Flemish oak armoire, with original metalwork. £980

A mahogany circular cloak tree in the Adam style with revolving door. £100

Restrained mid-18th century oak armoire from Normandy. £385

Early 18th century
walnut armoire.
£500

Early 19th century
gentleman's inlaid
mahogany wardrobe,
upper part with fitted
trays, 118cm. wide.
£110

Georgian mahogany
clothes press, 4ft.,
converted to hang-
ing wardrobe. £60

Victorian carved oak bedroom suite of:· wardrobe with mirror
centre 7ft 6in wide, dressing table 5ft wide and washstand 5ft
wide.
£300

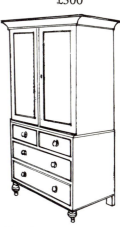

19th century gentleman's
mahogany wardrobe with
fitted trays, 132cm. wide. £85

Mahogany wardrobe with
two hanging compartments
and a cupboard and four
drawers, 6ft. 1in. wide. £30

Gentleman's mahogany
wardrobe, 4ft wide. £80

WASHSTANDS

Early 19th century mahogany corner basin stand with undershelf. £70

Edwardian inlaid mahogany washstand with cupboard and pull-out bidet, 19½ins. wide. £270

Late Victorian mahogany shaving stand with boxwood string inlay. £40

Late 18th century mahogany washstand on fine turned supports with a centre drawer and shaped cross stretcher. £85

George III mahogany washstand with fitted interior, 2ft. 8ins. wide. £75

19th century mahogany inlaid square basin stand with hinged cover, a cupboard below and cross stretchers. £85

George III mahogany toilet cabinet. £100

Late Victorian pine washstand with a tiled back. £25

George III mahogany washstand. £80

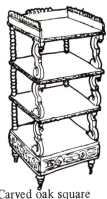

Carved oak square
four tier whatnot
with drawer in base,
1ft. 8ins.   £38

Mahogany, rosewood etagere
with three shelves and two
drawers below, on turned
legs, 3ft. 9ins. high.   £150

17in. wide, marquetry
three tier etagere with
brass gallery top and
drawer.   £90

Victorian walnut
whatnot of three
shelves, with turned
supports.   £60

Victorian inlaid walnut
four tier whatnot. £60

Victorian ebony and
amboyna wood mar-
quetry etagere with
ormolu mounts, £145

Bamboo cake stand,
circa 1900.   £30

19th century rosewood
whatnot stencilled
Taprell Holland & Son,
London, 49cm. wide. £500

19th century mahogany
oblong three tier whatnot
on turned supports.   £140

WINE COOLERS

Late 18th century Sheraton style mahogany wine cooler on fine turned legs. £195

Good quality George III mahogany wine cooler.   £500

18th century wine cooler with brass bandings.   £750

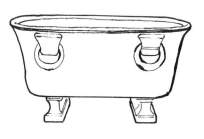

Sheraton period brass-banded cellarette. £300

Late Georgian mahogany wine cooler.   £300

18th century mahogany and brass-bound log basket, formerly a wine cooler.   £1,000

A late George III inlaid mahogany oval wine cooler, lead lined, with brass side handles and fluted legs.   £750

18th century oval brass-bound wine cooler.   £230

A late 18th century domed-top cellarette in mahogany, inlaid with conche shells.   £300

Regency mahogany work table, 30ins. wide when open. £80

Regency work table on claw feet. £310

Combined Victorian work and games table in walnut, 21ins. wide. £120

George III mahogany teapoy with boxwood stringing, three swept feet, 25½ins. tall. £275

Late 17th century walnut games table of outstanding quality, with the very rare open twist legs, 78cm. high, 115cm. wide, 61cm. deep. £2,500

Rare mid-19th century French work box in satinwood and kingwood, satin lined, 34ins. high. £1,325

Late 18th century rosewood veneered work table, 45cm. wide. £110

Victorian papier mache work table decorated with Chinese designs, 64cm. wide. £120

Egyptian parquetry games table. £220

WORKBOXES AND GAMES TABLES

Victorian burr walnut games table, the top inlaid with chess and backgammon boards. £220

Victorian burr walnut games and work table with heavily turned and carved legs and stretcher. £190

Early Victorian mahogany work table, fitted drawer with well below 21in. £130

Work table on pedestal base, early 19th century with marquetry of plants and an abbey scene. £155

Regency circular rosewood work table with rising top and fitted interior, 20in. diameter. £160

19th century pollared elm work table with brass claw casters.£145

Regency brass inlaid rosewood sewing table. £345

Late 18th century mahogany games and writing table, 75cm high x 109cm wide x 56cm deep. £1,600

English walnut teapoy containing twin lidded caddies and a glass bowl. £110

Regency, rosewood lady's work table with shaped platform base. £155

Games and work table with inlaid top and interesting slide-out well. £150

Late Regency burr walnut and oak work table fitted with two drawers. £130

Victorian inlaid walnut work table with folding top. £130

19th century French rosewood boudoir table of serpentine form. £330

Early 19th century inlaid and satinwood banded oblong work table on square tapered legs, 52cm. wide. £130

Regency games, writing and work table in calamander wood, about 1800. £1,450

19th century black export lacquer work table decorated with gilt chinoiserie scenes, 70cm wide. £110

An attractive Regency sewing table on splay feet with brass castors. £275

WRITING TABLES

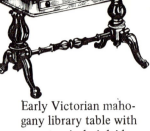

Early Victorian mahogany library table with an extensively inlaid rectangular top, 52½in. x 19in. £360

19th century ormolu mounted satinwood bureau plat. £1,295

Late 19th century French walnut parquetry bonheur du jour. £350

A Louis Phillipe bonheur du jour inset with Sevres porcelain plaques. £1,950

19th century Continental bonheur du jour inlaid with decorative scenes. £1,800

Late 19th century rosewood writing table with serpentine front. £250

Louis XV kingwood and marquetry table a ecrire, 17½in. wide. £750

Mid 19th century lady's mahogany writing desk. £200

Late 19th century satinwood worktable in the Sheraton style. £148

George III satinwood bonheur du jour, veneered in rosewood and mahogany. £1,150

Victorian ebonised and walnut banded writing table with brass beaded borders. £110

Sheraton style mahogany writing table, circa 1800. £520

Late 18th century tambour fronted mahogany desk, 69cm. wide. £775

Napoleon III bureau de dame, walnut crossbanded with kingwood ormolu fretwork, gallery top. £880

Regency mahogany writing cabinet, 127cm. high. £1,050

French kingwood bonheur du jour about 1850, 1.16 cm. high. £780

Small bureau plat with ormolu mounts and inlaid in rare timbers, 5ft 1in. wide. £675

Early Victorian writing table with leather lined top, on reeded legs. £55

19th century mahogany writing table with concave front and reeded legs, 54in. wide.　£365

Louis XVI style mahogany kneehole bureau plat with brass mounts, borders and gallery, 148cm. wide.　£540

Edwardian inlaid mahogany and satinwood banded oblong writing table on square tapered legs, 60cm. wide.　£85

Burmese padouk wood writing table.　£240

Ormolu-mounted Louis XVI style writing table on tapering legs with brass castors.　£800

Martin Carlin bureau plat and cartonnier with ormolu mounts.　£157,750

Fruitwood writing table with drawer, 36in. x 24½in., circa 1820.　£125

Edwards and Roberts walnut writing desk, circa 1860, on carved legs.　£425

Reproduction walnut writing table on cabriole legs, 42in. wide. £70

Small half-round lady's writing table with raised gallery back with velvet top, centre drawer with fretted front, 30in. x 20in. £130

Mahogany writing table with 'antique green' hide top, reeded moulding and dummy drawers at back, 43½in. wide, 20in. deep, 29in. high. £120

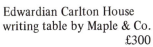

Edwardian Carlton House writing table by Maple & Co. £300

French tulipwood and kingwood serpentine bureau plat inlaid with floral marquetry, 3ft.3in. wide. £290

Victorian inlaid mahogany and rosewood banded writing table with spiral end supports, 102cm. wide.£70

Mahogany inlaid bow-front kneehole writing table with five drawers and the top inset with rexine, 4ft. wide. £75

Late Georgian mahogany bonheur du jour with line inlay, 2ft.6in.wide. £1,000

BEAKERS

Kothgasser beaker painted with bees and fish, circa 1815, 5.5ins. high.   £420

Newcastle slag glass tumbler in purple and white.   £4.50

Bohemian green glass mug with gilt overlay, dated 1886, 4.8ins. high.   £200

Late 17th century wheel-engraved ruby glass beaker, South German, 12.5cm. high.   £2,500

Egarmann beaker with three layers of colour in a chequered pattern, circa 1840.   £150

A beaker of grey Lithyalin glass by Friederick Egarmann of Blottendorf, 13ins. high, first half of 19th century.   £480

19th century Mary Gregory sapphire blue tankard, 6½ins. tall.   £58

Beaker from the Giles workshop.   £441

Early 19th century Bohemian red beaker decorated with gilt and white.   £300

Amber flash beaker
engraved with views
of German towns,
circa 1850.   £80

Early 19th century
enamelled glass
beaker decorated
by Anton Kothgasser,
12cm. high.   £1,995

Bohemian flashed
rosalin beaker with
waisted panel cut
sides, circa 1850.
£100

Early 19th century
Bohemian beaker by
Friederick Egarmann,
11cm. high.   £1,785

Bohemian milchglas mug
decorated with a roundel
enclosing a figure in
coloured enamel, about
1750.   £250

Lithyalin glass beaker
by Friederick Egarmann,
10.5cm. high, first half
of 19th century.   £780

Pink glass Mary
Gregory beaker.
£23

Pressed glass ale
can with geometric
decoration, circa
1860.   £7

An opaque white glass
beaker enamelled in
colours, 9cm. high.
£290

BOTTLES

German mineral water bottle in dark green glass. £3

Cobalt blue bottle marked 'Not to be Taken'. £2

Dark green glass pickle jar 1880. £6

Small green tinted glass sauce bottle. £0.75

Cobalt blue poison bottle. £1.50

Victorian blue glass night light. £5

Daffy's Elixir Cure All bottle. £28

Small mineral water bottle. £1

Codd's 'light bulb' bottle with black marble stopper. £15

Sheared top sauce bottle of green tinted glass. £1

Bung stopper mineral water bottle. £2

Green glass 'onion' bottle, circa 1885. £4

Victorian brown
glass spirit bottle.
£4

Amber glass
poison bottle.
£4

'Dumpy' green glass
mineral water bottle..
£4

Elegant green glass
beer bottle, circa
1890.   £1

Victorian green glass
night light.   £3.50

Brown glass beer
bottle.   £2

Prices Patent Candle
Co. cough medicine
bottle in cobalt blue.
£30

Brown glass
beer bottle.
£1

Victorian whisky bottle.
£4

Zara seal bottle.
£20

Warners green glass
safecure bottle for
diabetics.   £40

Rare 'Bitters' bottle
dated 1874.   £45

387

BOTTLES

H. Codd's cobalt blue marble stoppered bottle. £100

1 pint brown glass beer bottle. £3

Codd's amber glass mineral bottle. £30

Codd's glass mineral bottle with amber stopper. £12

Victorian octagonal glass ink bottle. £3

Victorian amber glass night light. £4

Early light amber glass 'Bovril' jar. £1

Small green glass poison bottle. £2

Victorian embossed black glass whisky bottle. £15

Cobalt blue bottle marked 'Poison'. £8

Amber glass 'Hair Tonic' bottle. £2

Clarke's clear fluid ammonia bottle. £5

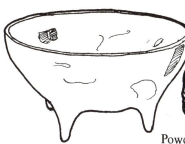

French Lalique glass
bowl on four feet,
24cm. diam., chipped.
£38

Powder bowl by Lalique
decorated with antelopes
in white glass, circa 1915.
£60

White glass sugar bowl,
possibly made on Tyneside.
£35

Edwardian green glass
dessert set comprising
six plates and a bowl,
25.5cm. diam.   £16

Rare caddy bowl
in cut blue glass,
circa 1810. £110

A Galle cameo glass bowl,
the pale pink body overlaid
in green and etched with
teasels, 19cm. wide.   £150

CASKETS

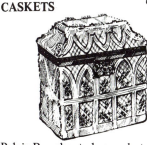

Palais Royal cut glass casket.   £75

Palais Royal cut glass casket and cover
with gilt metal mounts.   £100

Palais Royal cut
glass casket. £75

Amber glass casket with ormolu
mounts and engraved with scenes,
10cm. x 15cm., circa 1850. £125

Palais Royal cut
glass casket on
hoof feet. £110

DECANTERS

Opaque glass decanter by Mowart of Scotland, in deep blue, circa 1920. £15

One of a pair of Baccarat decanters with silver gilt caps, Paris 1819-38. £200

Bohemian glass decanter engraved with a panorama of the city of Prague, circa 1850, 8.5ins. high. £40

19th century bun-shaped decanter and stopper with slight disc cutting, 29cm. high. £4

English claret jug, with pillar cutting on body and stopper, about 1825, 10ins. high. £60

Mary Gregory green glass decanter. £30

One of a pair of cut glass square decanters and stoppers, 10ins. high. £24

Silver mounted green glass decanter by the Guild of Handicrafts Ltd., 1901, 20.5cm. high. £1,500

A pale green Prussian style decanter, with three-ring neck and lozenge stopper, circa 1840. £40

Decanter decorated in the London workshop of James Giles.   £840

19th century cut crystal decanter of shouldered shape, 33cm. high.   £22

Victorian decanter and stopper.   £6

Bottle-sized glass decanter.   £35

Pair of decanters with matching wine glasses from the Prince Regent Service.   £1,150

Ship's decanter with flute cutting and double-ringed neck, circa 1810.   £150

GOBLETS

Victorian overlay goblet 1850, cup-shaped bowl with crenallated rim, on a single knop and tall foot.   £380

Red flashed goblet with a view of the Crystal Palace.   £150

Dutch engraved Newcastle goblet engraved with two billing doves, circa 1750, 19cm. high.   £440

GLASS JUGS

Mary Gregory hand-painted glass cream jug. £10

Irish water jug, about 1790, impressed Cork Glass Co. round the pontil mark, 6in. high. £400

Late Victorian ornamental jug, made at Stourbridge about 1880. £44

Pink overlay jug made at Stourbridge, about 1850. £280

Mary Gregory red glass jug, 5½in. high. £28

A Lalique clear glass jug, the handle moulded with berries and foliage, 21cm. high. £30

Blue Bristol cream jug with gilding, about 1780. £125

Early English cream jug, about 1725, with strawberry topped feet, 3½in. high. £42

Venetian jug, about 1640, with dark turquoise rim and pinched lip. £300

English water jug
with cut swags,
about 1820, 11in.
high.   £60

Flat-bottomed Roman jug,
with a three comb handle,
1-2 century AD, 6in. high.
£120

Dark blue Bristol
cream jug, 1805,
3½in. high.   £50

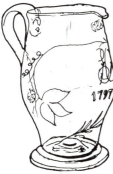

English ale jug,
engraved with hops
and barley and
dated 1797, 7in.
high.   £120

Decorated white glass
baluster cream jug,
possibly made on
Tyneside.   £38

Roman jug with
bulbous body,
about 2nd century,
3in. high.   £270

Cranberry cream jug, with
heart-shaped lip, clear handle and moulded feet, made
about 1870.   £36

Wrockwardine water
jug, late 18th century.
£70

Victorian cran-
berry glass jug,
14½cm. high.
£17

MISCELLANEOUS GLASS

'Birds and Fishes' window design by Webb. £320

Mary Gregory amber glass pin tray depicting a boy with a butterfly net. £50

Lithyalin tazza mounted with ormolu handles and stand, circa 1840. £110

Victorian cut glass candlestick. £4.50

Bristol blue glass sailor's love token. £28

A Sowerby's of Gateshead 'blanc de lait', slag glass ornamental basket, 8cm. wide. £8

Bohemian ruby glass flagon with ormolu mounts, 11ins. high. £160

A lace maker's glass lamp, 16.5cm. high. £75

Late 19th century hour glass egg timer in Mauchline stand. £8

Glass butter churn mounted on an iron stand. £18

A carved cameo amber glass plaque by G. Woodhall, 16.5cm. high. £1,500

Miniature ruby glass tea service with gilt decoration, circa 1860. £135

Rock crystal plaque by Giovanni dei Bernardi, mid-16th century, 10.8cm. x 8.9cm. £16,000

A ruby glass desk rule with silver mounts, 31cm. long. £20

Venetian 'Calcedonio' flask of shouldered hexagonal form, 17th century. £720

Victorian glass eyes. £6

Glass toddy stick. £0.25

A tobacco jar bearing 'The Jolly Japers'. £100

Webb cameo glass plaque carved by H.J. Boam, 1885. £5,800

Glass butter dish, cover and stand, circa 1810. £38

MISCELLANEOUS GLASS

A Waterford glass fruit bowl.   £80

Pair of apothecary jars, marked 'Castor Oil Seeds' and 'Cassia', with original contents, 20ins. high. £195

One of a pair of Irish salts, circa 1790.   £34

Small ruby glass box with metal mounts and Mary Gregory painting on lid.   £28

Mary Gregory enamelled dish with everted rim, circa 1880, 13¼ins. diam.   £85

Small shell design box with hinged lid.   £13

A cameo glass of smokey quartz colour, 9.5cm. high.   £400

A cut glass wine jug.   £85

Tiffany pendant coloured glass lightshade, 28ins. diam.   £1,900

Bristol blue glass box with metal mount, the top with gilded intaglio design.   £20

Art Deco dressing table set, circa 1930.   £85

One of a pair of Chinese cherry red wine cups, 18th century, 3ins. high.   £48

One of a pair of lustres with crystal drops and white overlay decoration, circa 1860.   £300

An unusual bird drinking fountain bearing 'The King-fisher', 17.8cm. high.   £220

A Daum match-holder of rectangular form, the pale blue frosted glass body enamelled with an Alpine scene, 4cm. high.   £42

Covered Bohemian comport, circa 1830.   £28

Victorian crimson glass epergne with centre trumpet, 60cm. high overall.   £45

Eglomise glass chemist's jar with St. George and the dragon.   £155

Pink, white and
blue Nailsea
flask, circa 1830.
£38

Pink and white
Nailsea tobacco
pipe, 41cm. long,
circa 1830.   £48

Pink and white
looped Nailsea
flask, circa 1830.
£38

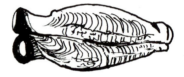

Nailsea flask in the form of a pair of
bellows.   £35

19th century Nailsea double flask with
white loop decoration.   £38

Glass walking stick,
152cm. long. £20

Nailsea bell of red and
blue mottled covering
on a white ground. £75

Glass church warden
pipe of clear glass
with a blue bowl,
122cm. long.   £45

Mid-19th century spun glass tableau of three peacocks, 47cm. high.   £70

Victorian spun glass single-masted fishing smack with a small blue rigged vessel, 36cm. high.   £75

Victorian spun glass house, complete with glass dome and wooden stand, 51cm. high. £100

Lalique car mascot 'The Spirit of the Wind'.   £320

Rare Lalique panel entitled 'L'oiseau Du Feu', moulded in relief, 17ins. high. £1,900

One of a pair of frosted glass bookends in the form of elephants, signed J. Hoffman, 14cm. high.   £26

A sea green and yellow pate de verre figure of Loie Fuller signed A Walter Nancy, 20.5cm. high.   £320

Late 19th century amber carving from Konigsberg, 9ins. high.   £350

PAPERWEIGHTS

Clichy glass bouquet paperweight identifiable by the pink ribbon tying the stalks. £2,000

Clichy paperweight with millefiori arrangement of two rows of florettes. £320

Saint Louis 'crown' glass paperweight. £650

Clichy pansy flower delicately coloured with leaves of pale purple and lemon. £680

Side view of Sentinel, an avant-garde paperweight. £12

Baccarat wheat-flower with pointed yellow petals and black markings. £950

American sandwich paperweight with one deep pink flower with pointed petals. £245

Modern but very rare Scottish paperweight by Paul Ysart, sgnd. PY. £200

Rare Baccarat paperweight showing a butterfly hovering over a flower. £1,250

Dahlia head glass
paperweight by
Saint Louis. £950

Modern Scottish
paperweight by
Perthshire Paper-
weights Ltd. £45

Bouquet paperweight
by Baccarat, superb
quality and condition.
£2,000

Baccarat glass paper-
weight, rare because
of its intricate work.
£950

Side view of Vortex
by Colin Terris
depicts a whirlpool
movement.   £20

Close millefiori
weight by Baccarat
dated B1847. £385

Glass paperweight,
typical of the Clichy
factory, in three
colour combination.
£750

Fine St. Louis
upright bouquet
paperweight,
7.5cm.   £440

High quality Saint
Louis bouquet of
fruit set in a bas-
ket of white latti-
cinio.   £240

SCENT BOTTLES

Green Bohemian glass scent bottle with three overlaid panels, 4.5ins. high. £75

19th century scent bottle in a pierced gilt metal mount inset with four landscape vignettes, 12cm. high. £24

Green overlay scent bottle with silver mounts. £18

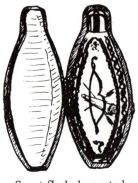

Bohemian glass scent bottle of three layers, 10ins. high. £85

Scent flask decorated with gilt in the design of quiver and arrows Bristol decoration. £110

Bohemian scent bottle with painted overlay and gilt decoration, 19cm. high. £90

A green and clear glass scent bottle with a silver top. £16

Chinese carved amber snuff bottle, 2½ins. high. £600

Double-ended ruby glass scent bottle with silver tops, circa 1860. £19.50

Elegant scent bottle possibly decorated in London. £892

Victorian overlaid scent bottle. £95

Victorian egg-shaped scent bottle, silver mount and cap, by Mappin Bros., Birmingham, 1887. £30

Clichy patterned millefiori scent bottle and stopper, 16.5cm. high. £945

Edwardian bottle for lavender salts with plated top. £6

Mid-19th century Victorian scent bottle. £17

Scent bottle made in Newcastle-upon-Tyne around 1780, slightly cracked. £49.25

Scent flask and smelling salts bottle by Sampson Mordan & Co., circa 1880, 7cm. high. £140

Scent bottle made in Newcastle-upon-Tyne around 1780. £78.75

GLASS VASES

German clear glass vase in a silver plated pewter case by Crivit. £15

Moser iridescent glass vase in graded mulberry tinged with pink. £28

Miniature cameo vase by Galle. £95

One of a pair of opaline glass vases with flowers in colours on a turquoise ground, 39.5cm. high. £850

Burgun and Schwerer wheel carved vase in bluebell purple and gilt. £400

Edwardian celery vase engraved with ferns, 26cm. high. £16

A Loetz peacock blue iridescent glass vase, 25.5cm. high. £190

A Legras cameo glass vase of quatrefoil shape, the frosted glass body overlaid in purple, 13cm. high. £85

One of a pair of M. Gregory cranberry glass vases, 5in. tall. £28

A Galle cameo glass
vase of uniform shape,
the grey, orange body
overlaid in orange, 9cm.
high.   £60

Dark green Art Nouveau
rippled glass vase in a
brass case with lily pad
design.   £22

A Galle cameo glass
small baluster vase, the
olive green body over-
laid in darker green. £78

Red glass Bohemian
vase with gilt decor-
ation and painted
panels, 19cm.high.
                £150

14th century two-handled
Syrian vase of glass enamelled in colours, 30.5cm. high.
              £5,460

Green glass tulip
vase with tear drop
decoration.   £6

Blue and white carved
cameo glass vase, 20.5cm.
high.   £1,500

Cameo footed vase set
with four cabachons
by Daum, circa 1905.
                £285

Galle cameo glass
vase, overlaid in
brown, 43.5cm.
high.   £400

GLASS VASES

Bohemian vase overlaid with white panels and decorated with gilt, 5.5in. high. £60

Iridescent green blue vase with tear drop decoration. £6

Richardson overlaid glass vase, 11in. high. £135

Slim Art Nouveau vase in pale blue glass. £5

Pair of vases in the manner of Mary Gregory, late 19th century. £50

A Vienna vase with a portrait of Sarah Bernhardt, 40.5cm. high. £240

Clutha glass vase in olive green with white and blue striations, circa 1895. £75

Three handled Art Nouveau glass vase in green. £8

A Galle cameo glass vase of tall slender baluster form, the grey, orange body overlaid in crimson, 35cm. high. £230

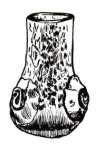

Art Nouveau vase decorated with snails in fiery orange and silver blue. £26

Pair of 18th century Venetian vases. £120

Art Nouveau glass vase in pale lime green with brown bullrushes rising from the base. £40

Mary Gregory pink glass vase of globular shape. £30

A pair of Bohemian green and gilt vases, 17in. high. £400

Large Mary Gregory vase of pink glass. £68

A Galle cameo glass vase overlaid in brown, 32cm. high. £260

Iridescent green and yellow Loetz glass vase with applied snake decoration. £23

Green glass Bohemian vase with portrait on panel and gilt decoration, 19cm. high. £65

WINE GLASSES

Extremely rare bright olive green wine glass, the rim of which is heavily gilded, 1750, 16.5cm. high.　£200

Dram or spirit glass with moulded cup bowl on a plain stem, 1780, 9.9cm. high.
£25

Facet stem wine glass with round ogee bowl, diamond cut stem and plain foot, 1780, 15.8cm. high.　£35

Engraved cordial glass with trumpet bowl set on plain drawn stem and conical foot, 1745, 17.8cm. high.
£80

Opaque twist wine glass with flared funnel bowl set on a double series opaque twist stem on a high conical plain foot, 1770, 13.8cm. high. £40

Engraved cordial glass with small bowl moulded to half height, 1770, 17.1cm. high.　　£90

U bowl ale glass with arch moulded decoration and knopped stem, circa 1840.
£7

A magnificent Beilby armorial goblet inscribed 'W. Beilby Jr.', dated 1762, 8¾ins. high.
£19,500

U bowl ale glass engraved with hops and barley, circa 1840.　£11

Victorian Bohemian 'documentary' stained-glass goblet, engraved on one side, with faceted stem and circular foot, 1851. £80

'Captain' glass with large ogee bowl supported on a heavy double series opaque stem, 1760, 17.2cm. high. £130

A Dutch engraved Royal armorial goblet with the Royal arms of England, 20.5cm. high. £420

Mixed twist ale glass with straight sided bowl on a mixed twist stem with a plain conical foot, 1770, 19.1cm. high. £90

Bohemian round funnelled bowled goblet engraved with figures of a Boar Hunt, circa 1740. £290

Opaque twist wine glass with pan top bowl flared at the rim, 1770, 14.6cm. high. £45

Wine glass vertically moulded funnel bowl decorated with eight panels, 1750, 15.8cm. high. £85

Conical bowled goblet engraved with a continuous stag hunt, circa 1730, 8 in. high. £22

Faceted champagne flute with plain round funnel bowl, 1790, 17.1cm. £40

WINE GLASSES

Sunderland Bridge rummer*, with the initials G.A.H. 1800, 12.7 cm. high. £60

Ale rummer engraved with hops and barley circa 1880. £20

Plain firing glass with trumpet bowl set on thick flat foot, 1740, 8.8cm high. £35

Cordial wine glass with small straight sided bowl, 1770, 13.9 cm high. £75

Wine glass with flared 'tulip' bowl, 1760, 16.5 cm high. £50

Opaque twist wine glass with ogee bowl vertically ladder moulded for its whole height, 1770, 15cm. high. £40

Opaque twist wine glass with octagonal moulded bowl, 1770, 15.2cm. high. £110

Mixed twist wine glass with a waisted bell bowl, 1755, 18.7cm. high. £90

Capstan stemmed ale glass with arch decoration, circa 1840. £10

Rummer engraved with a view of St. Nicholas' Church, Coventry, 1820, 15.2cm. high. £90

Tot glass with stylised engraving. £1

One of a pair of English goblets, finely engraved and initialled WD, circa 1800. £55

Wine glass with funnel bowl, vertically moulded and ladder ribbed to its full height, 1770, 15.2cm. high. £50

Large gilded goblet with ogee bowl on plain columnar stem and conical foot, 1750, 18.3cm. high. £160

Engraved mixed twist wine glass, 1760, 15.2cm. high. £90

Opaque twist wine glass with funnel bowl, 1760, 15.4cm. high. £35

German wine glass in Continental opaque white glass from 18th century. £270

Rare opaque twist wine glass with drawn trumpet bowl, 1770, 17.1cm. high. £25

WINE GLASSES

Deceptive glass with capstan stem, circa 1810. £6

Short ale glass with lemon squeezer foot, circa 1800. £12

Engraved rummer of traditional shape with the initials S.J., 1800, 14cm. high. £30

Opaque twist wine glass with deep ogee bowl, 1770, 16.2cm high. £35

Late 18th century rummer engraved with a gentleman fishing, 11.5cm. £16

Mixed twist wine glass with round funnel bowl, 1760, 14.6cm high. £90

U bowl ale glass with moulded cut thumb-print decoration, circa 1850. £9

Elegant German goblet, about 1780, decorated with coloured enamel. £400

Opaque twist mead glass with cup-shaped bowl incurved at the rim and gadroon mould-ing on the lower half, 1750, 13.9cm high. £200

U bowl ale glass with arch decoration, circa 1850.   £7

Incised twist bright emerald green wine glass,, 1750, 13.3cm high.   £130

Opaque twist firing glass set on double series twist stem, 1770, 10cm high.   £40

Opaque twist ale glass with tall round funnel bowl, 1760, 20.3cm. high.   £95

Engraved ruby sherry glass, circa 1825.   £7.50

Cordial glass with bowl engraved with flowers and leaves, 1780, 16.5cm high.   £90

Airtwist cordial glass with fine drawn trumpet bowl, 1745, 14cm high.   £80

Opaque twist wine glass with medium-size bucket bowl, 1760, 16.5cm. high.   £40

Mixed twist wine goblet with very large ogee bowl, 1760, 19.1cm. high.   £100

WINE GLASSES

Faceted wine glass with slightly flared ogee bowl, and a petal cut and scalloped foot, 1770, 15.2cm. high. £50

Large ale rummer with lemon squeezer foot, circa 1810. £50

Beilby wine glass with conical bowl enamelled in white, 1780, 15.2cm. high. £160

Airtwist ale glass, with round funnel bowl engraved with a single hop and two leaves, 1750, 19.7cm. high. £85

Pair of Mary Gregory green glasses depicting a boy and a girl. £30

Opaque twist wine glass, gilded, with ogee bowl, 1770, 14.6cm. high. £175

A plain stem wine glass with bulbous knop and ogee bowl, circa 1750. £37

Beilby wine glass with ogee bowl enamelled in white with a band of baroque rococo scrolling, 1770, 15.2cm. high. £210

German white glass enamelled in colour, 15cm. high. £270

Pressed glass ale with simulated capstan stem, circa 1870. £4

Coaching glass with faceted ball knop joined to an ogee bowl by a collar, 1820, 12.6cm. high. £30

Beilby enamelled wine glass with gilded rim, 1770, 17.4cm. high. £425

One of a pair of Jacobite wine glasses, engraved with a six-petalled rose, an open and closed bud and the motto 'Fiat', about 1750. £540

'Last drop' ale tumbler, circa 1870. £25

Engraved ale or champagne flute, 1780, 19.7cm. high. £50

Opaque twist wine glass with plain ogee bowl set on vertically drawn opaque stem, 1760, 15.8cm. high. £90

A Dutch engraved Newcastle goblet with the Arms of Van Brederode of Holland. £400

Lynn wine glass, the ogee bowl with five horizontal rings, 1760, 13.6cm. high. £135

HAIR ORNAMENTS

Tiara in pinchbeck and Strass
paste, circa 1810.   £75

Engraved tortoiseshell
hair comb.   £8.50

Art Nouveau comb
of pale coloured
horn.   £26

Two pronged comb
made of stained
horn.   £24

Hair comb of tortoiseshell
surmounted by French jet,
circa 1830.   £880

French comb of jet in the
form of a lovebird with
outstretched wings.   £30

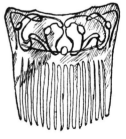

18 carat gold hair slide made
in the Etruscian style.   £55

One of a pair of French
haircombs of horn
adorned with silver
lilies.   £225

English tortoiseshell comb
with flowing gold design
set with turquoises.   £125

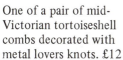

Georgian pinchbeck tiara decorated with false pearls, turquoises and paste diamonds. £75

One of a pair of mid-Victorian tortoiseshell combs decorated with metal lovers knots. £12

One of a pair of Victorian tortoiseshell combs decorated with a gold feather-like design set with rose diamonds. £46

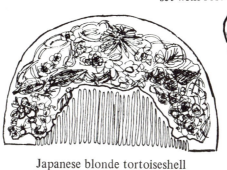

Japanese blonde tortoiseshell hair ornament and pin, inlaid with gold, silver and mother-of-pearl. £135

English tortoiseshell comb with gold design set with turquoises. £125

Pacific North-West coast wood comb, possibly Salish, 15cm. high. £650

Victorian horn comb decorated with ivy leaves in blue and green enamel. £11

Pinchbeck tiara decorated with filigree work. £75

Art Nouveau tortoiseshell hair comb. £9.50

A Victorian officer's pill box hat of The Honourable Artillery Corps Infantry. £52

A Victorian officer's patrol cap of the Monmouthshire Regiment, with braided peak. £48

A Victorian officer's blue cloth ball topped helmet of The Royal Artillery. £45

A good brass fireman's helmet, brass helmet plate with fire fighting devices. £66

A good Italian cabasset c.1600, formed in one piece, pear-stalk terminal to crown. £65

A Victorian officer's black cloth spiked helmet of the Royal London Militia. £60

A good Nazi police shako, patent leather peak and crown, green cloth covered body. £30

A good brass fireman's helmet of the Oxford Fire Brigade. £75

An other rank's fur cap of a rifle regiment, corded red boss bears Kings Crown badge of Queen Victoria's Rifles.£20

A post 1902 officer's blue cloth spiked helmet of The Wiltshire Regiment. £60

A late Victorian officer's patrol cap of the Gloucestershire Regiment, bearing a fine gilt and enamel badge with braided bullion peak. £74

A Victorian officer's blue cloth spiked helmet of The 4th Volunteer Battalion, The Cheshire Regiment. £44

A good other rank's shako of The Highland Light Infantry, diced border with Kings Crown badge. £70

A scarce Saxon Jaeger shako, brass and silver plated helmet plate, leather chinstrap, black hair plume. £80

A Prussian Cuirassier other rank's steel helmet, inside of skull stamped 'C.D. Juncker 1916'. £105

A rare Bavarian pressed tin infantryman's pickelhaube, brass helmet plate. £70

A good brass fireman's presentation helmet, the peak mounted with copper plaque. £105

A post 1902 officer's blue cloth spiked helmet of The Army Service Corps. £42

Pair of brass callipers by Culpeper. £400

19th century sextant by Troughton & Simms. £260

An 18th century circular universal equatorial dial by Adams. £275

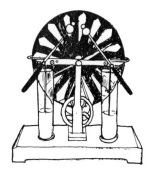

American Dover pattern whisk in iron with a turned wood handle, circa 1904. £2.50

Wimburst machine for producing electricity, 14in. high. £85

Mid 19th century American brass Altizimuth theodolite by N. & L. E. Gurley, 1ft. high. £100

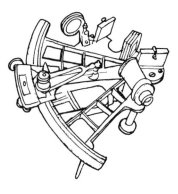

Late 19th century brass binocular microscope by A. C. Collins, 1ft.6in. high. £170

19th century brass sextant by A.F. Parkes & Sons.£150

Mahogany cased single draw brass telescope, circa 1820. £155

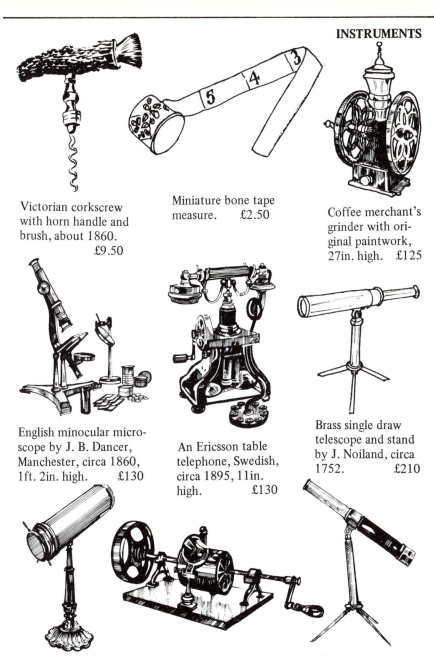

Victorian corkscrew with horn handle and brush, about 1860. £9.50

Miniature bone tape measure. £2.50

Coffee merchant's grinder with original paintwork, 27in. high. £125

English minocular microscope by J. B. Dancer, Manchester, circa 1860, 1ft. 2in. high. £130

An Ericsson table telephone, Swedish, circa 1895, 11in. high. £130

Brass single draw telescope and stand by J. Noiland, circa 1752. £210

A London Stereoscope Co. jewel kaleidoscope, circa 1860. £105

Rare tin foil phonograph, circa 1879. £2,100

Early 19th century brass kaleidoscope by W. Harris, 1ft. long. £170

Crimean War set of
surgeon's instruments
by 'Sumner & Co.,
Liverpool', circa 1855.
£285

Pocket sundial
and compass
combined by
M. Butterfield
of Paris, early
10th century.
£275

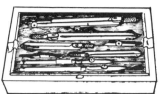

A set of architect's
drawing instruments
by Thornton Ltd.,
in mahogany case.
£19

Late 19th century
brass microscope by
R. and J. Beck.
£250

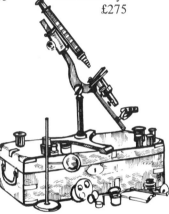

Andrew Ross microscope with
accessories, circa 1839.   £500

A fruitwood noct-
urnal dial signed
W. Broughton and
dated 1679. £720

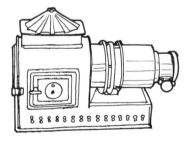

Baird lantern slide projector
(enlarger) with electric light
and wood tripod stand. £7

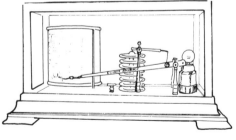

Barograph in stained wood case.
£38

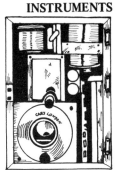

Early 19th century lacquered brass opaque solar microscope by W. Jones.   £320

19th century brass opaque solar microscope by Cary of London.   £320

Early 19th century 30 hour chronometer by Dent of London.   £430

Brass microscope by Culpeper of an original 1725 design.   £200

Binocular version of the 'Watson' Edin. microscope.   £90

Binocular microscope by Dancer, circa 1880.   £150

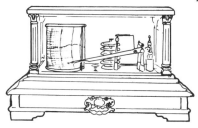

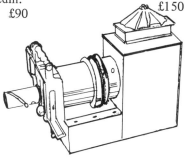

Barograph in oak case with drawer, 15in. wide.   £57

Baird magic lantern, the slide with coloured plates.   £18

INSTRUMENTS

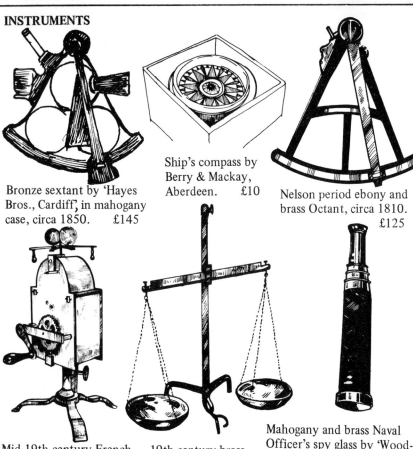

Bronze sextant by 'Hayes Bros., Cardiff', in mahogany case, circa 1850.   £145

Ship's compass by Berry & Mackay, Aberdeen.   £10

Nelson period ebony and brass Octant, circa 1810.   £125

Mid 19th century French mechanical roasting jack in brass and sheet iron.£25

19th century brass bankers' scales. £35

Mahogany and brass Naval Officer's spy glass by 'Woodward, Clements Inn Strand', in leather case.   £60

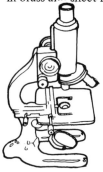

Microscope by C. Baker, London, (9184) in case.£32

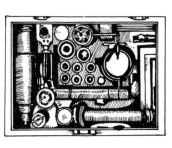

A brass compound universal microscope circa 1820. £320

Wanzer lock stitch sewing machine on marble base.   £15

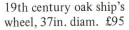

Constellations from the
Gemma Frisus universal
astrolabe.   £57,000

19th century oak ship's
wheel, 37in. diam. £95

Mahogany and brass single
draw telescope on stand,
circa 1820.   £155

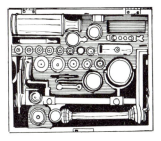

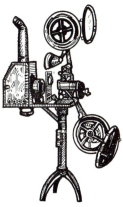

Early Victorian Scottish
butter churn in pine, 48cm
high x 34cm wide x 43cm
deep.   £40

Early 19th century brass
microscope by A. Abrahams
of Liverpool.   £380

An early
cinematograph
projector. £185

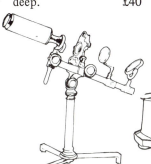

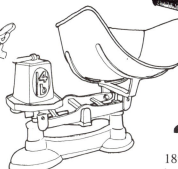

Georgian brass
compound micro-
scope by Gilbert
& Sons, London.
            £300

Late Victorian grocer's
scales.   £32

18th century oxidised
brass reflecting tele-
scope signed S. Johnson,
London.   £260

INSTRUMENTS

French blue lacquered metal opera glasses, circa 1900. £10

Ebony and brass octant circa 1810, 14in. long. £145

Astronomical telescope engraved H. Hughes & Sons, London. £165

Watson 'Fram' brass microscope, circa 1890. £50

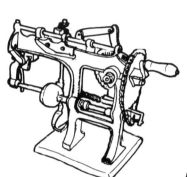

Apple corer made around 1890-1910 works on same idea as a sewing machine. £75.80

Smith and Beck microscope, in case. £42

Lambert typewriter marketed by The Gramophone and Typewriter Ltd., circa 1903. £90

English microscope by Powell & Lealand, 1872. £450

Early 19th century Culpeper type microscope with trade label of William Harris. £180

A brass theodolite
by Cary of London.
£230

19th century cased
marine chronometer.
£520

An 18th century brass
Georgian reflecting
telescope by J. Short
of London.   £500

Victorian brass
microscope by
Baker of Hol-
born.   £45

Burr walnut table
model pedestal
stereoscope.£600

Small 19th century
brass microscope.
£10

Surveyor's sighting
crosshead and com-
pass by W.S. Jones,
London, circa 1840.
£85

Nicely made brass microscope
by Negretti and Zamba , circa
1865.   £70

Late 19th century
brass pocket micro-
scope by T. Rowley.
£10

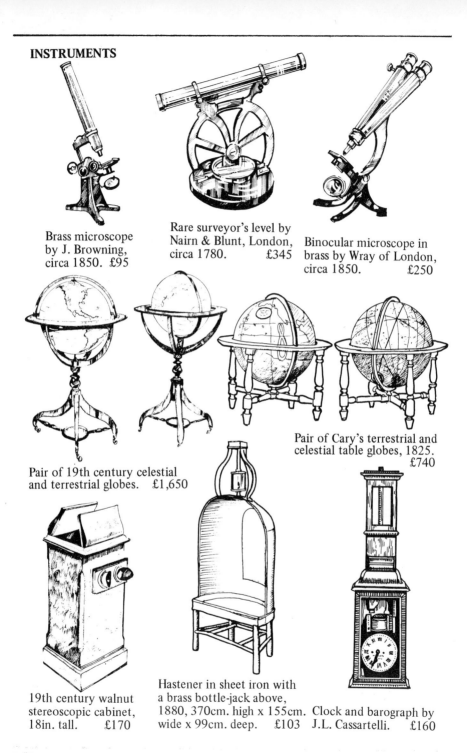

INSTRUMENTS

Brass microscope by J. Browning, circa 1850. £95

Rare surveyor's level by Nairn & Blunt, London, circa 1780. £345

Binocular microscope in brass by Wray of London, circa 1850. £250

Pair of 19th century celestial and terrestrial globes. £1,650

Pair of Cary's terrestrial and celestial table globes, 1825. £740

19th century walnut stereoscopic cabinet, 18in. tall. £170

Hastener in sheet iron with a brass bottle-jack above, 1880, 370cm. high x 155cm. wide x 99cm. deep. £103

Clock and barograph by J.L. Cassartelli. £160

19th century
novelty tape
measure. £5

19th century spyglass by
G. Adams in a horn and
ivory case.   £150

Victorian brass silver
scales on a mahogany
base.   £80

Pair of Cary celestial and terrestrial
dated globes, each with a compass
in the stand.   £1,550

Pair of celestial and terrestrial
globes.   £800

Brass surveyor's level
by Adie & Son, Edin-
burgh, circa 1850.£78

George III celestial
globe by Dudley
Adams, 18in. diam.
£850

Rare inclinometer
engraved 'Dover
Charlton', Kent.
£385

19th century steel griddle iron.   £23

Victorian cast iron door stop, 9 in. high.   £10

A box iron by Kenrick, size 6, circa 1870. £14

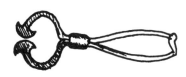

Steel sugar cutters, circa 1790. £12

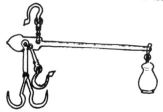

Steel yard as used by farmers and butchers to weigh heavy loads. £25

Early 18th century iron hanging rush light and candle holder, 4ft. long extending to 6ft.   £68

17th century steel steak fork, ram's horn top, circa 1660.   £35

Fireside trivet in wrought iron with heavy pierced brass top and turned fruitwood handle, circa 1750.   £38

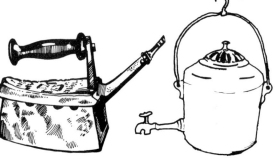

William Cross & Sons 'Hot Cross' gas iron.   £6

2½ gallon iron fountain.   £17.50

Swedish steel vegetable chopper. £24

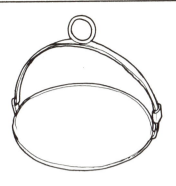

19th century iron griddle. £15

Collection of hand-wrought flesh forks. £18.45 each.

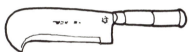

Small, Victorian butcher's cleave. £4.50

Victorian, cast iron, butcher's cleave. £4.50

18th century meat fork. £32

Polished steel harpoon from the whaler 'Harmony 1821', 45 in. long. £128

Petrol heated iron, by Coleman, model 8 'Instant Lite'. £15

Tinned iron whisky dipping measure. £5

18th century plate warmer. £60

IVORY

Victorian ivory sewing reel. £4.50

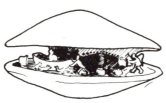

One of a pair of Japanese ivory shells, interiors carved in landscapes. £52

Chinese ivory thimble, about 1920. £3

Chinese ivory figure of a girl holding a fan and a flower, 18½cm. high. £24

Pair of German ivory figures of children on circular plinths, 19cm. high. £100

French ivory bust of a girl, with ormolu drapery, signed A. Leonard, 24cm. high. £120

19th century Japanese ivory figure of a sage, 25cm. high. £50

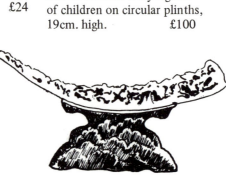

19in. ivory tusk, carved to show a procession of travellers. £110

Large Chinese ivory group with a figure of a man, eagle and monkey, 38cm. high. £140

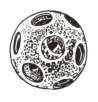

Enamelled gold and paint on ivory snuff box by James Morriset, 1779, 8.9cm. wide. £8,400

19th century Chinese ivory concentric pierced ball. £20

Chinese ivory card case with carved panels. £16

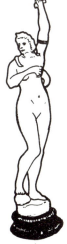

Italian ivory figure of 'Salome', 26cm. high. £90

French ivory figure of Christ, on a rouge marble base, 26cm. high. £140

Chinese ivory figure of a man with musical instruments, 31cm. high. £130

Late 18th century Chinese ivory game of Bilboquet. £44

Early 19th century fan with ivory sticks. £5

Chinese ivory figure of a boy on a see-saw, 17cm. high. £75

IVORY

Whale tooth engraved with a sailing ship at anchor and a sailor with his concubine, initialled by J.A., 4in x 2in. £110

An ivory octagonal two division tea caddy. £140

Inscribed whale tooth with vignette of murder on reverse, 6in x 1¾in. £95

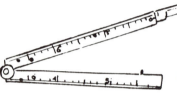

Carved Indian bone chess man. £7

Folding ivory ruler with pen blade. £15

Whale tooth engraved with the 'Death of Samuel Comstock' and 'John Tabors Ride', 6¼in. x 2in. £140

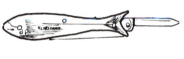

Sheffield made ivory penknife with perpetual calendar. £30

Indian carved bone chess man. £7

Victorian penknife with ivory fish handle. £10

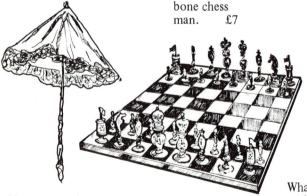

Victorian pink parasol with lace border and ivory handle.£12

Chinese ivory chess set complete with black and gold chessboard. £230

Whale tooth engraved with sailing ship and inscribed 'The Inflexible at Lake Champlain 1776', 4½in. x 2in. £120

Whale's tooth, etched
'Taking whale, Nero,
1870', 5½in.   £50

Whale tooth, whaling
tools on reverse, 5in.
x 2in.   £70

19th century Japanese carved ivory figure
of Daruma, signed Hayashi, 7¼in. high.
£190

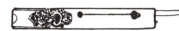

French ivory pen machine, circa 1840. £20

19th century scrimshaw whale's
tooth depicting a sailing ship.
£75

Whale tooth decorated with a
study of six figures, 6¾in. x
2¼in.   £80

Indian bone
chess man.
£7

Inscribed whale tooth,
5½in. x 1¾in.   £40

Early 19th century French
ivory penknife with retract-
able blade.   £5

Chinese ivory figure of
a boy with mask, 8cm.
high.   £22

13½in. tall whale tooth
section, carved to show
dragons and sea horses.
£90

Whale's tooth, etched
seascape inscribed
'Brig Britannia', 4¼in.
£36

IVORY

Finely carved and pierced ivory Ryusa netsuke of a Phoenix with kiri leaves and stylised waves. £54

Oriental carved ivory 'Flying Fish Dragon', 15in. long. £500

Japanese ivory table seal with group of three kylons. £46

Victorian ivory souvenir of the Isle of Wight. £10

Set of four 18th century Flemish ivory statuettes, 11.8cm. to 14cm high. £546

Tortoiseshell dish inlaid with ivory and hardstones, 21in. diam.£1,000

Art Deco ivory and bronze figure by Gregoire. £250

Mother-of-pearl oval shaped ash tray with etched ivory cover of the sailing ship 'Taurus'. £46

IVORY

Late 19th century sectional Japanese ivory group, 14in long. £210

Victorian ivory brooch.£5

Edwardian set of ivory cocktail sticks. £10

19th century Japanese ivory carving of a travelling salesman carrying baskets, 10¼ in. tall. £825

Javanese Pelog Rebab with head, neck and tail spike of delicately turned ivory. £170

19th century French carved ivory group, 9in. high. £1,900

Chinese ivory figure of a girl holding a fan, 12½cm. high. £18

Carved ivory shelf ornament by Harumitsu. £850

Mid 18th century ivory carved bodkin case. £24

JADE

19th century jade figure of a crouching dog, 3½in. wide. £300

Ming period jade figure of a single horned mythical beast, 7cm. high. £450

18th century figure of a bird in pale celadon jade. £440

Chinese green jade recumbent horse, 14cm. wide, on a wooden stand. £95

One of a pair of Chinese green jadeite bowls, 5½cm. diam. £90

18th century pale jade group of a ram and young, 8cm. long. £1,200

18th century recumbent chimera in burnt jade. £340

Jade ewer and cover, 7½in. high. £600

Small Chinese jade figure of a monkey. £15

Late 18th century green jade fish, 2.1/8in. long. £10

Chinese jade figure of a man, 2½in. high. £14

18th century jade carving of a carp swimming amidst lotus plants, 9in. wide. £1,250

18th century Ching period jade group of two birds, 2½in. wide. £250

Chinese jade group of two maidens. £594

18th century jade figure of a bird slightly turning its head, 6.6in. long. £1,200

A carved jade fabulous animal, 10in. long. £780

18th century circular white jade bowl, 5½in. wide. £820

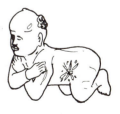

A spinach jade fertility baby pillow, 41cm.x 48cm. £725

Antique necklace, rose diamond loops with collet centres, circa 1820. £1,300

Victorian pearl, diamond and enamel necklet. £1,050

An antique diamond collet necklace. £6,400

Turkish amber necklace threaded with silver beads. £150

Top quality 15 carat gold necklace. £200

Rose diamond bracelet with a message 'Thou art for me'. Gold clasp which opens to show a lock of hair. £290

Continental silver gilt chatelaine set with garnet and pearls. £90

Berlin iron filigree necklace and bracelet signed by Devaranne, about 1830. £160

Austro-Hungarian silver gilt necklace with matching earrings, circa 1870. £95

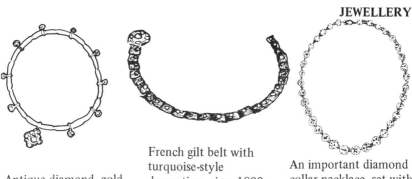

Antique diamond, gold and enamelled necklet. £1,300

French gilt belt with turquoise-style decoration, circa 1890. £28

An important diamond collar necklace, set with thirty-five graduated brilliant cut diamonds. £30,160

Victorian brooch of superb quality and condition, about 1840. £220

Gold bracelet of heavy links with heart locket, set with turquoises and ruby. ·£300

An antique cabochon emerald and diamond parure. £6,000

A diamond necklace. £1,250

18th century Chinese mandarin amber necklace. £250

A diamond negligee pendant. £6,000

JEWELLERY

Diamond frog brooch, late 19th century.
£300

Early 19th century brooch.
£1,150

An emerald and diamond cluster ring of cushion shape, the step cut emerald weighing 4.47cts. £5,655

A diamond and emerald clover leaf brooch.
£7,600

Moss agate brooch in gold frame. £35

A mid-Victorian diamond and emerald brooch.
£950

Amber ring in a gold setting, with a good speciment of an embalmed insect.£85

Victorian diamond crescent brooch.   £1,875

Mizpah brooch of twin-hearts in 9 carat gold.   £14

A diamond moth brooch with ruby eyes.   £850

9 carat gold ring with an anchor, cross and heart.
£24

Mid-19th century brooch. £1,250

Heart brooch, sapphire and diamond, mid 19th century.   £4,500

Silver, jasper and enamel flower pendant by Alex. Placzek.   £30

An antique diamond crescent and star brooch.   £2,800

A cut-steel bird brooch.   £15

2nd century Roman gold medallion and chain.   £690

Victorian silver shell and beetle design brooch.   £37.50

A Victorian diamond sunburst brooch with pendant fitting.   £740

Strap and buckle brooch of silver with pink and grey Aberdeen granites, circa 1870.   £37

Silver and enamel 'daisy' pendant by Alex. Placzek. £25

Gold, ruby, emerald and enamel pendant in Holbeinesque taste.   £2,050

Expanding Roman bracelet made from sheet gold.   £370

19th century French sapphire and diamond ring.   £1,400

A diamond and sapphire double clip brooch. £1,410

An antique diamond tremblant spray brooch. £3,600

Diamond and pearl brooch with a pink pearl drop. £1,325

An antique diamond spray brooch in the form of an open crescent with stars bursting from the centre. £1,320

An Art Deco diamond and sapphire brooch with a central triangular cut diamond. £660

Multi-coloured diamond basket of flowers brooch. £1,800

A ruby and diamond double clip. £900

Georgian jewel with sprig of flowers, snake twisted in the stalk, and heart hanging from its mouth. £88

High quality silver brooch, late 19th century, Victorian, with flowers decorated in gold overlay. £26

An antique diamond Maltese Cross brooch. £1,000

Early 19th century carved Baltic amber brooch. £110

A Victorian diamond star brooch, the mount gold with silver settings. £750

Silver bar brooch with stylised versions of faith, hope and charity. £13

A diamond, ruby and flower brooch. £1,100

Metal brooch with 'Regard' spelt out in paste stones. £14

A diamond leaf spray brooch. £540

Third century Roman gold earrings made of sheet gold with square sectioned wire. £175

An antique diamond flower spray brooch, the stones pave set in silver, the mount gold. £790

Pendant in the shape of a padlock with a crystal compartment to hold a lock of hair, made of 9 carat gold studded with pearls. £95

An antique jewel, the nubian carved from translucent brown hardstone. £4,800

One of a pair of emerald and diamond clips of Art Deco design. £7,200

Baltic amber ring in a silver setting. £65

Victorian amber flower brooch. £27

A diamond and emerald brooch. £8,200

JEWELLERY

Florentine mosaic and goldstone, gold-mounted brooch. £95

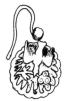

Silver shell-shaped earrings with love-bird motif.   £12

A platinum ring set with three brilliant cut diamonds.
£1,800

A diamond square cut single line bracelet, the sixty-one stones mounted in platinum, signed Cartier.   £1,510

A diamond and blade opal brooch in the form of a stylised swallow in flight.
£660

Pair of Victorian pinch-beck and red paste ear-rings.   £5

Yellow navette diamond ring, 5.48cts., circa 1930.
£5,200

Sapphire and diamond bracelet, modern. £1,700

Enamelled clover with a pearl centre, on 18 carat gold.   £25

Pair of antique diamond ear-rings. £2,200

Tie pin motif, in the form of a question mark set in 18 carat gold.   £26

An antique three coloured gold and enamel bracelet set with eleven pictorial plaques.£790

Sapphire and diamond cluster ring. £600

Silver earrings in the shape of acorns. £30

Pink sapphire ring on gold shank. £200

A white gold bar brooch set with a solitaire diamond. £900

Metal brooch, the detailed cuffs and prominent wedding band of which denote love and marriage. £19

Victorian sapphire and diamond bracelet. £1,450

Sapphire and diamond ear-rings, circa 1930. £1,600

One of a pair of emerald and step cut diamond drop earrings. £12,250

A diamond flexible bracelet. £5,000

Unusual 'Dearest' ring, stones dangling with perfect flexibility from a gold plaited band. £100

Pair of diamond ear clips. £580

Cupid's arrow brooch, with rose diamonds, 1920's. £42

A flexible diamond bracelet set with brilliant cut diamonds, the centre one of 2.2cts. flanked by stones of about 1ct. £6,600

JEWELLERY

An Art Deco emerald and diamond ring. £1,500

Berlin ironwork bracelet by Geiss. £150

A Victorian diamond circular brooch with pendant fitting. £1,550

Ch'ien Lung period amber ring.   £25

A black pearl, pearl and diamond cluster tear shaped negligee pendant. £200

9 carat gold suite of brooch and ear-rings. £109

A diamond and pearl trellis brooch. £1,300

A diamond pendant of target design.   £500

19th century cross in Berlin ironwork. £47

German brooch with enamel cover to a notebook of a lover's letters.   £48

19th century silver and hardstone brooch in the form of an anchor. £5

Victorian square shaped copper ship's cargo inspection oil lamp with hinged lid. £20

Victorian brass Corinthian column oil lamp with etched cranberry coloured globe. £44

Victorian brass railway style candle bracket lamp with chimney and coronet. £34

Japanese carved wood hexagonal hanging lantern with opaque and decorated glass panels, 61cm. high. £28

Brass oil lamp with pedestal stem. £28

One of a set of four Colza lamps on metal stands. £600

A night light holder bearing various scenes. £80

19th century electric lamp, the base with a bronze eagle. £12

One of a pair of Norwegian ship's lanterns marked Stybord and Bagbord, 23in. high. £95

LAMPS

Small Edwardian
tin carrying
lamp.   £3

Edwardian metal
carrying lamp. £4

Victorian brass
chamber candle
lamp with cone
snuffer.   £16

China vase shaped
oil lamp with brass
neck.   £55

Victorian brass hanging
oil lamp complete with
ribbon white shade.£24

Victorian brass column
lamp, the clear globe
with embossed design.
                    £28

Victorian ship's navig-
ation oil lamp in copper.
                    £32

Victorian brass lace maker's
lamp with reflector and
chimney.   £34

Victorian brass and
copper ship's engine
room lamp.   £18

Brass travelling lamp with plated reflector.   £12

Galle glass table lamp, signed, about 1900, 35cm. high.   £530

Bull's eye lantern with green and red shutters, circa 1870.   £7.50

Victorian brass pedestal oil lamp fitted with a frosted and etched globe.   £25

George III bronze-framed porch lantern.   £400

Large Victorian oil lamp with pink column and 9in. etched shade.   £40

Onyx pillar table oil lamp with cloisonne enamel and brass mounts.   £75

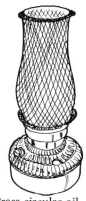

Brass circular oil lamp with crimson glass shade, 20in. £18

Brass reading lamp with plated reflector.   £12

LAMPS

CHANDELIERS

A French lantern-shape electric light, circa 1910, 97cm. high. £60

Superb Adam style chandelier, circa 1785. £6,000

Edwardian chandelier, circa 1902. £125

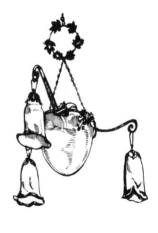

Late 19th century Venetian glass chandelier, 61cm. high. £75

Gilt metal chandelier with three tiers of twenty-one electric lights, 213cm. high. £200

Highly coloured Belgian chandelier by Muller, 61cm. high. £200

CHANDELIERS

One of a pair of 17th century French ormolu chandeliers. £355

Gilt metal and cut glass bowl electric chandelier. £140

A large Edwardian salon chandelier with a fountain of glass drops, 107cm. high. £500

FLOOR LAMPS

Early 19th century brass Corinthian pillar floor lamp, 145cm. high. £120

Victorian brass electric floor lamp on hoof feet. £90

19th century carved oak floor lamp. £20

LEAD

Neo-classical lead jar, circa 1780.   £50

Superb mounted figure of Henry, Duke of Lancaster, in full armour, by Ping.   £30

Mid-19th century lead jar with cast and applied decoration. £30

One of a pair of 18th century lead terrace vases.   £245

One of a pair of cast lead circular plant tubs with flowers and scrolls in relief, 13¼ins. diam. £100

One of a pair of English lead urns, circa 1800, 1ft. 6ins. high x 1ft. 6ins. max. width.   £75 each

One of a pair of French gilt spelter female figures with cupids, 48cm. high.   £40

Pair of 19th century lead figures in period costume, 53ins. high.   £660

Late 18th century lead figure, 2ft. 8ins. high.   £250

Early 19th century French padlock with oak leaf decoration on key escutcheon cover.   £10

George III brass door lock, 7ins. wide, with keeper and key.   £38

Old Spanish padlock and key.   £9

Victorian cast iron door knocker, circa 1850, 8ins. high.   £12

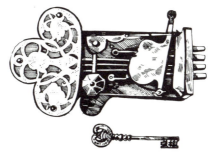

16th century steel door lock with key, from the Bohemia's Castle of Dux, where Casanova's body was finally laid to rest, 19½ins. wide.   £399

17th century bar padlock and key. £28

17th century engraved door lock and key.   £28

Louis XVI ormolu door lock. £85

French steel-cased door lock with heavy ormolu trim, brass handles, and escutcheon plate, circa 1790.   £58

MARBLE

19th century white marble statuary bust of a girl, draped, 68cm. high. £44

One of a pair of French marble urn-shaped vases with female mythological figure handles in ormolu, 17½in. high. £240

Antique marble bust of Caesar. £580

Indian marble statuary goddess painted red and gold, 42cm. high. £30

Pair of Italian terracotta garden seats, about 1840, 1ft.10½in. high x 2ft.2in. wide x 1ft.3in. deep. £295

Mid 19th century figured white marble and ormolu mounted jardiniere. £295

Carved marble figure of 'A Girl with a Kid' with circular plinth by R.J. Wyatt. £525

Pair of carved stone caryatids from a fireplace, circa 1760, 57ins. high. £480

Late 19th century stone sundial, 3ft. high. £18.50

A sculptured white marble figure of the Apollo Belvedere, 1.39m. high. £980

Italian green ma[...] male figure on a [...] 30cm. wide.

Chinese white marble stele, 62.2cm. high, A.D. 570. £27,000

English 18th ce[...] bench, 1ft.6in. [...] wide x 1ft.4in. [...]

Italian marble garden urn on plinth, 47in. high, 38in. wide. £400

One of three [...] dicular Gothic [...] carved in high [...] overall.

Early 19th century French padlock with oak leaf decoration on key escutcheon cover. £10

George III brass door lock, 7ins. wide, with keeper and key. £38

Old Spanish padlock and key. £9

Victorian cast iron door knocker, circa 1850, 8ins. high. £12

16th century steel door lock with key, from the Bohemia's Castle of Dux, where Casanova's body was finally laid to rest, 19½ins. wide. £399

17th century bar padlock and key. £28

17th century engraved door lock and key. £28

Louis XVI ormolu door lock. £85

French steel-cased door lock with heavy ormolu trim, brass handles, and escutcheon plate, circa 1790. £58

MARBLE

19th century white marble statuary bust of a girl, draped, 68cm. high.
£44

One of a pa[ir]
marble, urn[s]
with female
figure hand[les]
17½in. high

Indian marble statuary goddess painted red and gold, 42cm. high. £30

Pair of Italian ter[racotta]
about 1840, 1ft.1[in]
wide x 1ft.3in. de[ep]

Carved marble figure of 'A Girl with a Kid' with circular plinth by R.J. Wyatt. £525

Pair of carved
from a firepla[ce]
57ins. high.

MIRRORS

Georgian mahogany toilet mirror, tulip wood stringing, 18in. wide. £42

19th century Venetian carved and pierced gilt-framed oval wall mirror.
£75

Victorian mahogany dressing glass with drawer in the base.
£18

Edwardian mahogany framed dressing mirror, 89cm. high. £10

Regency style convex mirror in giltwood ball pattern frame.
£60

19th century upright dressing table mirror with gilt bird in the cresting, 3ft 6in. £48

Mahogany oval cheval mirror. £38

Overmantel mirror in carved gilt frame of Adam design, 4ft 6in. wide. £42

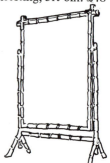

19th century ebonised and gilt bamboo pattern, upright mirror. £39

Mahogany oblong dressing glass with three drawers in the base, 20½in. wide. £28

18th century mahogany and parcel gilt mirror 1.27m. high. £1,500

Mahogany inlaid mirror, three drawers in base, circa 1800. £130

One of a pair of Italian giltwood girandoles, mid 18th century. £300

Charles II stumpwork mirror panel. £1,300

Victorian gilt plaster wall mirror. £50

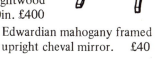

George II walnut and giltwood overmantel, 38in x 70in. £400

Victorian mahogany cheval mirror. £95

Edwardian mahogany framed upright cheval mirror. £40

MIRRORS

Early 19th century mahogany and parcel gilt wall mirror, 44in. high, 27in. wide. £340

Late 19th century walnut dressing glass, 12½in. high. £45

Eastern carved wood oblong wall mirror. £5

Victorian mirror, framed in tortoiseshell and ebony. £145

Early Georgian giltwood mirror, the frame carved with garter motto. £1,417

19th century mahogany oblong bevelled wall mirror, 83cm. wide. £42

Georgian cheval glass in a turned mahogany frame with brass candle holders. £90

One of a pair of Georgian carved giltwood upright wall mirrors, 115cm. £480

19th century ebonised and gilt bamboo pattern, framed cheval mirror. £38

George I carved
giltwood mirror
with broken arch,
39½ins. high. £1,000

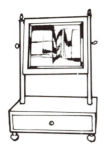

19th century oblong
mahogany dressing
table mirror with
drawer, 35cm.   £22

Unusual shaped Georgian
mirror with small oval
mirror above   £60

George II giltwood
wall mirror, 37in.
high, 19½in. wide. £130

Victorian oval
wall mirror in a
gilt frame, 3ft.
high.   £20

George III walnut framed
upright bevelled wall
mirror, 84cm. high.   £50

Regency style gilt-
wood upright pier
mirror, 60cm. wide.
          £50

19th century wall mirror
in an elaborately carved
frame, 176cm. wide. £80

19th century gilt
framed wall mir-
ror, 76cm x 106cm.
          £75

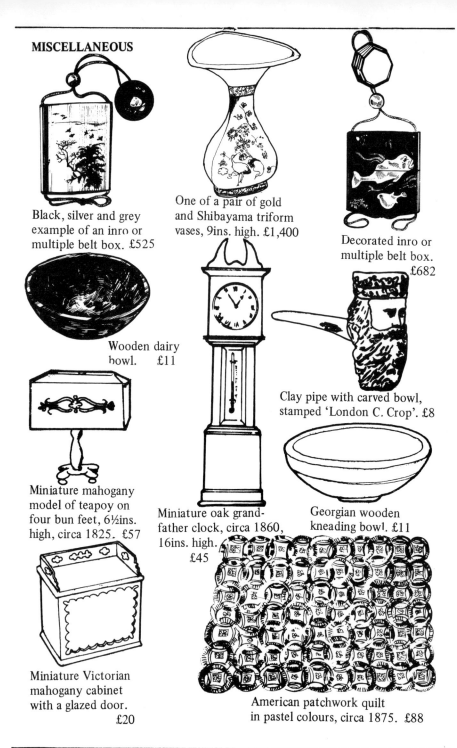

MISCELLANEOUS

Black, silver and grey example of an inro or multiple belt box. £525

One of a pair of gold and Shibayama triform vases, 9ins. high. £1,400

Decorated inro or multiple belt box. £682

Wooden dairy bowl. £11

Clay pipe with carved bowl, stamped 'London C. Crop'. £8

Miniature mahogany model of teapoy on four bun feet, 6½ins. high, circa 1825. £57

Miniature oak grandfather clock, circa 1860, 16ins. high. £45

Georgian wooden kneading bowl. £11

Miniature Victorian mahogany cabinet with a glazed door. £20

American patchwork quilt in pastel colours, circa 1875. £88

Flemish woven tapestry, circa 1600, 3.44m. high. £2,900

An unusual French Empire peat burning fire. £150

One of a pair of gold and Shibayama vases signed Yaschika, 12½ins. high. £3,000

An Italian alabaster circular tazza on a gilt metal base, 30cm. diam. £36

Vase of wild strawberries by Carl Faberge in semi-precious stones and a rock crystal vase, 16.5cm. high. £36,000

Japanese souvenir rickshaw, about 1900. £4

Unusual box in the shape of a grandfather clock, Dutch, circa 1902. £125

Candelabrum of Blue John and ormolu by Mathew Boulton. £880

Neo classical carved pine chimney-piece, about 1785. £2,200

Stevengraph 'William Prince of Orange crossing the Boyne'. £240

MISCELLANEOUS

Three Persian hide water vessels in sizes. £10

Panorama of the Isle of Wight, circa 1820, 2.7m. long. £275

English needlework picture with a vignette of Christ and the Women of Samaria, circa 1660. £550

Victorian bead purse. £3

Five manicure tools, in blue leather bag, 4in. long. £35

Victorian Tunbridgeware clothes brush. £8

French parcel-gilt mounted malachite cup, about 1840, 23.6cm. high. £260

Victorian walnut and brass book slide. £9

Solid agate teapot marbled in yellow and brown. £780

Victorian miniature basket, about 4in. across. £1

19th century beadwork tea cosy. £9

An alabaster figure of an elephant on an oblong base, 22cm. long. £16

An 11½in. musical necessaire, in the form of a grand piano. £160

Stevenograph 'HMS Majestic'. £65

Bottle of Toraji Szamarooni, vintage 1938. £5

Early Scottish horn spoon. £7

Bottle of Dom Perignon champagne, vintage 1943. £24

Solid agate silver shaped sauceboat. £1,300

A leather tankard. £70

The coronation of King George and Queen Elizabeth, drawn by Mary McNeie, 1938, 216m. long. £30

MODELS

A scale model of a 1910 delivery van, 87cm. long. £100

'Heinrici' model hot air engine, 18ins. high. £110

Victorian model of a butcher's shop, circa 1865. £250

Fine model of the Yarmouth drifter 'Everest', about 1860-75, signed Charles Saunders. £200

Carved giltwood model of a stagecoach with two horses, 56cm. wide. £48

Scale model of a fairground organ. £390

Victorian model greengrocer's shop, 13½in. high, circa 1840. £95

19th century model of a gypsy caravan. £60

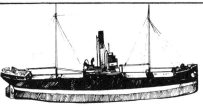

A ship builder's model of the steamer 'S.S. Hookwood', 6ft. long.   £720

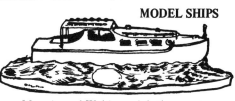

Mappin and Webb model silver motor launch, 1965, 45.7cm. long.   £400

20th century English three-masted model ship, 3ft. 2ins. wide.   £200

Fully-rigged model of the 74-gun man-o'-war 'Royal George', 1782.   £840

Wooden model of a clinker-built fishing boat with anchor and oars, 13ins. long.   £32

A large ship builder's model of the 'R.M.S. Orcades', 8ft. long.   £620

Bone prisoner-of-war model of three-masted man-o'-war.   £3,600

French prisoner-of-war bone model of a man-o'-war, early 19th century, 91cm. long.   £4,200

3½in. gauge model of the Royal Scot.   £520

3½in. gauge working model of a 4-4-0
trans-American locomotive and tender.   £300

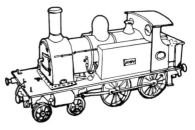

Steam model locomotive.   £800

4½in. gauge scale model of a coal-
fired locomotive 'Jimpy'.   £390

Working model of the Great Northern locomotive
No. 7 Scorpion, overall length 170cm.   £1,500

A Tammany Hall iron mechanical bank.   £35

American painted iron mechanical money box with figures of Punch and Judy, 7½in.   £70

An automated 'Jolly Nigger' money bank.   £15

Late 19th century American cast iron 'Punch and Judy' money box, 7½ins. high.   £130

A rare cold painted cast iron baseball money box, 9½ins. wide.   £110

MOULDS

An unusual chocolate mould, possibly German in the shape of a lion.   £10

A pelican-shaped chocolate mould, possibly German.   £9

An unusual chocolate mould in the shape of a dog, possibly of German manufacture.   £10

MUSICAL BOXES AND POLYPHONES

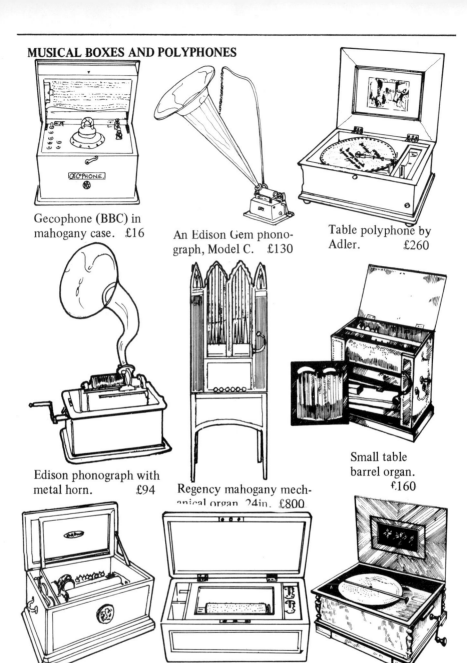

Gecophone (BBC) in mahogany case. £16

An Edison Gem phonograph, Model C. £130

Table polyphone by Adler. £260

Edison phonograph with metal horn. £94

Regency mahogany mechanical organ, 24in. £800

Small table barrel organ. £160

Late Victorian musical chest in burr walnut and ebonised case, patent K. Prowse & Co. Lon. £885

Mahogany inlaid music box with one drum, 14½in. wide. £80

Stella table polyphone with 22 metal discs. £750

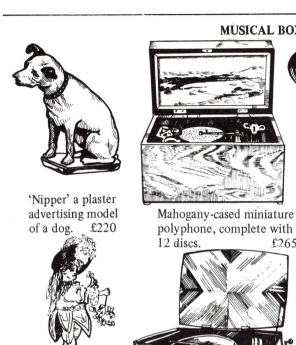

'Nipper' a plaster advertising model of a dog. £220

Mahogany-cased miniature polyphone, complete with 12 discs. £265

Berliner gramophone by Kammerer & Reinhardt of Waltershausen, Germany, circa 1890. £1,150

Musical automaton by E. Jumeau, 21in. high. £680

A superb Stella disc musical box, circa 1901. £2,550

Edwardian table gramophone with metal horn. £90

An Edison Bell 'Domestic A' gramophone by Pathe Freres, circa 1901. £160

A swiss organ musical box playing six airs, 66cm. wide. £560

An early 20th century 'Trademark' type English gramophone. £360

MUSICAL BOXES AND POLYPHONES

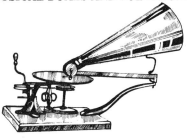

A Gramophone company hand driven style No. 2 gramophone with 7in. diam. turntable, 1898-1901. £520

Late 19th century Swiss cylinder musical box playing ten airs, 1ft.9in. wide. £120

A C.T. Bates church barrel organ playing ten hymns, circa 1840, 5ft.9in. £320

A Big Ben picture automaton, 27in. x 22in. £130

German, late 19th century polyphone with seven metal discs, 1ft.9in. wide. £260

Late 19th century Stella polyphone in an inlaid case, 29in. wide, with seven discs. £320

A large German Stella disc musical box with six discs of 17¼in. diam, circa 1900. £500

Swiss late 19th century upright cylinder musical box, 2ft.2in. wide. £400

Rare German hand driven gramophone by Kammerer and Reinhardt, 1890-95. £950

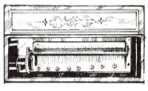

19th century musical box with four interchangeable cylinders. £585

17in. doll, whose head moves as her hands play the piano, which is really a musical box. £480

A Nicole Freres key wound cylinder musical box, 1ft. 6in. wide, Swiss, circa 1900. £400

His Master's Voice Horn gramophone, circa 1915. £130

A Mermond Freres interchangeable cylinder musical box with four cylinders, 3ft.3in. wide. £800

MUSICAL INSTRUMENTS

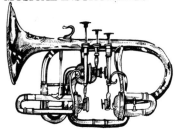

Mid 19th century brass cornopean by H. Kohler, London, 13ins. long. £350

Mid 19th century North Italian violin case with fruitwood marquetry inlay, 31¼in. long. £230

Silver mounted violin bow by Eugene Sartory, Paris, 55gm. £420

An important 18th century treble recorder by T. Stanesby, Jnr., London, 19¾in. long. £2,300

An unusual carved Viola da Gamba bow, probably English, 27in. long, 64gm. £170

Native string instrument with hide and shell ornament. £10

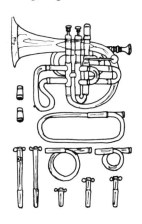

A cornopean by F. Pace, Westminster, circa 1835. £270

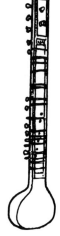

A small early 19th century sitar. £45

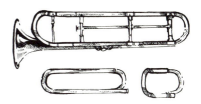

Hunting horn made by Phipps and Robinson, London 1792. £575

Brass slide trumpet by Hawkes and Son, London, with two tuning crooks. £130

Gold and tortoiseshell mounted violin bow by Malcolm M. Taylor, 65gm. £320

Rare and important late 17th century treble recorder by Joseph Bradbury, 30½ins. long. £2,900

Silver mounted violin bow by Eugene Sartory, Paris, 57gm. £620

Inlaid table harp, circa 1815. £115

Royal Scots 4th/5th Battalion (Queen's Edinburgh) drum. £75

Five keyed serpent by B. Huggett, circa 1835, 74cm. high. £409

A violincello piccolo bearing a manuscript label J. Steiner 1669, back 23in. long. £620

A tenor oboe by T. Cahusac, third quarter of 18th century. £1,150

An Indian Esrar from the early 19th century. £80

Blackman flute in case. £30

French brass euphonium. £10

One of a pair of Thai bronze drums, 48cm. high. £720

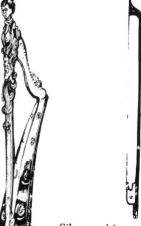

A single action harp by Erard Freres of Paris, circa 1790. £820

Flute in mahogany case. £30

A North Italian hook harp, dated 1776, 67in. high. £260

Silver and ivory mounted violincello bow by W.E. Hills & Sons, 75gm. £480

A viola by Johann Blasius Weigert, Linz, 1724, length of back 16¼ins. £850

A violin by Paul Bailly, Paris 1890, back 14ins. long. £520

A violincello by Giuseppe Pedrazzini, Milano, 1922. £2,600

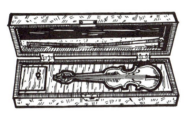

Miniature violin by John Shaw, Manchester 1905. £1,600

Viola by Joannes Franciscus, Pressenda, 1826. £8,200

An Italian violin labelled Santino Lavazza, circa 1800, 14ins. long. £850

19th century violin 23½ins. long. £34

Violin by Joseph and Antonius Gagliano, Naples, about 1790. £3,200

A fine cello by George Panomo, London, circa 1830. £5,400

A violin probably by a later member of the Gaudagnini family, 1756. £2,600

A viola by J.B. Weigert, Linz, 1724, length of back 16¼ ins. £850

An Italian viola attributed to E. Ceruti, Cremona 1847. £650

A violin by G. Pollastri, Bologna 1932, length of back 14in. £1,250

Violin by T. Eberle, Naples. £4,200

A fine unlabelled French violin, circa 1840, back 14in. long. £1,100

An Italian violin by G. Scarampella Varese, 1902, back 14½in. long. £1,150

A French violin labelled J. B. Vuillaume, length of back 14½in. £1,300

A violin by Joseph Rocca, Turin 1844, length of back 14in. £3,600

An unlabelled violincello with varnish of golden brown, back 19½in. long. £6,200

A violin partly by A. Stradivari, 1713, back 14in. long. £7,800

An English violin by N. Cross, London, circa 1730-40, back 14in. long. £260

An early Italian violincello by A. M. Pesaro, 1690, back 30in. long. £1,100

A violin by A. G. Bergamer, back 14¼in. long. £600

An Italian violin by A. Lorenzi, 1793, back 14¼in. long. £700

An English violincello by T. Kennedy school, back 29in. long. £780

A violin by G. Guarneri, Cremona 1707. £17,500

A Scandinavian Hardanger fiddle, dated 1877. £380

NETSUKE

Japanese ivory netsuke of a dancing man.   £30

Shozan or Shogyoku, man with a crook and scriber, signed.   £60

18th century ivory netsuke of a recumbent Sennin.   £90

Kyuchi or Shusai peasant holding a fowl with a feedbox, signed.   £64

A fine carved ivory Ryusa netsuke with Hotei seated, two children and two others on reverse.   £58

Ivory netsuke depicting a group of two pups.   £380

Carved wood Manju netsuke.   £30

Koichi, actor, signed.   £85

18th century netsuke of a family of hares by Tametaka.   £770

Shozan dancer with a fan, signed.   £85

Japanese ivory netsuke of a man.   £25

Shogyoku, actor, signed.   £85

19th century Japanese
ivory animal netsuke.
£28

Standing horse
netsuke. £340

Sanichi peasant woman
feeding a fowl, signed.
£100

Masayuki, actor with
a fan, signed. £85

Good carved ivory Shunga
netsuke signed Vukimasa.
£130

Masayuki, actor,
signed. £64

Japanese carved
ivory netsuke
of a monkey.
£24

Carved ivory netsuke
of a stylised head.
£28

Carved wood netsuke
in the form of a Shishi,
sgnd. Tadatoshi.
£1,350

Shozan dancer
with fan. £60

Issan, finely dressed
woman holding a
fan, signed. £60

Japanese fisherman
Sanichi, signed.£46

NETSUKE

Mitsuyuki musician, signed. £85

Shozan or Shogyoku actress, signed. £85

Shozan dancer, signed.   £85

Japanese ivory netsuke of a man and gourd. £20

18th century netsuke of a stylised tiger by Tomotado. £4,400

Japanese ivory netsuke of a man in a ceremonial dress with sword. £28

Fine ivory netsuke of a seated dog, signed Tomotanda. £525

Early 19th century carved ivory netsuke. £80

Actress holding her mask, signed. £85

Shozan actor. £58

19th century netsuke of an actor, signed. £60

Tomohura, sculpture, signed. £85

484

Masayuki,
depicting
old age,
signed.£85

Woman
carrying
a vessel.
£85

Early 19th
century
Masayuki,
man with
hat, signed.
£62

Shozan
dancer
with open
fan, signed.
£62

Man with
a sword,
signed. £85

Carved wood
netsuke of a
monkey with
her young,
signed Harumi
tsu.   £220

Japanese ivory
netsuke of a
gourd with a
horse head.£35

Mitsuyuki,
actress,
signed. £85

Masayuki,
actor,
signed.£60

Shogyoku,
woman
carrying
fish in a
basket,
signed. £85

Woodcutter,
signed. £62

Kyuichi or
Shusai,
musician,
signed. £62

PEWTER

French 19th century pewter, lidded, double litre measure, 10in. £90

Pewter Prismen Kann or lidded flask, by F. Cane, Appenzell, Swiss, early 19th century, 36cm. high. £330

Victorian half-pint tankard of baluster form, the domed cover with shell thumbpiece, 4¾ins. high. £32

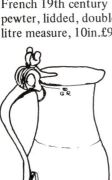

Jersey pewter wine measure of typical form, about 5½in. high. £170

18th century pewter flat topped tankard with ball thumbpiece. £220

18th century flagon with attractive hinged lid, made by J. Weber of Zurich. £230

Large 19th century lidded Scottish measure. £25

19th century. Normandy flagon. £150

French 19th century pewter, lidded litre measure, 8in. £40

Victorian pint tankard of tapering cylindrical form, with scroll handle and spout, 4½ins. £24

A Swiss Glockenkanne, inscribed 1748, 25cm. high.
£340

18th century flagon of baluster form with domed cover, 10½in. high. £60

German pewter tankard with broad foot.
£170

19th century quart tankard of baluster form with scroll handle and spout, 6½ins. £21

19th century pewter straight sided tankard, with lid and curled decorated thumbpiece.
£110

Late 18th century tappit hen of unusual waisted form with domed cover. £205

19th century Swedish tapering lidded pewter tankard with ball thumbpiece. £105

Early 19th century one gallon harvest measure with scroll handle, 11½in. high.£115

PEWTER

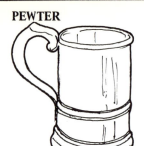

Pewter pint mug with reeded band and base stamped WR., 15½cm. high. £30

An early oval pewter shaving bowl. £74

18th century Bar-Sur-Aube pewter wine pitcher, 30cm. high. £550

Pair of embossed pewter plates. £64

Set of Irish haystack measures in pewter. £80

An early embossed pewter jug. £56

An early oval fluted pewter jardiniere. £360

North German pewter flagon by H. Helmoke of Lubeck, circa 1656. £1,000

18th century pewter charger, 12½in. diam. £42

18th century pewter Normandy flagon, 12in. high. £230

Late 18th century water cistern with tap, 9in. high. £150

One of a pair of mid-17th century pewter candlesticks, 9½ins. high. £8,000

Pair of 20th century Chinese pewter horse-heads, 16ins. high. £65

Pair of early pewter embossed plates. £115

One of a pair of Japanese pewter pricket altar candlesticks with pierced stems, 52cm. high. £40

Pewter relief of 'The Battle of Rocroi' signed Reuerand, 1859, 12.5cm. x 7.5cm. £66

An Irish pewter gallon measure by J. Austen. £370

PEWTER

An Oxford pewter ale or cider jug of quart capacity, circa 1800. £190

Liberty pewter and enamel tobacco-box with sides cast with rows of stylised leaves and set with blue-green enamel cabochons, 4¾in. £40

19th century Scottish pewter lidded measure. £18

Swedish or Baltic pewter tankard with flat top and ball thumbpiece, 18th century, 8in. £220

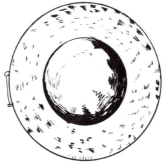

Pewter Cardinal's hat dish, French, about 1700, 15½ in. diam. £210

Rare Cromwellian pewter tankard with a wide flared foot, 9¾ins. tall. £1,250

19th century pewter goblet. £12

A pewter spoon rack by A. Heiddan, Lubeck, circa 1820. £140

19th century pewter tankard. £16

19th century Japanese
pewter Ting, 28½cm.
£28

Late 19th century
thistle measure
with Glasgow tree.
£20

Scottish pewter flagon,
18th century, interior
base marked with a
Tudor rose with crown
and Edin., 8½in. £135

Swiss Glockenkanne,
about 10in. high, with
wriggled decoration.
£240

18th century pewter
charger with deep cen-
tral bowl, 13in. diam.
£24

Charles I bun shaped
covered flagon.
£1,000

German pewter tankard,
10in. tall with engraved
body.   £200

Broad rimmed pew-
ter charger, 21¾in.
diameter, circa 1675.
£1,400

18th century wine
measure by Andre
Utin of Vevey.£280

Marshall and Rose baby grand pianoforte in mahogany case, 4ft 6ins. long. £320

An Asherberg boudoir grand pianoforte, 7 octave, in a rosewood and marquetry case, 203cm. long. £600

Coin in slot barrel piano playing ten dance tunes, in a birchwood case. £460

An enormous Imhof and Mukle orchestrion, 12ft. 6ins. high. £8,500

Early 19th century upright grand piano by Broadwood £200

Boudoir grand piano by John Broadwood, in a satinwood inlaid mahogany case. £1,400

A Steinbeck baby grand pianoforte in a rosewood case, 122 cm. long. £350

Monington and Weston baby grand pianoforte no. 56600, in a mahogany case, 5ft 3in. long. £300

Regency table piano by Muirwood & Co., Edin., 167cm. wide. £135

A Collard and Collard boudoir grand pianoforte in a mahogany case, 156cm. long. £280

An English 19th century 'Competion' pipe organ with sixty-one keys and twelve stops, 7ft. high. £380

Miniature Victorian piano and stool by D. Hillman. £45

Kaim and John upright grand pianoforte, 6½ octave, in rosewood inlaid case. £60

Late 18th century grand piano by Broadwood. £2,700

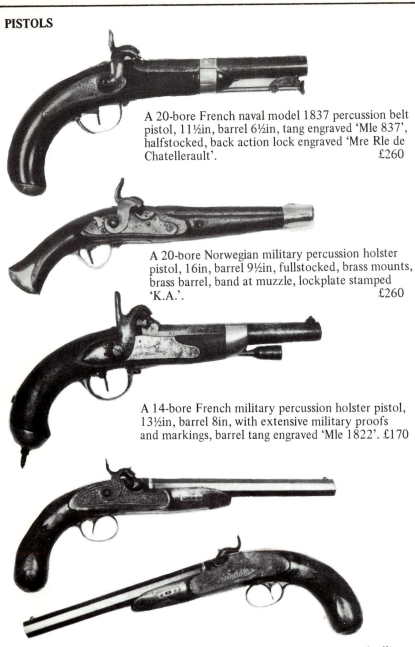

A 20-bore French naval model 1837 percussion belt pistol, 11½in, barrel 6½in, tang engraved 'Mle 837', halfstocked, back action lock engraved 'Mre Rle de Chatellerault'.   £260

A 20-bore Norwegian military percussion holster pistol, 16in, barrel 9½in, fullstocked, brass mounts, brass barrel, band at muzzle, lockplate stamped 'K.A.'.   £260

A 14-bore French military percussion holster pistol, 13½in, barrel 8in, with extensive military proofs and markings, barrel tang engraved 'Mle 1822'. £170

A pair of 45-bore Austrian percussion duelling pistols by M. Nowotny, 15in, octagonal twist smooth-bore barrels 9in, engraved 'M. Nowotny in Wien' scroll engraved breeches.   £600

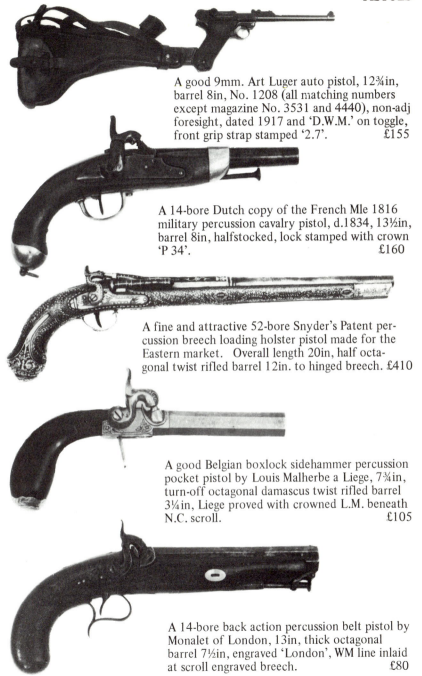

A good 9mm. Art Luger auto pistol, 12¾in, barrel 8in, No. 1208 (all matching numbers except magazine No. 3531 and 4440), non-adj foresight, dated 1917 and 'D.W.M.' on toggle, front grip strap stamped '2.7'. £155

A 14-bore Dutch copy of the French Mle 1816 military percussion cavalry pistol, d.1834, 13½in, barrel 8in, halfstocked, lock stamped with crown 'P 34'. £160

A fine and attractive 52-bore Snyder's Patent percussion breech loading holster pistol made for the Eastern market. Overall length 20in, half octagonal twist rifled barrel 12in. to hinged breech. £410

A good Belgian boxlock sidehammer percussion pocket pistol by Louis Malherbe a Liege, 7¾in, turn-off octagonal damascus twist rifled barrel 3¼in, Liege proved with crowned L.M. beneath N.C. scroll. £105

A 14-bore back action percussion belt pistol by Monalet of London, 13in, thick octagonal barrel 7½in, engraved 'London', WM line inlaid at scroll engraved breech. £80

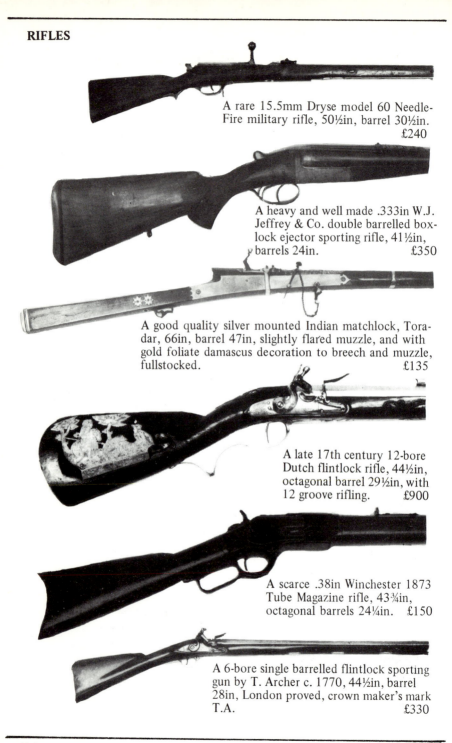

A rare 15.5mm Dryse model 60 Needle-Fire military rifle, 50½in, barrel 30½in. £240

A heavy and well made .333in W.J. Jeffrey & Co. double barrelled box-lock ejector sporting rifle, 41½in, barrels 24in. £350

A good quality silver mounted Indian matchlock, Tora-dar, 66in, barrel 47in, slightly flared muzzle, and with gold foliate damascus decoration to breech and muzzle, fullstocked. £135

A late 17th century 12-bore Dutch flintlock rifle, 44½in, octagonal barrel 29½in, with 12 groove rifling. £900

A scarce .38in Winchester 1873 Tube Magazine rifle, 43¾in, octagonal barrels 24¼in. £150

A 6-bore single barrelled flintlock sporting gun by T. Archer c. 1770, 44½in, barrel 28in, London proved, crown maker's mark T.A. £330

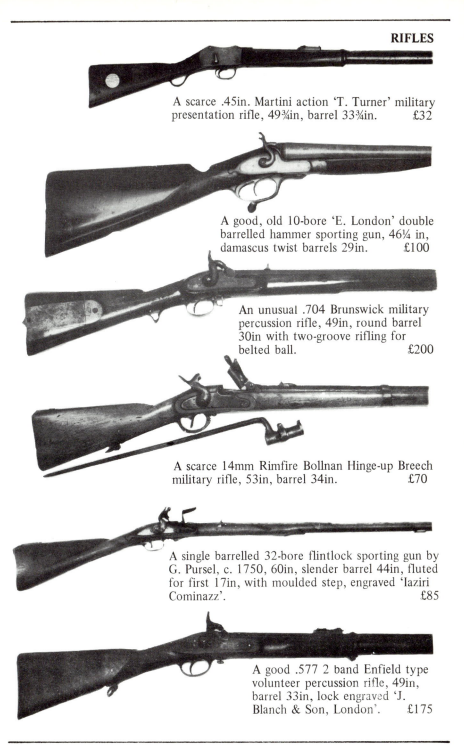

A scarce .45in. Martini action 'T. Turner' military presentation rifle, 49¾in, barrel 33¾in.   £32

A good, old 10-bore 'E. London' double barrelled hammer sporting gun, 46¼ in, damascus twist barrels 29in.   £100

An unusual .704 Brunswick military percussion rifle, 49in, round barrel 30in with two-groove rifling for belted ball.   £200

A scarce 14mm Rimfire Bollnan Hinge-up Breech military rifle, 53in, barrel 34in.   £70

A single barrelled 32-bore flintlock sporting gun by G. Pursel, c. 1750, 60in, slender barrel 44in, fluted for first 17in, with moulded step, engraved 'Iaziri Cominazz'.   £85

A good .577 2 band Enfield type volunteer percussion rifle, 49in, barrel 33in, lock engraved 'J. Blanch & Son, London'.   £175

RUGS

North-West Persian rug. £1,300

Eastern bordered rug, 6ft. 6in. x 4ft. 3in. £135

Eastern bordered rug, 6ft. x 4ft. 3in. £50

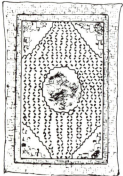

Chinese carpet of about 1770 with pattern of Fo-dogs, in the centre a medallion, 7ft. 2in. x 4ft. 11in. £2,200

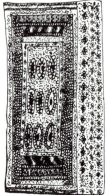

Bokhara rug, crimson and blue ground, bordered, 6ft. x 4ft 1in. £55

Khotan rug, about 1950, with vase and pomegranate type design, 12ft. 4in. x 5ft. 10in. £1,800

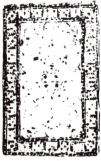

Kirman Persian rug with an ivory, blue and rose ground, 2m. x 140cm.£110

A silk Hereke rug woven partly with a silver thread on wine red field. £7,200

Caucasian bordered rug, 5ft. 5in. x 4ft. £105

Fine Shirvan rug,
59in. x 45in.£500

Antique Chinese rug
in tones of Imperial
blue, 7ft.8in. x 5ft.
4½in.   £75

A Mochtachem Kashan
carpet with tomato red
field, 3.95m. x 3.05m.
£5,200

Chinese rug about 1850,
9ft.3in. x 6ft.1in., has a
dragon motif in brown
on a blue field.   £950

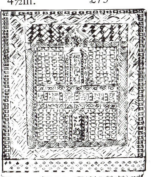

A finely woven Tekke
Hatchli prayer rug, with
orange field, 1.44m. x
1.30m.   £640

Mongol saddle
rug, 1.27m. x
61cm.   £399

A Teheran rug,
6ft.6in. x 5in.
£1,350

Eastern bordered
rug, 4ft.8in. x 3ft.
9in.   £52

18th century Chinese
carpet on an ivory
field, 9ft.6in. x 8ft.1in.
£1,700

RUGS

A silk Tabriz prayer rug with terra cotta Mihrab, 1.79m x 1.23m.   £4,200

Chinese silk antique carpet, 8ft.6in. x 6ft.3in.   £750

Derbend rug, 5ft.11in. x 3ft.9in.   £70

An early 18th century Paris chinoiserie tapestry, 2.09m. x 4.60m.   £3,000

Afshar prayer rug, 5ft.4in. x 2ft.8in. £28

16th century Flemish tapestry, 22ft. x 8ft.   £5,200

Caucasian bordered rug, 7ft.5in. x 4ft. 10in.   £50

19th century Gashgai rug, 8ft.10in. x 5ft. 4in.   £100

Good quality Ispahan rug. £1,600

A finely knotted
Kashan carpet,
4.32m x 3.15m.
£1,800

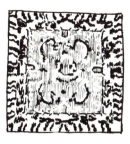

Late 18th century
Chinese rug.   £150

Shirvan rug, 117cm. x
94cm.   £550

An early 18th century
Paris tapestry, 2.84m.
x 4.80m.   £2,400

Seychour antique
runner, 10ft.8in.
x 3ft.8in.   £360

16th century Flemish
tapestry woven with a
landscape.   £5,200

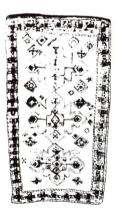

Eastern bordered
rug, 6ft.6in. x 3ft.
9in.   £38

Turkey bordered rug,
the blue field with
tree motif, 4ft.10in. x
4ft.5in.   £8

Caucasian bordered
rug, 5ft.6in. x 3ft.
9in.   £20

Fine hand-painted Tavern sign 'The Oddfellows Arms' in blackwood frame, 43ins. x 35ins. £68

Hand-painted red pottery butcher's shop sign of a bull's head, 19ins. high. £165

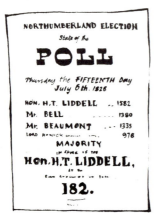

Election result printed on pink silk, 1826. £7.75

A large Royal Coat of Arms cut in four pieces, painted in true heraldic colours, circa 1860, 51ins. x 40ins. £650

19th century double-sided sheet iron Tavern sign 'The Prince of Orange'. £145

A Crosse and Blackwell advertising plaque stamped 'TJ and J Mayer', 24cm. x 32cm. £440

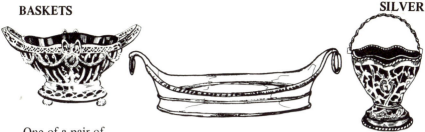

One of a pair of
George V silver
gilt baskets of
oval form, London
1922, 78ozs.
£1,150

George III boat-shaped basket
by John Schofield, London 1797,
20ozs. 3dwt.   £250

George III sweet-
meat basket by
S.B., London,
1771, 5ozs. 10dwt.,
excluding liner. £19

George IV silver
cake stand by
Mackay of
Edinburgh, 1829.
£300

Victorian silver bon-
bon dish by Yapp
and Woodward,
Birmingham, 1846.
£90

George III swing-
handled cake basket,
maker's mark I.W.,
1810.   £380

Circular fruit basket
by Benjamin and
James Smith, London,
1809, 55ozs. 8dwt.
£680

Circular silver dessert
basket by J.P., F.P.,
London 1905,
24ozs. 11dwt.   £250

Silver swing-handled
basket by R.I.,
London 1797. £222

BEAKERS

Queen Anne silver beaker on rim foot by T. Elston, Exeter, 1703, 3¼ins. high, 2ozs. 5dwt.   £340

Plain tumbler cup made by Joseph Stokes in 1699, weighs 4ozs., 2¾ins. high.   £720

19th century Dutch silver, circular beaker engraved with inscription, 7cm. high.   £20

Silver beaker, about 1693, was probably made by Robert Timbrell, 2¾ins. high.   £2,150

Late 17th century English silver beaker and spice box, 5ozs. 7dwt. £2,350

Plain silver beaker engraved with a Coat-of-Arms, about 1800, 4ins. high.   £200

One of a set of four silver beakers made by John Crouch in London in 1809, 3½ins. high, 6ozs. 10dwt. each beaker.   £1,125

Late 17th century German silver beaker, Augsburg, circa 1680, 4ozs. 19dwt, 3½ins. high.   £520

18th century Continental silver beaker.   £650

Deep silver bell-shaped beaker, made in Jersey about 1740, 3½ins. high, weighing 3ozs. 10dwt. £330

17th century German silver beaker decorated on the matted ground with three vignettes of contemporary figures and a musician. £800

Silver gilt beaker by Jakob Priester, Augsburg, circa 1700, 5ozs. 7dwt. £550

Beaker by H.B., London, circa 1680, 9½cm. high. £400

Small Commonwealth silver beaker by Gilbert Shepherd, London 1689, 1oz. 5dwt. £380

Silver beaker, 1682, maker's mark 'IC', pellet below, 3½ins. high and weighs almost 4ozs. £1,200

BELLS

Victorian silver table bell by E. & J. Barnard, 5ins. high. £310

Pierced and chased circular table bell. £18

Small George III silver bell, possibly by William Cox. £240

BOWLS

19th century silver punch bowl. £300

Victorian circular silver bowl and spoon, London 1886, 6oz. 15dwt.   £28

George III punch bowl by R. Keay of Perth, 1817, 28cm. diam.
£410

Victorian silver punch bowl.
£240

Silver-gilt metal bowl dated London 1777, maker I.H.
£325

Scottish silver bowl of octagonal form by Cunningham & Simpson, Edinburgh, 1806, 18oz.8dwt. £260

George II silver bowl by Alexander Bland, 1735, 30¾oz. £5,200

Silver baluster shaped sugar bowl and cover, 7in. high, 12.25oz., by J. Kentember, 1771.
£450

George II Scottish sugar bowl by William Aytoun, Edinburgh 1746, 7oz. 13dwt.   £520

Large Victorian circular rose bowl, embossed with scrolls, flower heads and foliage, 10in. diam, 37oz. 10dwt. £195

A Guild of Handicrafts silver and green enamel bowl by Charles Robert Ashbee, 11.5cm. high. £680

An Eastern silver chased and embossed rose bowl, 23cm. diam., 15oz. £28

Queen Anne monteith bowl by Richard Syng, London 1704, 49oz. 6dwt. £1,950

Silver sugar basin with swing handle by R. Hennell, London 1786, engraved with a Coat of Arms. £250

One of a pair of silver gilt two-handled bowls by Digby Scott and Benjamin Smith, London 1806, 46oz. 2dwt. £750

Sugar bowl, 1786, blue liner, London, by H. Cowper. £350

Silver sugar bowl and cover by G. Jones, London 1727, 7.5oz. £520

Ornamental shell-shaped sugar bowl and cover by Christian Hilland, 1739, 9.4oz. £1,250

BOWLS

Circular dessert basket by Parker and Wakelin of London, circa 1770, 16ozs. 10dwt.   £320

19th century Oriental plated bowl.   £10

A plain circular silver bowl, 20.5cm. diam., 22ozs. 5dwt. £76

Circular silver quaich design sugar bowl with pierced handles, 3ozs. 5dwt.   £13

William III wine taster, London 1695, 3ozs. 3dwt.   £800

George III bowl by Peter, Anne and William Bateman, London 1805, 6ozs. 12dwt.   £200

18th century German silver-covered sugar box, 5ins. wide, circa 1760, 7ozs. 1dwt.   £320

Two-handled silver-gilt bowl by Claude Payne, French, 12cm. diam., 9ozs. 6dwt.   £9,000

George II Irish circular bowl and cover by Thomas Williamson, Dublin 1735, 168ozs. 6dwt.   £2,100

Silver Georgian patch box, almond-shaped and engraved with leaves and a shield enclosing the initials 'EB'. £32

Circular silver pill box, imported by H.C.F., London 1903. £40

High quality silver box with simple design, Birmingham 1892. £33

Round silver pill box with kitten enamelled on the lid. £48

Dutch silver box, Leevwarden, circa 1750, 22ozs. 10dwt. £1,650

Silver-gilt Art Deco box with enamel target design. £28

Cut glass biscuit box of Art Nouveau design with a plated stand and cover. £10

Silver trinket box with inlaid tortoiseshell lid. £20

Oval silver box having porcelain lid with picture of a lady. £35

BUCKLES

16th century German silver gilt buckle, circa 1540, 3½ins. wide.
£580

A tortoiseshell buckle with pique ornamentation of exotic birds and flowers.
£30

A Liberty silver and enamel buckle in the manner of Jessie M. King, Birmingham, 1908.
£130

BUTTER KNIVES

William IV child's knife, Birmingham 1836, by George Unite, 5½ins. long.
£10

Irish butter knife by Samuel Neville, Dublin 1810.
£30

Scandinavian butter knife by G. Jensen, Copenhagen, 1960. £17

One of twenty-four George III silver gilt cheese knives by Robert Garrard, London 1814.
£360

Butter knife by George Unite, Birmingham, 1893.
£18

Butter knife by Samuel Pemberton, Birmingham, 1802.
£17

BUTTER DISHES

Silver butter shell, Parker & Wakelin, London 1766.
£110

One of a pair of Victorian shell-shaped silver butter dishes, London 1893, 2oz. 15dwt.
£20

One of a pair of George II butter shells, 4ins. wide, by Edward Wakelin, London, 1756, 5ozs. 8dwt.
£150

510

Set of six George IV silver buttons embellished in relief with birds, a hare and hound, 1in. diam., by W.W., London, 1823.   £120

Part of a selection of silver buttons with sporting scenes, circa 1795, six large and eleven small buttons by Susannah Barker.   £740

CADDY SPOONS

Caddy spoon by Joseph Taylor, 1796.   £34

George IV silver King's pattern caddy spoon with fan and scroll decorated bowl, Birmingham 1824, by Joseph Taylor.   £35

Bright cut caddy spoon by Thos. Wallis.   £32

Caddy spoon by J. Betteridge, Birmingham 1830.   £28

Silver caddy spoon with oblong bowl, Joseph Willmore, Birmingham 1822.   £37

Caddy spoon with fluted bowl by Hester Bateman.   £89

A Victorian caddy spoon with a waisted bowl and engraved handle, circa 1860.   £35

Caddy spoon by G. Baskerville, London 1798.   £30

A caddy spoon with fiddle pattern engraved bowl, 1835, London.   £38

CANDLESTICKS

Sterling silver candelabrum of three lights, 28cm. high. £10

One of a pair of sterling silver dwarf candelabra on circular bases, 12cm. high. £30

19th century silver plated five-light candelabrum, 69cm. high. £69

One of a pair of early 19th century German three-light candelabra, 22ins. high, by Friedrich Carl Busch, Hanover, circa 1850, 31ozs. 4dwt. £360

A large plated candelabrum of Adam design for five lights, on tapering stem and square base, 67cm. high. £90

One of a pair of Sheffield plate table candelabra. £78

One of a pair of Victorian silver candelabra, 10½ins. high. £110

Three-branch table centre in the form of an oak tree with stags at base standing on embossed mirror base, 27ins. high. £190

One of a pair of South American three-light candelabra by B.S.A., town mark M, circa 1775, 133ozs. 3dwt., 15ins. high. £1,600

One of a pair of George III silver candlesticks by J. & T. Settle, Sheffield, 1817. £340

One of a set of four George III silver table candlesticks on square cast bases, London 1780, by John Crouch and Thomas Hannam, 76.5ozs. £1,000

One of a pair of George II candlesticks by William Grundy, 1749. £1,500

One of a pair of silver dwarf candlesticks on oval shaped bases. £44

One of a pair of George III cast silver candlesticks by William Cafe, London, 1764, 9ins. high, 31ozs. £560

One of a pair of Russian silver dwarf candlesticks. £80

A pair of three-branch candelabra sold with four table candlesticks by T., J., and N. Creswick, Sheffield, 1829, 17½ins. high. £680

One of a set of four table candlesticks by James Langlois, London 1749, 73ozs. 4dwt. £1,100

One of a pair of George IV cast silver candlesticks, Sheffield hallmark 1828, makers T.J. and N. Creswick, 29cm. high. £390

CANDLESTICKS

One of a pair of silver candle-sticks, 4½in. high, Birmingham 1908.
£40

One of a pair of George III candle-sticks by W. Cope, 1765, 26cm. high, 44oz.
£750

One of a pair of silver dwarf candle-sticks, 13.5cm. high.
£13

One of a pair of Russian silver candlesticks, 30oz.
£215

One of a pair of Louis XVI silver candlesticks by J. Besnier, Paris 27cm. high. £16,363

One of a pair of George III silver table candlesticks by W. Cafe 1761/63, 40oz. 19dwt.
£560

One of a pair of George II silver table candlesticks by R. Rew, London 1757.
£650

One of a pair of early George III table candle-sticks by E. Coker, London 1762, 10in. high.
£540

One of a pair of George III table candlesticks by E. Coker, London 1762.
£800

One of a pair of early George III table candlesticks by E. Coker, London 1762, 10¼ in. high.   £750

One of a pair of silver encrusted candlesticks. £75

One of pair of Victorian plated table candlesticks, 10½ins. high.   £28

One of a pair of table candlesticks by Cradock & Reid, London 1823.   £900

One of a set of four Sheffield plate candlesticks, 12ins. high, circa 1765.   £525

One of a pair of table candlesticks by John Carter, London 1768, loaded 12¼ in. £600

One of a set of four table candlesticks by J. Cafe, London 1755, 111oz. 4dwt. £1,900

One of a pair of table candlesticks by G. Nash, London 1734.   £850

One of a pair of silver candlesticks by John Green & Co., Sheffield, 1784, 12½ins.   £575

CARD CASES

Victorian silver
card case.   £38

Birmingham silver
gilt card case, 1863,
4ins. high.   £65

Silver card case,
Birmingham,
1907.   £25

Victorian inlaid
tortoiseshell
card case.   £15

Plain Victorian
silver card case.
£10

Attractive mother-
of-pearl card case.
£15

Chinese ivory
carved card
case, about 1900.
£20

Metal inlaid mother-
of-pearl card case.
£12

Tortoiseshell and
silver pique box,
Queen Anne.
£80

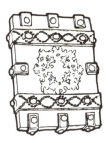

Victorian walnut and ivory mounted card case, 10½cm. tall. £11

Visiting card case embossed with golfer, Birmingham, 1906. £30

Engine-turned card case by Hilliard and Thomason, Birmingham, 1858 . £30

Chinoiserie decorated tortoiseshell card case. £18

Tortoiseshell, gold and silver pique purse, about 1795. £60

Early Victorian, European leather necessaire with an ivory plaque depicting a romanticised rural domestic scene. £70

Victorian mother-of-pearl card case. £15

Ivory and gold pique patch box, mid-18th century. £40

Tortoiseshell and mother-of-pearl card case. £18

CASTERS

Silver sugar dredger, Birmingham, 1911.   £44

Set of three George I silver casters of plain baluster form by Simon Pantin, London, 1714, 23ozs. 6dwt.   £740

George II sugar caster by David William, Jnr., London 1730, 10ozs. 14dwt., 7ins. high.   £600

17th century sugar caster, London Hallmark, William III, date 1696, by Andrew Raven.   £575

Silver caster by Henry Brind, London 1742.   £225

Octagonal sugar caster by Samuel Welder, 1716, 5¼ins. high, 4.15ozs.   £222

Set of three George I casters by Samuel Welder, London, 1722, 12ozs. 6dwt.   £480

Silver salt cellar, the beak holds the rodent finial spoon, 3in. tall, with three companion pepperettes. £170

CENTREPIECES

CENTREPIECES

The Macready Testimonial, a large silver centrepiece.
£9,900

Attractive Old Sheffield Plate centrepiece with cut glass bowl, circa 1850.
£375

Solid silver epergne with original cut glass, 28ins. high. 1909, 99ozs. £625

Chinese centrepiece in silver and mother-of-pearl, 24ins. high.
£65

George III epergne by Emick Romer, London, 1770, 91ozs. 19dwt., 17¼ins. high.
£700

Dutch silver gilt mounted nautilus cup, Amsterdam, 1598, 288mm.
£5,818

CHAMBERSTICKS

George I chamberstick by Colin McKenzie, Edinburgh, 1718.
£400

One of a pair of George III silver chambersticks by Roberts & Co., Sheffield, 1809, 21ozs.
£390

Sheffield plate chamberstick, circa 1810.
£39

CHALICES

Silver chalice by Charles Fox, 1839. £85

An ornate 18ct. gold chalice, the panels decorated with animals and fruit, 15ozs. 15dwt., 10½ins. high. £2,000

A Victorian chalice, plain circular bowl on a chased knopped stem with circular-shaped base, 18ins. high, Edinburgh, 1880, 9ozs. 5dwt. £48

CLARET JUGS

19th century cut glass claret jug with plated mounts. £70

Silver ewer with 'electro texture' handgrip. £70

Long-necked silver mounted claret jug, made in London, 1872, by E.C. Brown, 11½ins. high. £295

19th century silver mounted glass claret jug. £250

Silver mounted claret jug, made by James Powell and Son, London, 1904. £375

Victorian silver-plated claret jug with an engraved crystal base. £100

A Faberge cigarette case enamelled in white and green with gold mounts.
£1,100

Dutch silver tobacco box by Hendrina Das, Amsterdam, 1761, 5ins. wide. £750

Oblong silver pocket cigarette case with enamelled portrait of a nude, 4ozs. 5dwt.
£28

Dutch silver tobacco box with serpentine ends by Hendrina Das, Amsterdam, 1746, 5¼ins. long. £1,100

Art Nouveau silver cigarette box by Omar Ramsden and Alwyn Carr, 5¾ins. long. £340

Plated cigarette box with hinged cover, 17cm. wide. £4

Oblong silver cigarette box with engraved inscription, 11.5cm. wide.
£8

Miniature treasure chest in silver, Art Nouveau design, Birmingham, 1904.
£48

Early 18th century, Norwegian, silver casket by Harmen Antoni Reimers of Bergen, circa 1715, 2¼ins. wide, 2ozs. 4dwt. £950

COASTERS

Pierced Sheffield plate wine coaster, circa 1790.   £35

One of a pair of John Tapley bottle stands, maker's mark, London 1948.
£430

One of a pair of Sheffield circular wine coasters with chased borders.
£22

Sheffield coaster with shell and foliate border, circa 1815.   £35

One of a pair of coasters by Richard Morton and Co., Sheffield, 1777.
£265

One of a set of four 19th century French decanter stands, 24½ozs.   £500

One of a pair of Sheffield circular wine stands with chased borders.
£28

One of a set of four circular wine coasters by Thomas Jackson II, London, 1774, 4¾ins. diam.   £580

One of a pair of silver gilt wine coasters, the sides formed by over- lapping arches, by J.P., F.P., London, 1904, 25ozs. 16dwt.
£200

George III baluster coffee pot by L.H., London 1766, 31ozs. 16dwt.   £680

William IV coffee jug complete with burner by Charles Gordon, London 1832   £430

18th century Italian coffee pot by D.C., circa 1770, 15ozs. 17dwt. £650

George II silver coffee pot by John Burdon, 1741, 25.5ozs.   £1,000

Early Victorian coffee pot, London 1841, 26ozs.   £440

George II tapered cylindrical coffee pot by Ayme Videau, London 1746, 24ozs. 8dwt. £1,500

Silver hot water jug, London, 1878.   £95

George II coffee pot with wooden side handle, about 1740, 18cm. high.   £115

Vase-shaped plated coffee jug, circa 1770, 11½ins. high.   £145

Vase shaped silver coffee pot, probably Portugese, circa 1780, 19ozs. 15dwt., 9½ins. high. £160

Plated coffee pot by Matthew Boulton and Co., circa 1810, 8¾ins. high. £145

Coffee pot by Stephen Smith, London 1879. £298

George III baluster coffee pot by W. and R. Peaston, London 1762, 23ozs. 13dwt. £700

George III silver coffee pot. £460

Plated coffee pot, 10¾ins. high, circa 1765, unidentified maker's mark. £180

George II plain silver baluster coffee pot, by Alexander Johnston, London 1759, 11ins. high, 27ozs. 3dwt. £570

George IV coffee pot, 9½ins. high, marked on body, lid, finial and handle, by Benjamin Smith, London 1829, 33ozs. 17dwt. £430

Queen Anne coffee pot by Robert Peake, London 1702, 23ozs. 10dwt. £1,600

George III coffee pot
by E.R., London 1762,
29ozs.   £400

George III coffee pot by
J.E. Terrey, London
1817, 30ozs. 9dwt.,
with leaf capped handle
and domed lid.   £500

Paul Storr coffee
jug, London 1815.
                    £1,040

George III vased shaped
coffee pot with domed
hinged cover by William
Grundy, London 1761,
27ozs. 15dwt.   £450

Baluster coffee pot
by B. Smith, London
1840, 8½in. high,
21oz.8dwt.   £385

George III silver coffee
pot by J.S., London
1761, 29ozs.   £650

George II coffee pot
by Thomas Mason,
London 1728, 28ozs.
10dwt., 10ins. high.
                    £1,000

George III coffee pot
by William Grundy,
1771.   £650

George II coffee pot
by Isaac Cookson,
Newcastle, 1744,
27ozs. 15dwt. £700

CREAM JUGS

Cowrie shell cream jug with silver mounts. £13

Barrel shaped cream jug by Smith and Hayter, London 1792, 4ozs. 3dwt. £130

Cream jug by Hester Bateman, London 1782. £235

Cream jug of lozenge outline by Peter Podie, London 1801, 5½ins. high, 9ozs. 15dwt. £420

George III oval milk jug, by Urquart and Hart, London 1803, 4¼ins. high, 5ozs. 4dwt. £95

Baluster shaped cream jug with curved lobes by Ayme Videau, London 1760, 5½ins. high, 6ozs. 15dwt. £270

George III cow creamer by John Schuppe, London 1773, 4ozs. 3dwt., 4ins. high. £1,250

Oval body cream boat by Christian Hilland, London 1738, 5ozs. 19dwt., 4¾ins. wide. £420

George II cream jug, 4½ins. high, circa 1730, 6ozs. 10dwt. £85

Helmet shaped cream jug by Thomas Law, Sheffield, 1779, 3ozs. 6dwt., 4½ins. high.
£190

George III silver cream jug by Peter and Anne Bateman, circa 1780.
£140

Unmarked 18th century silver cream jug, circa 1720, 3½ins. high, 5ozs. 7dwt.
£95

Baluster body cream jug by John Collins, London 1828, 8ozs. 12dwt. 4¾ins. high.
£230

Oval bodied cream jug by Paul de Lamerie, London 1740, 5¼ins. wide, 6ozs. 11dwt.
£1,000

Pedestal cream jug, maker BM, London 1780.
£96

Vase shaped silver cream jug, London 1901, 12ozs. 10dwt.
£46

George III silver-gilt cream boat, 5ins., maker's name rubbed, London 1753, 5ozs. 2dwt.
£140

George III cream jug, 5½ins. high, by Richard Ferris of Exeter, circa 1790, 3ozs. 13dwt.
£105

CREAM JUGS

George IV cream jug by William Ely, 1827, 7ozs. £95

Silver cream jug by George Smith, London, 1785. £88

George II cream boat, 5¼ins., by Dorothy Mills and Thomas Sarbitt, London, 1744, 3ozs. 18dwt. £140

CRUETS

George III cruet stand by Robert Hennell, 1790. £120

George III egg cruet for six, marked John Emes, London, 1804. £340

Cruet with three casters and two glass bottles by Samuel Wood, London, 1744/46, 42ozs. 17dwt. £700

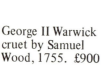

George II Warwick cruet by Samuel Wood, 1755. £900

Georgian five bottle pierced silver cruet by Thomas Dealtry, London 1776. £230

Mid-18th century five-bottle Warwick cruet with silver mounts and frame. £240

Plated double-handled prize cup, 10ins. high. £2

Silver gilt cup and cover made for Richmond races in 1804 by Richard Cooke, 130ozs., 18ins. high. £2,000

Large Victorian prize cup with scrolled handles, London 1893, 57ozs. 5dwt., 26.5cm. high. £110

Silver dram cup, made in 1653, may have been a wedding cup, 3ins. high, 2ozs. in weight, maker's mark ET with a crescent below. £3,150

Hammered silver cup by C.R. Ashbee, London, 1901. £480

Late 16th century parcel gilt pineapple cup by Martin Dumling, Nuremburg. £1,600

Superb Charles II parcel gilt two-handled cup and cover, bearing the maker's mark IA, 1667. £6,200

The 1920 Ascot Gold Cup, 15in. high, maker's mark S.G., London 1920, 69oz. 11dwt. in 18 carat gold. £3,100

Commonwealth two-handled cup and cover, marked on base and lid, maker's mark A.F. in a shaped shield, London, 1653. £14,983

DISHES

Victorian silver bon-bon dish, 2ozs. £9

Unusual George III Irish dish ring, 7½ins. diam., apparently by Joseph Jackson, Dublin, probably 1778, 11ozs. 2dwt. £800

George III oval entree dish and cover by William Bennett, London, 1800, 46ozs. 15dwt. £340

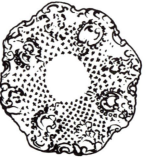

One of a pair of George III circular vegetable dishes and covers by William Burwash and Richard Sibley, London, 1810, 124ozs. 8dwt. £680

Victorian pierced and embossed, circular-shaped sweetmeat comport, 21cm. diam., Sheffield 1894, 7ozs. 5dwt. £36

One of a pair of entree dishes and covers by Emes and Barnard, London, 1810, 91ozs. 18dwt. £620

Dutch silver brazier, the circular body pierced with foliate designs by Mennotijssen Leeuwarden, circa 1735, 11ozs. 12dwt. £320

One of a pair of 19th century electro-plated oval hot water well dishes, stamped H.W. and Co., 26½ins. overall. £280

Early 19th century Dutch sweetmeat dish bearing the two crests of Admiral Lord Nelson by Nathaniel Teuter, Amsterdam, 1805, 4ozs. 18dwt. £440

18th century Dutch
sweetmeat bowl,
4¾ins. wide, by Jan
Buysen, Amsterdam,
1790, 5ozs. 2dwt.
£400

Dish cross by Samuel
Herbert and Co.,
London, 1765,
13ozs. 7dwt.   £230

Victorian, elm quaich
with silver mounts,
Inverness 1880, by
Ferguson and McBean.
£24

Plated circular
muffin dish.
£6

George IV dessert dish
by R. Gainsford,
Sheffield, 1829, 25ozs.
8dwt.   £380

Old Sheffield silver
sweetmeat stand.
£39

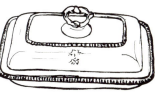

One of a pair of
entree dishes by
William Frisbee,
London, 1799,
96ozs. 1dwt.
£550

An oval plated double-
handled breakfast dish
with revolving cover,
on four supports. £34

One of a set of four
entree dishes and
covers by Benjamin
Smith, London, 1808,
213ozs.   £1,750

FLATWARE

Silver-gilt seal-top spoon, initialled
TC over TD on the base, 1606.£420

Silver spoon made in 1555,
5¾ in. long.   £800

Charles I child's slip top spoon
by E.H., London 1633. £480

St. Matthew, a Charles I apostle
spoon, makers mark I.F., London,
1641.   £340

Large silver Puritan spoon with a
slightly splayed top made in 1663.
                              £345

19th century silver tablespoon.
                              £23

George III fiddle pattern tablespoon
by R. Keay, Perth, circa 1795. £15

George III fiddle pattern tablespoon
by J. Sinclair, Wick, circa 1810. £52

Charles I silver gilt seal top spoon,
makers mark E.H., London 1635.
                              £350

One of a pair of 16th century lion
dejant spoons, English Provincial,
circa 1565.   £900

Georgian silver mustard spoon,
1796-7 marked 'k', head of the
lion and 'l.h. Co.'.   £5

Charles I silver gilt apostle spoon,
makers mark D, Exeter, circa
1639.   £480

Silver spoon slipped in conventional
manner and initialled on the slant B
over I over A, London mark for
1649.   £450

One of a pair of late 18th century
berry spoons with husk engraving
along the stems, by different
makers.   £35

James I seal top spoon,makers
mark C, London 1609.   £320

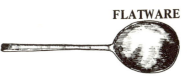

Commonwealth slip top spoon,
makers mark S.V., London 1654.£240

A James I seal top spoon, London
1615.   £175

18th century silver spoon of the
Hanoverian pattern, 16¼ in. long
made by J. Gordon of Aberdeen.£420

Unusual crested tablespoon made in
1761, makers mark WC with a mullet
between.   £750

Small Puritan style spoon, hallmarked for 1653.   £493

St. Bartholomew, a Mary Tudor
apostle spoon, London 1555. £900

St. Andrew, Charles I apostle
spoon, makers mark D, London
1635.   £340

Late 15th century English
diamond point spoon. £530

One of a pair of berry spoons,
London circa 1780.   £30

A Charles I seal top spoon, London
1629.   £160

Silver serving spoon by Peter and
William Bateman, London 1813.
                               £43

Victorian silver berry spoon. £24

17th century lions head finial
spoon, English Provincial, circa
1630.   £230

FLATWARE

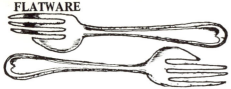

Pair of 18th century oyster forks, Old English thread. £35

Pair of George IV pickle forks, 4½in. long, Dublin 1824, by M. West. £25

Elizabeth I Apostle spoon, St. John, London 1590. £680

Early silver spoon probably English, Roman occupation or Anglo-Saxon period. £380

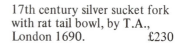

Feather edge sifter spoon with fluted bowl, by Joseph Rodgers and Sons, Sheffield, 1909. £10

17th century silver sucket fork with rat tail bowl, by T.A., London 1690. £230

Silver toasting fork by Joseph Willmore, 1806. £70

Silver gilt sifter spoon, London 1872. £38

Victorian fiddle pattern flatware service by Jack Bond, 1842. £1,500

A canteen of Kings Husk pattern, nearly all by Mary Chauner, 1838, 333½oz. £2,900

Mid Victorian silver travelling knife and fork. £10

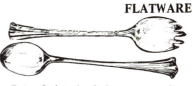

Pair of plated salad servers made in 1920's. £3.75

Silver and ivory corer, 1811. £44

Hand hammered silver jam spoon, London 1824. £6

Late 17th century sucket fork by I.S. London, circa 1690. £260

One of a set of six teaspoons, London 1852. £28

Victorian silver plated sugar sifter spoon. £3

Two pairs of fiddle-pattern salt spoons, by C. Eley, London 1826. £8 per pair

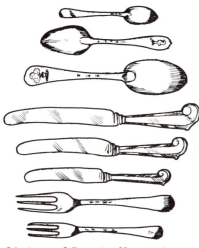

84 pieces of Georgian Hanoverian pattern table silver by different makers between 1720 and 1760, 79oz. 4dwt. £2,300

44 pieces of table silver by Omar Ramsden, London 1926-38, 54oz. 8dwt. (excluding knives). £680

CASED SETS

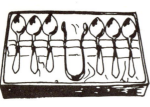

Cased set of six plated spoons and soup ladle. £5

Cased set of six silver coffee spoons and sugar tongs with fluted handles. £11

Set of six silver teaspoons and a pair of sugar tongs with shaped handles, 3ozs. 10dwt.   £13

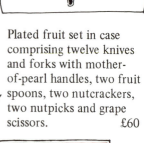

Cased set of twelve fish knives and forks with ivory handles. £18

18th century travelling set for two companions. £950

Plated fruit set in case comprising twelve knives and forks with mother-of-pearl handles, two fruit spoons, two nutcrackers, two nutpicks and grape scissors.   £60

Silver egg cup, spoon and napkin ring in case, 2ozs. 5dwt.   £12

Silver folding two-pronged fruit knife and fork, 5¼ins. long, 1889.   £20

Cased set of twelve silver coffee spoons.   £22

George III goblet
by James Sutton,
London, 1781.
£120

18th century Italian
chalice dated 1745,
11ins. high, Naples,
15ozs. 14dwt. £260

Mid 17th century
silver wine goblet,
6ins. high, 6ozs.
9dwt.   £4,000

Georgian silver
goblet, London,
1823, 12ozs.
£130

George III vase-shaped
goblet on a short stem
with circular base,
16.5cm. high, Edinburgh,
1817, maker G.M.H.,
12ozs.   £95

Louis XIV silver
chalice by Christopher
Silvert, circa 1710,
11ozs. 5dwt.   £380

One of a pair of silver
goblets by Emes and
Barnard, London, 1816,
29ozs.   £430

18th century Italian
silver chalice, maker
S.S., Turin, 1764,
10½ins. high,
13ozs. 1dwt.   £220

Silver goblet by
William Bateman,
London, 1822.
£236

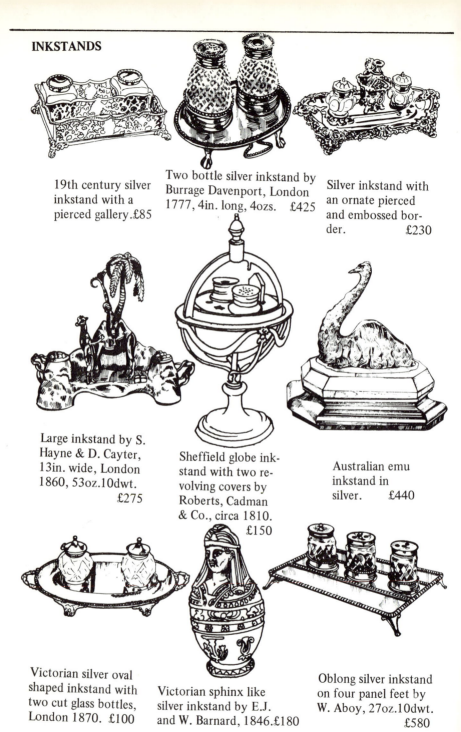

19th century silver inkstand with a pierced gallery. £85

Two bottle silver inkstand by Burrage Davenport, London 1777, 4in. long, 4ozs.   £425

Silver inkstand with an ornate pierced and embossed border.   £230

Large inkstand by S. Hayne & D. Cayter, 13in. wide, London 1860, 53oz.10dwt.   £275

Sheffield globe inkstand with two revolving covers by Roberts, Cadman & Co., circa 1810.   £150

Australian emu inkstand in silver.   £440

Victorian silver oval shaped inkstand with two cut glass bottles, London 1870. £100

Victorian sphinx like silver inkstand by E.J. and W. Barnard, 1846. £180

Oblong silver inkstand on four panel feet by W. Aboy, 27oz.10dwt.   £580

Oblong silver inkstand by R. Hennell II, London 1822, 25oz.16dwt., 8½in. wide. £380

Silver ink pot in tne form of a cairn terrier seated before his plate of bones, by I.S.Hunt, 1851. £300

Three bottle inkstand by E. Aldridge and F. Stamper, London 1755, 20oz.18dwt., 10¼in. wide. £380

Victorian parcel gilt silver inkwell by E. C. Brown, 1867, 4½oz. £500

Large silver inkstand by John Parker, 16½in. wide, 204oz. £5,850

Silver ink pot in the form of a boxer dog guarding his master's beer by I.S. Hunt, 1851. £460

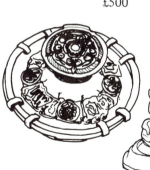
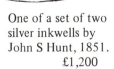
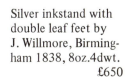

Hammered inkwell of capstan form by O. Ramsden, London, 1920, 6in. diam. £150

One of a set of two silver inkwells by John S Hunt, 1851. £1,200

Silver inkstand with double leaf feet by J. Willmore, Birmingham 1838, 8oz.4dwt. £650

JARDINIERES

One of a pair of Louis XV jardinieres and stands, in silver. £363,636

A circular Sheffield jardiniere with chased border. £6

Victorian semi-fluted silver jardiniere, with lion mask and ring handles, London, 1891, 30ozs. £130

JUGS

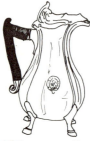

18th century Dutch hot milk jug by Martinus Van Stepele, The Hague, 1759, 10ozs. 13dwt. £950

American silver pitcher by Ebenezer Moulton, Boston, circa 1800, 22ozs. 17dwt. £600

Plated and engraved vase-shaped hot water jug with beaded border. £6

Silver plated hot water jug with stags horn handle, circa 1900. £9

George II Irish, covered jug by Erasmus Cope, Dublin, 1736, 33ozs. 8dwt. £1,800

Exquisite hot milk jug by Emes and Barnard, London 1808. £235

An oval plated hot water kettle on stand with two spirit lamps.   £34

Spherical silver tea kettle with stand, 1737, London, 41ozs. 15dwt. £620

George III tea kettle by D. Smith and R. Sharp, London, 1760.   £380

A partly fluted oval, plated hot water kettle.   £6

Circular plated kettle on foliage supports.   £19

Plated and engraved, partly fluted circular hot water kettle.   £7

Silver plated kettle and lampstand by Butt of Chester. £67

George II silver tea kettle on stand with burner by Edward Wakelin, London, 1747. 76ozs. 12dwt., 14¾ins. high.   £750

George II tea kettle and stand by John Jacobs, London 1747.   £480

LADLES

19th century silver ladle. £32.

Silver cream ladle, J Whipple & Co. Exeter, 1878.   £23

Bright cut ladle by R. Keay, Perth, 1790.   £48

George III silver toddy ladle, Birmingham, 1809, by J. Willmore, 6½in. long.   £45

George III silver toddy ladle by A. Davidson, Montrose, circa 1810.£75

Unmarked Regency punch ladle with turned rosewood handle, 9½in. long.   £35

Silver punch ladle with wooden handle by W. Justus, 1739. £150

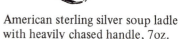

American sterling silver soup ladle with heavily chased handle, 7oz.   £40

Continental silver punch ladle, engraved with chased handle. £12

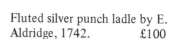

Fluted silver punch ladle by E. Aldridge, 1742.   £100

Pair of Onslow pattern cream ladles by F. Higgins, 1899. £32

Pair of fiddle pattern cream ladles by J. Bell of Newcastle, 1829.   £70

Vesta match case showing King Edward VII, 1901.   £40

Metal match case in the form of a Gladstone bag.   £30

Silver match case with floral decoration.   £20

Silver match case with fluted decoration.   £15

French Art Nouveau silver smoker's set, circa 1900.   £75

Golfer match box by Sampson Morden & Co., 1891.   £175

Angel match box holder, Birmingham, 1903.   £8

Vesta match case advertising Otto Monsteds Margarines.   £80

Metal match case depicting a coiled snake.   £40

MINIATURE SILVER

Small silver sander masquerading as a watering can, by T. Johnson, 1882. £150

Miniature silver rickshaw. £10

Miniature silver rider on rocking horse. £5

Continental silver-metal viola. £16

German silver miniature model of a sedan chair. £75

One of a pair of miniature English hallmarked silver mirrors. £6

An unusual silver box in the form of a violin, with hinged front. £32

Set of four miniature silver chairs. £34

Miniature silver man with a ladder. £5

Silvered children's rattle. £14

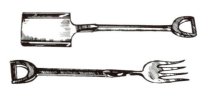

Silver spade and trowel, 1872, 10ins. long. £135

Miniature silver watering can with decorative embossed rustic design. £14

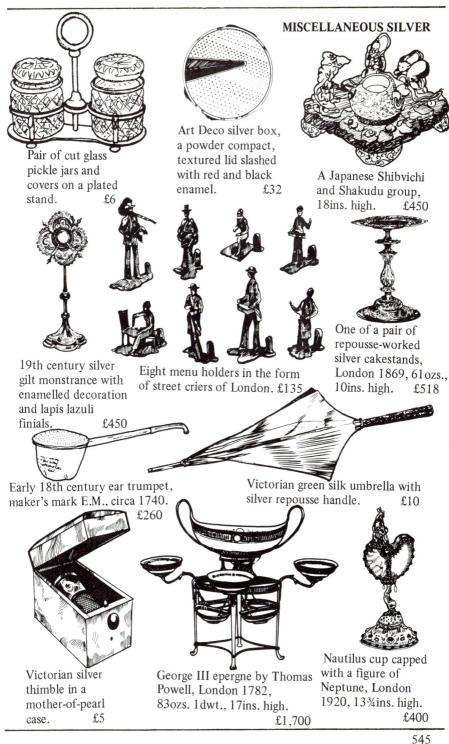

Pair of cut glass pickle jars and covers on a plated stand. £6

Art Deco silver box, a powder compact, textured lid slashed with red and black enamel. £32

A Japanese Shibvichi and Shakudu group, 18ins. high. £450

19th century silver gilt monstrance with enamelled decoration and lapis lazuli finials. £450

Eight menu holders in the form of street criers of London. £135

One of a pair of repousse-worked silver cakestands, London 1869, 61ozs., 10ins. high. £518

Early 18th century ear trumpet, maker's mark E.M., circa 1740. £260

Victorian green silk umbrella with silver repousse handle. £10

Victorian silver thimble in a mother-of-pearl case. £5

George III epergne by Thomas Powell, London 1782, 83ozs. 1dwt., 17ins. high. £1,700

Nautilus cup capped with a figure of Neptune, London 1920, 13¾ins. high. £400

MISCELLANEOUS SILVER

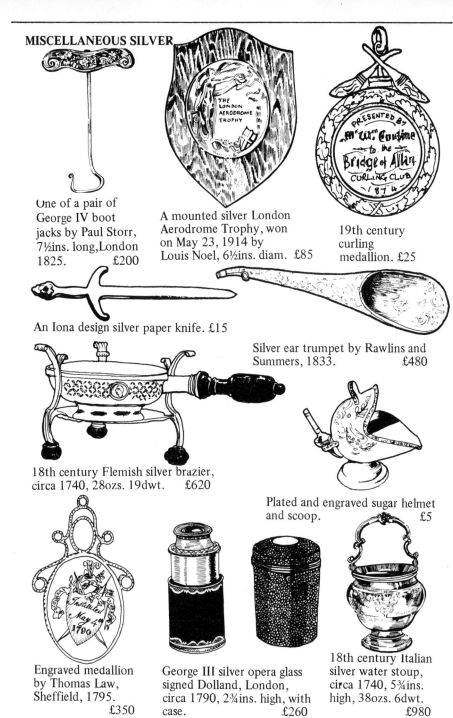

One of a pair of George IV boot jacks by Paul Storr, 7½ins. long, London 1825. £200

A mounted silver London Aerodrome Trophy, won on May 23, 1914 by Louis Noel, 6½ins. diam. £85

19th century curling medallion. £25

An Iona design silver paper knife. £15

Silver ear trumpet by Rawlins and Summers, 1833. £480

18th century Flemish silver brazier, circa 1740, 28ozs. 19dwt. £620

Plated and engraved sugar helmet and scoop. £5

Engraved medallion by Thomas Law, Sheffield, 1795. £350

George III silver opera glass signed Dolland, London, circa 1790, 2¾ins. high, with case. £260

18th century Italian silver water stoup, circa 1740, 5¾ins. high, 38ozs. 6dwt. £980

A fine three-piece hunting set, modelled in solid silver, comprising the master and two hunt servants, London 1882, 182ozs.   £2,500

Plated snail design table ornament.   £19

Silver bookmark 5ins. high, makers mark HSB, 1891   £75

18th century gold lacquer cockerel and hen, 33cm. and 21cm. high.   £720

Silver figure of St. Michael as a Roman warrior, probably made in Naples, circa 1745.   £1,400

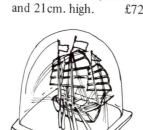

A silver and parcel gilt figure of a knight with an ivory face, 34cm. high.   £370

An Oriental silver model ship on a wooden stand with glass domed shade. £36

Silver statuette of an officer of the Inniskillen Dragoon Guards.   £350

MUGS

Victorian christening
mug, London 1864.
£68

A Paul Lamerie
mug, 1727, 14½ozs.
£1,750

Child's mug by
Thomas Daniel,
1818.   £65

Queen Anne mug
by William Fawdrey,
London, 1708.
£180

Engraved silver mug by
Thomas Folkingham,
1714, 4½ins. high,
10ozs. 8dwt.   £625

Silver mug made by
Wakelin & Taylor in
1779, weighing
12ozs. 18dwt. £365

Silver mug by Stewart
Lewis & Co., circa 1860,
9cm. high.   £75

Silver mug by Paul
Storr, London 1813.
£285

A silver beer mug by
Thomas Jackson,
London, 1806, 11cm.
high.   £175

Scottish snuff mull,
circa 1790.   £99

Scottish snuff mull,
circa 1800.   £77

Scottish horn snuff
mull with silver
thistle mount. £22

Scottish horn snuff
mull with a silver
and onyx cover. £40

Scottish snuff mull,
circa 1760.   £132

Scottish snuff mull
with silver thistle
mount.   £28

Scottish snuff mull
with a silver mount.
            £20

Scottish mull,
circa 1820,
10cm. long.
      £55

Scottish horn and
silver mounted snuff
mull with agate top.
         £52

MUSTARDS

Mustard pot,
Birmingham,
1895.   £28

George III mustard
pot by Hester Bateman,
London, 1783,
3ozs. 8dwt.   £500

George III silver
mustard pot,
London, 1816,
possibly by
D. Hennell, 3.9 ozs.
£100

NAPKIN RINGS

Victorian shaped and
engraved napkin ring,
by Wakley and Wheeler,
London, 1895.   £7.50

Silver plate napkin
ring in the form of
a belt.   £3.50

Circular napkin ring
makers EJH and HH,
Chester, 1906.   £6

NUTMEGS

Oval nutmeg grater
by Thomas Willmore,
1790.   £200

Box-type nutmeg
grater by William
Elliott, 1825. £120

George III silver
nutmeg grater by
Phipps and Robinson,
1795.   £195

George III silver pepperette, London 1809 by Stephen Adams.   £70

One of a pair of silver pepperettes by William Bateman, 1822, 5ins. high, 7½ozs.   £350

One of a pair of peppers, makers F. & S., Birmingham, 1907.   £28

George II bun pepperette by J. Daniel, London 1750.   £120

925 silver-metal, model of a duck, pepperpot.   £17

Silver pepper caster by Robert Hennell, London 1789. £60

PEN AND FRUIT KNIVES

Silver pen-knife with mother-of-pearl fish-head handle, hallmarked 1897.   £10

Silver pen-knife with mother-of-pearl spiral handle, hallmarked 1897.   £10

Pocket fruit knife and patent orange peeler, in mother-of-pearl handle holder.   £40

Silver pen-knife with mother-of-pearl handle, hallmarked 1897.   £10

PORRINGERS

Restoration silver porringer and stand, maker's mark RF, London, 1662, 52ozs.   £10,500

Charles II silver porringer and cover by P.R., London, 1683, 19ozs. 15dwt. £1,400

Commonwealth silver porringer by R.W., London, 1655, 6ozs. 9dwt., 2¾ins. high.   £1,050

Commonwealth two-handled porringer, 1652, maker's mark I.H., 9.2cm. high.   £950

QUAICH

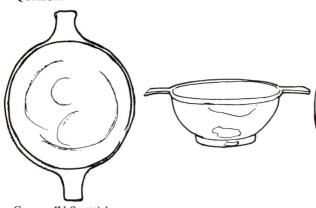

George IV Scottish quaich by J.H., Edinburgh, 1821, 2ozs. 4dwt.   £155

Circular silver prize quaich with engraved inscription, 3ozs. 5dwt.   £15

18th century Scottish quaich by James Taylor, Glasgow, circa 1775, 3ozs. 10dwt.   £250

One of a pair of triangular salts, Brook and Son, Edinburgh, 1928.
£24

Silver oval salt tray, Watson Fenton and Bradbury, Sheffield, 1795.   £90

One of a set of four oval silver salts by D. & R. Hennell, London, 1768, 16ozs. 14dwt.   £280

Salt cellar by Paul A. Bateman, London, 1792.
£37

One of a pair of Paul Storr salt cellars, London, 1820, 17½ozs.   £520

One of a pair of silver salts, Birmingham, 1896, original green liners.
£22

George IV salt cellar with heavily chased flowers and scrolls by J. McKay, Edinburgh, 1823, 3ozs. 15dwt.
£45

French salt cellar, circa 1860, provincial mark.
£12

One of a pair of George II circular salts by Edward Wood, London, 1746, 7ozs., 3¼ins. diam.   £74

Silver salt cellar by John Foglino, London, 1845.
£45

One of a set of six salts by Paul Storr, and one of six gilt spoons by Eley and Fearn, 1801, 25ozs. £1,050

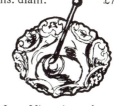

Late Victorian salt with decorated borders and matching spoon, by Wm. Devenport, Birmingham, 1901. £10

SALVERS AND TRAYS

Victorian silver salver. £380

Victorian silver tray by E.B. & J.B., London 1854, 82ozs.   £700

William III silver tazza, London 1700, 5ozs. 15dwt.   £170

George II silver tray by Eliza Godfrey, London 1746, 20ins. diam., 100ozs.   £800

A circular shaped plated salver with chased border, 32cm. diam.   £17

Silver charger by Louis Mettayer, London 1720, 68cm. diam. 234ozs.   £7,000

Victorian two-handled silver tea tray, London 1840.   £850

Silver waiter by Crouch and Hannam, London 1788. £195

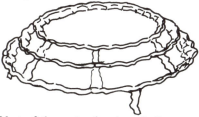

George III tray by William Bouldstridge, 1812, 145¾ozs. £1,000

Queen Anne silver tazza, London 1708, 13ozs. 10dwt. £300

Nest of three circular shaped silver salvers with escalloped borders and hoof feet, with London and Sheffield hallmarks, 20cm., 24.5cm. and 31cm. diam. , 63ozs. 10dwt. £300

One of a pair of George III silver salvers by Thomas Hannam and John Crouch, London 1801, 26ozs., 8ins. diameter. £280

7 inch waiter with shell and scroll pattern made by James Morrison, 1745. £180

One of a set of sixteen, 18th century silver dinner plates engraved with Royal Armorials, by Robert Calderwood, Dublin, circa 1760, 289oz. 18dwt. £2,000

Silver pen tray with Chester hallmark, 1901. £30

Old Sheffield Plate snuffer tray, circa 1798. £26

SALVERS AND TRAYS

Circular salver by Robert Makepeace and Richard Carter, London, 1777, 39ozs. 12dwt.   £460

Heavy oval salver by Charles Favell and Co., Sheffield, 1902, 165ozs., 27ins. wide.   £900

Victorian silver oval-shaped dish by John S. Hunt, London, 1844, 88½ozs., 22½ins. x 18ins.   £560

George III oval salver by William Sharpe, London, 1817, 18ozs. 17dwt.   £250

Victorian silver dish with embossed border by William Bateman and Daniel Ball, 35ozs., 1840.   £145

George III silver salver made by William Robertson, Edinburgh, 1793.   £420

Massive silver two-handled tray, London, 1909, 240ozs.   £1,020

Silver trinket tray by William Fountain, London 1794.   £48

Irish silver circular plate possibly by Erasmus Cope, Dublin, 1725, 13ozs. 13dwt.   £580

One of a set of twelve French silver gilt dinner plates by Odiot, Paris, circa 1830, 185ozs. 10dwt. £1,750

George III silver salver by Edward Capper, London, 1771, 33½ozs., 13ins. diam.   £350

Circular salver by Robert Jones and John Schofield, London, 1763, 29ozs. 10dwt.   £300

George III silver waiter.   £190

Irish salver, Dublin 1794, 48ozs. 5dwt.
                                    £440

George II salver by Joseph Sanders, London, 1733, 11ozs. 16dwt. £270

18th century Dutch silver snuffer stand and snuffers by Jan Ponct of Bremen, Amsterdam, 1756, 9ozs. 18dwt. £2,300

SAUCEBOATS

One of a pair of George III mint sauceboats, 1774, maker George Smith. £950

One of a pair of mid-18th century sauceboats, London, 37ozs. 17dwt., rubbed marks. £550

Silver sauce boat on hoof feet by John Pollock, 1755. £175

Silver sauceboat by William Shaw and William Priest, London, 1756. £170

One of four sauceboats by T. & F. Guest and F. Craddock, London 1806, 96ozs. 11dwt. £1,450

One of a pair of silver helmet-shaped sauceboats, 1750. £1,300

Plain silver sauceboat with inset coin on three hoof feet, 2ozs. 10dwt. £19

One of a set of four George III sauceboats, covers and stands probably by Benjamin Smith, London, 1807, 250ozs. £7,600

Small cream jug, John Gilbert, Birmingham, 1913. £15

Pair of sauceboats by John Jacob, circa 1735, 36¾ozs. £1,000

Cream jug by Robert Garrard, London, 1843. £96

Silver cheese scoop with ivory handle by TF, 1808. £90

Small long-handled silver scoop, Birmingham, 1904. £10

Marrow scoop, Samuel Pemberton, Birmingham, 1802. £32

Silver cheese scoop with ivory handle by William Ely and William Fearn, 1804, 10¼ ins. long. £80

Combined silver marrow scoop and table spoon by Elias Cachart, 1750. £85

George III butter knife, engraved silver blade, stained green ivory handle, Birmingham, 1800. £38

Silver cream scoop with rat-tail and wood handle. £15

Marrow scoop by Samuel Godbehere. £45

Victorian silver cheese scoop with ivory handle £30

Silver marrow scoop by E.B., London, 1745. £75

SKEWERS

Silver meat skewer by Wallace and Hayne, London 1819. £55

Pair of silver meat skewers by Peter and Ann Bateman, 1798. £60

Meat skewer by Wallis and Hayne, London, 1819. £60

Silver skewer, 1902. £20

SLICES

Silver fish slice by John, Henry and Charles Lias, 1848, 12ins. long. £36

Early butter knife by Thomas Wallis, London 1798. £18

Thread and shell butter knife by Hayne and Cator, London, 1855. £15

Silver fish slice by I.S., 1807. £25

Cast silver fish slice by William Trayes, 1837, 7ozs. 14dwt. £350

Mother-of-pearl handled butter knife by J.C., Birmingham, 1853. £10

Butter knife with cast hunting scene by H. & A. Ltd., London, 1917. £20

Silver fish trowel by Richard Williams, 1770, 13ins. long. £275

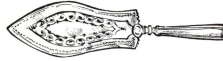

Silver fish slice by Peter and Ann Bateman, 1798. £120

Butter knife by Richard Crasley, London, 1796. £18

Fiddle butter knife by Jonathan Hayne, London, 1825. £12

Fiddle-pattern fish slice by Jonathan Hayne, 1834, 12ins. long, 5ozs. £55

A plated fish slice and fork. £7

Silver fish slice and fork with ivory handles. £15

Late 18th century Russian silver snuff box, Moscow, circa 1785, 4ins. wide. £360

Papier mache snuff box with mother-of-pearl decoration. £6

An antique Continental rock crystal shaped snuff box with gold mounts, 2¾ins. wide. £370

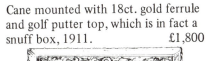

Good quality silver snuff box by Thomas Shaw, 1828. £60

Victorian lacquered box decorated with mother-of-pearl. £2

Cane mounted with 18ct. gold ferrule and golf putter top, which is in fact a snuff box, 1911. £1,800

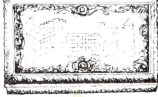

Snuff box by S.P., Birmingham, 1781. £155

Good quality snuff box by N. Mills, 1838. £510

Victorian oval shaped snuff box by Nathaniel Mills, Birmingham 1843. £210

SNUFF BOXES

Louis XVI octagonal gold snuff box, Paris 1774, 8.3cm. wide. £6,825

Snuff box, by Wm. Purse, London, 1810. £76

18th century gold and tortoiseshell pique work circular snuff box, 2in. diam. £190

Victorian lacquered papier mache oval snuff box with silver mounts. £14

George IV silver gilt snuff box. £125

Late 18th century polished and shell carved agate snuff box with gold mounts, 2½in. wide. £740

Table snuff box with engine turned sides by T.H., J.H., Chester 1819, 4in. wide. £550

Mussel-shell shaped snuff box in silver. £28

George IV silver snuff box, Birmingham 1827, by J. Betteridge, 3½in. x 1¾in. £85

Cowrie shell snuff box with silver mounts. £13

George IV oval snuff box by Edward Cornelius Farrell, London 1822, 2¾ins. wide. £380

Early 18th century Boscobel oak silver snuff box, unmarked, circa 1700, 3¼in. wide. £380

Queen Anne silver patch box, with the image of Queen Anne and the initials QA on cover, London, circa 1707, by T. Kedder. £85

18th century gold and enamel snuff box with lid painted by Richter. £1,300

Victorian papier mache snuff box. £8

Louis XV tortoiseshell and gold pique snuff box decorated all over with pique work of decreasing size, about 1725. £330

A mid 18th century English snuff box of pudding stone mounted in gold. £2,000

Cowrie shell snuff box, maker P.A., circa 1720. £95

STIRRUP CUPS

Fine heavy example of a fox-head stirrup cup, 1883, by Francis Higgins, 5½ins. high, 11ozs. 2dwt. **£1,125**

Late 19th century stirrup cup in dog-mask shape, by Robert Hennell IV, 7ins. long, 14ozs. 12dwt., in pair with a whippet. **£850**

Gilt fox head stirrup cup, London 1806, 7ozs. 16dwt. **£1,500**

TANTALUS

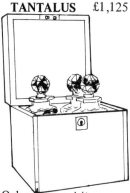

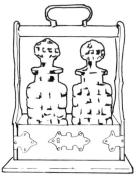

Oak square spirit case, fitted with three glass decanters and cut stoppers, and two plated spirit labels. **£30**

Oak tantalus spirit frame with two glass decanters and stoppers. **£34**

Coromandel and brass mounted liquor casket fitted with four cut glass decanters. **£110**

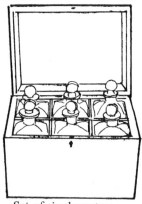

Set of six decanters, circa 1795. **£120**

A Victorian three-bottle tantalus with brass mounts. **£60**

Mahogany medicine case fitted with glass jars, mortar and pestle, etc., 8¼ins. wide. **£55**

One of a pair of silver tankards by Jeronymus Wessel, Stockholm, circa 1670, 16.6cm. high, 63ozs. 4dwt. £4,000

Georgian silver tankard, maker W.G., London, 1778, 10ins. high, 52ozs. £860

Charles II provincial peg tankard by James Plummer, York 1681, 21ozs. 10dwt. £1,600

George III silver tankard, 1766, 30ozs. £700

Charles II silver tankard, 21½ozs. £980

Large silver tankard by William Spring, 1708, weighing 38ozs. £5,200

One of a pair of George II silver quart tankards by Thomas Heming, London, 1746, 68ozs., 7½ins. high. £2,600

Dutch silver mounted horn tankard with medallion portrait of William and Mary. £520

17th century Norwegian silver tankard. £580

TANKARDS

William and Mary cylindrical tankard by I.Y. London, 1691, 24oz. 10dwt.　　　£920

Charles II cylindrical tankard. £1,680

George II silver tankard by S. Blachford of Exeter.　　£530

Queen Anne silver tankard.　　£820

Charles I tankard by T.I., London 1639, 29oz. 13dwt, 7¾in. high.　　£6,800

George III baluster tankard by Hester Bateman, London 1784, 8in. high, 23oz. 14dwt. £850

Small silver tankard by John Plummer, mid 17th century, 6¾in. high. £2,750

George III baluster tankard by John Payne, London 1760, 9in. high. £1,050

William and Mary cylindrical tankard by B. Pyne, London 1689, 23oz. 2dwt. £2,000

Silver tankard by Paul Solanier of Augsburg, circa 1690, 13oz.
£1,550

Swedish silver tankard with figure medallion lid and scroll thumbpiece by C.P. Tellander, Jonkoping, circa 1749, 16oz. £1,850

A Tsar Alexander II silver tankard in the Art Nouveau manner, 17oz. £150

American cylindrical tankard by J. Hurd, Boston, circa 1730, 25oz., 7½in. high.
£3,800

Baluster tankard by Peter and Anne Bateman, 24½oz.
£704

George III silver baluster tankard by P. and A. Bateman, London 1795, 24oz. 18dwt. £680

Silver baluster tankard, circa 1764, 5¾in. tall.
£230

Georgian silver tankard. £500

Fine example of a baluster mug made by L. Laroche in 1740, 3¾in. high.£300

TEA CADDIES

Silver plated tea caddy. £38

Early 19th century silver tea caddy, 12ozs. £170

George III tea caddy, marked on base and cover, by Robert Hennell, London, 1782, 4ins. high, 13ozs. 2dwt. £440

18th century Dutch silver tea caddy, maker's mark I.B., Amsterdam, 1726, 8ozs. 7dwt. £950

George III two-division tea caddy by Daniel Pontifex, London 1797, 19ozs. 13dwt., 7ins. high. £420

One of a set of three silver tea caddies by William Vincent. £960

George III plated tea caddy. £16

George III shaped oval tea caddy by T. Chauner, London, 1785, 12ozs. 4dwt. £580

A silver Portuguese tea caddy by P.I.E. Porto, circa 1810. £245

Pair of tea caddies and a mixing bowl by Samuel Taylor, London 1755, 27ozs. 15dwt., in a veneered rosewood case. £750

Pair of George III silver caddies by Parker and Wakelin, London 1767, in a Japanese lacquered case. £2,700

Set of three George II silver gilt tea caddies by Alexander Johnston, London 1754, 34ozs. 13dwt., in a silver mounted tortoiseshell case. £1,400

TEA AND COFFEE SETS

Scottish three piece tea set by G. McHattie,
Edinburgh 1825, 51oz.2dwt.   £430

Georgian tea set by R. & D. Hennell, London, 1800, 41 oz. 10 dwt.,
comprising teapot and stand, milk jug, sugar basin and slop bowl £440

Unusual three-piece tea set by R. Hennell II,
London 1819, 76oz.12dwt.   £850

Victorian silver four-piece coffee service.£820

Silver teapot and stand, milk jug and sugar
basket, by P. & A. Bateman, 1791, 4, 5,
30oz.1dwt.   £780

Four piece silver tea service, Birmingham,
88oz.   £370

Victorian silver tea and coffee service,
London 1870, 59½oz.   £720

Plated three piece chased circular teaset.£22

TEA AND COFFEE SETS

A fine silver tea service by Benjamin Smith, 1814, bearing a contemporary crest. £1,300

Victorian four piece tea and coffee set by E.J. and W. Barnard, London 1850 and 1851, 74oz. £920

Fine quality 19th century Indian three piece silver tea service, 43oz. £150

Four piece silver tea and coffee set, partly oblique, with chased shell and gadrooned border, 59oz. 15dwt. £335

Silver George IV tea service of three pieces, by John Angell, 1823 and 1825.   £460

George III tea and coffee service, York 1808/1812, 60oz. £540

George IV silver three piece tea set by Pearce and Burrows, 1827.
£500

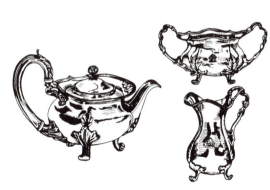 

George IV matching four piece tea and coffee set by Benjamin Smith, London 1825, 95oz. 12dwt.   £950

Four piece silver tea and coffee set by Garrard & Co., 83¾oz.   £700

Silver tea set and tray by Omar Ramsden and Alwyn Carr, London, 1912/13/14, 66oz. 18dwt. not including tray.   £1,550

Four piece silver tea and coffee service hallmarked Sheffield 1902, 84oz.   £330

Oblong shaped four piece silver tea and coffee set with fluted panels and border, on hoof feet, 58oz. 15dwt.   £380

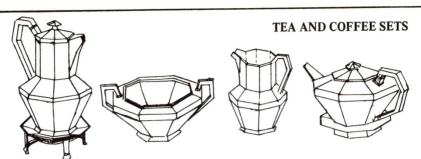

Early Victorian hexagonal tea and coffee set by John Figg, 1839, comprising teapot and stand, coffee jug and burner, sugar and creamer, 89oz. £2,050

Silver tea and coffee set, London 1901, with an oval tray, Sheffield 1902. £940

Victorian silver gilt tea service. £820

Victorian four-piece silver tea-service, 1884, 46oz. £400

TEA AND COFFEE SETS

Part of a circular silver three-piece teaset, 19oz. 15dwt. £50

Part of a four-piece teaset comprising two teapots and two sugar bowls, maker S.S., circa 1825, 121ozs. 7dwt. £460

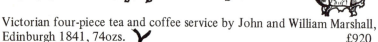

Victorian four-piece tea and coffee service by John and William Marshall, Edinburgh 1841, 74ozs. £920

Victorian four-piece tea and coffee service by Jas. and Albert Savory, the coffee pot by Hyam Hyams, 1848, 79ozs. 10dwt. £820

Russian silver teaset and tray. £460

An Oriental silver coffee set of three pieces with chased dragon design, 22ozs. 10dwt. £60

George III teapot and stand by Henry Chowner, London 1789, 17ozs. 16dwt., 5½ins. high. £420

Late 18th century engraved silver oval teapot and stand. £475

Circular silver flat-shaped teapot, 10ozs. 10dwt. £12

George III oval teapot engraved with garlands of flowers by Hester Bateman, London 1782, 16ozs. 15dwt. £230

Georgian silver teapot with ornate embossing by Charles Wright, London, 1771, 30ozs. £200

Part of a Scottish three-piece teaset by George Fenwick, Edinburgh, 1809, 42ozs. £480

A plain plated oval teapot on paw feet. £13

Teapot and stand by Hester Bateman, London, 1790, 20ozs. 1dwt. £720

TEAPOTS

Part of a three piece tea set by J. Angell and Sarah and John Blake, London, 1817, 50oz. 17dwt.   £400

Silver teapot made by Paul Storr in 1838.   £315

Rococo style silver teapot by Fuller White, 1762.
£450

George I bullet shaped teapot by Thomas Morse, London, 1723, 13oz. 19dwt.   £600

Bullet shape silver teapot by Isaac Cookson, circa 1745.
£950

Teapot by Savory, London, 1880.   £199

George III silver teapot by Thomas Watson, Newcastle, 1790, 21oz., 6¾in. high.
£130

Victorian plated oval teapot.
£7

George III silver teapot by
John Walton, Newcastle,
1818.   £300

Rare silver teapot by Isaac
Robouleau.   £1,800

Good George IV teapot, 7in.
high, by Benjamin Smith,
London, 1829, 35oz. 2dwt. £260

German bullet shaped silver
teapot, makers mark I.W.,
Augsberg 1725.   £680

Silver teapot by Paul Storr,
20oz. 9dwt, 1834.   £186

George II bullet shaped teapot
by Francis Pilsbury, London,
1731, 11oz. 9dwt.   £300

An unusual Victorian silver teapot
depicting drinking scenes by E.F.,
London, 1844, 29oz.   £250

William IV silver teapot by I.T.,
London, 1835, 28oz.   £240

TOILET REQUISITES

One of a pair of Irish silver toilet boxes and covers, Dublin 1700, by Thomas Boulton, 3¾ins. diam., 12½ozs. £520

Four piece, lady's dressing table set with enamelled mounts. £5

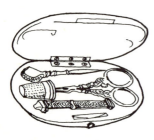

Ebony oval etui case with recesses for scissors, etc., in French hallmarked gold and silver. £65

Six-piece silver mounted manicure set in case. £9

Ornate silver set of dressing table equipment. £52

A coromandel and mother-of-pearl inlaid dressing case with glass and plated fittings. £38

19th century plated toast rack. £9

Victorian six division silver toast rack on ball feet, Birmingham 1898, 9ozs. 5dwt. £26

Toast rack by Walker and Hall, 1899, 7ozs. £32

TONGS

Georgian silver sugar tongs, 1799. £8

King's pattern silver grape scissors by Mary and Charles Reily, 1826. £60

Pair of George II silver-gilt rocaille sugar nips, circa 1740, unmarked, 4ins. long. £75

George III sugar nips, 1765. £35

Victorian apostle set of caddy spoon, moist sugar spoon and sugar tongs, by Elkington & Co., Birmingham 1874-5. £86

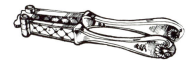

Victorian silver nut crackers by Edward Edwards, 1841. £180

Silver gilt grape scissors, London, 1882. £135

TONGS

Silver asparagus tongs by William Chawner, 10½ins. long, 5.5ozs., 1832.   £95

Early 18th century silver sugar tongs by L.E., London, circa 1710.   £180

Silver rococo period nips enhanced with gilding, 1745.   £85

Asparagus tongs by Mappin and Webb, Sheffield 1894.   £48

Sugar tongs by Hester Bateman.
                                        £39

Cast and shaped scroll-decorated tongs by Thomas Wallis, London, circa 1778.   £20

George I style nips, by Thos. Bradbury & Sons, London 1860.
                                        £18

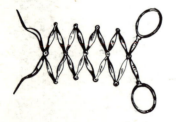

Cast butterfly nips, Victorian plate.
                                        £7

Pair of Scottish lazy tongs by Hamilton and Inches, 1906, 48cm. fully extended.   £100

Silver asparagus servers by Thomas Northcote, 1790.
                                        £75

Silver asparagus tongs by
G.W. Adams, 1864.   £65

Sugar tongs by Hester Bateman,
circa 1780.   £40

Pierced silver sugar tongs, John Munns,
London, circa 1756.   £35

Open-work tongs with acorn bowls,
by William Sheen, London, circa 1760.
                                            £30

Feather edge tongs, maker I.H.,
circa 1775.   £13

Late Victorian silver nips, circa 1880.
                                            £48

Irish silver nips with flower engraved
box hinge, Dublin, 1765.   £70

Chased leaf tongs, by W. & J. Deane,
London, circa 1765.   £22

Plain shaped tongs by Peter and
William Bateman, London, 1812. £16

Scissor nippers, by Stephen Adams,
London, circa 1760.   £34

TUREENS

One of a pair of George III sauce tureens and covers by John and Edward Edwards, London 1812, 45ozs. 4dwt. £550

One of a pair of Louis XV soup tureens and stands by Thomas Germain. £456,000

George IV oval-shaped soup tureen and cover by John Houle, London, 1820, 105ozs. 4dwt. £1,800

One of a pair of George III sauce tureens and covers made by John Robins, London, 1791. £700

Butter cooler and stand by Philip Rundell, London, 1819, 54ozs. 11dwt., 10¼ins. diam. £1,850

George III oval soup tureen and cover by William Sumner, London 1808, 127ozs. 3dwt. £2,150

An oval plated double-handled soup tureen with liner, cover and bead border. £60

George IV silver soup tureen and cover by Fentem Danby and Webster, Sheffield, 1827, 69ozs. 15dwt. £820

One of a set of four George IV tureens and covers by Joseph Angell II, London 1824, 121ozs. 3dwt. £980

Soup tureen and cover by Richard Cooke, London, 1808, 54ozs. 12dwt. £620

George III silver soup tureen hallmarked Edinburgh, 1796, 85ozs. £800

Shaped oval silver soup tureen and cover by J. Watson & Co., circa 1830, 16ins. overall width. £370

Part of a 101-piece silver service by J. Mortimer and J.S. Hunt, London, 1842. Total weight 3,100ozs. £26,000

18th century German silver soup tureen and cover by Johann J. Bruglocher, the elder, Augsburg 1737-39, 89ozs. 13dwt. £3,600

Silver soup tureen, cover and stand by Jacques-Nicolas Roettiers, Paris, 1770, the stand 50cm. wide. £103,333

One of four silver soup tureens, Dublin 1750. £1,900

URNS

A fine Sheffield vase-shaped tea urn with scrolled handles and chased and gadrooned borders, 42ins. high.   £150

Elaborate silver tea urn, London, 1816, 98ozs. £460

Early 18th century German silver gilt coffee urn by Georg Daniel Weiss, Nuremburg, circa 1715, 26ozs. 9dwt.   £1,250

Early 18th century coffee urn probably Flemish or Dutch colonial, 29ozs. 15dwt., 12¼ins. high. £880

George III silver tea urn by Henry Chowner, London 1790, 38ozs. 7dwt., 14½ins. high. £700

Unusual George II pear-shaped chocolate urn.   £3,780

VINAIGRETTES

William IV oblong engine-turned vinaigrette, Birmingham 1833, 2cm. wide.   £34

George III gold vinaigrette set with a gold citrine.   £600

Victorian oblong vinaigrette, engine-turred, by Nathaniel Mills, Birmingham, 1845, 3cm. wide. £58

Silver gilt vinaigrette, by Joseph Willmore, Birmingham, 1807.   £65

Gold vinaigrette by W. and P. Cunningham, Edinburgh, 1814. £800

Silver vinaigrette by Nathaniel Mills.   £190

Copy of the Warwick Vase by Paul Storr, 1823, 143½ozs. £2,500

Pair of George III tea vases by Samuel Taylor, London, 1762, 14ozs. 13dwt. £330

Art Nouveau silver flower vase with embossed cherubs, 20.5cm. high. £48

Large trumpet-shaped silver flower vase, 20.5cm. high. £7

Three covered sugar vases by Thomas Daniel, London 1777, 31ozs. 9dwt. £500

One of a pair of 18ct. gold vase-shaped cups and covers, 9½ins. high, London 1911/13, 33ozs. 12dwt. £1,650

WINE COOLERS

One of a set of four Sheffield wine coolers, makers Creswick & Co., circa 1815. £340

One of a pair of George IV rococo wine coolers by Benjamin Smith, 15¾ins. high. £9,750

Sheffield vase-shaped double-handled wine cooler, 26cm. high. £36

WHISTLES

Silver police whistle, dated 1888. £30

Scottish thistle whistle, 1906.　£32

Smooth silver whistle by Sampson Mordan and Co., 1903.　£25

Victorian silver rattle with ivory teether and whistle.　£45

Bulbous-shaped whistle in chased silver, 1901.　£30

Victorian carved jet whistle.　£25

Good quality bosun's call, dated 1818.　£120

Small Victorian silver whistle of bulbous form.　£18

Victorian silver whistle and penknife, London 1879.　£68

Silver dog whistle, Birmingham 1898.　£35

19th century silver whistle with niello decoration.　£49

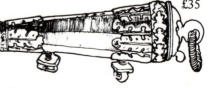

Good quality silver military whistle and case with Tudor rose decoration.　£95

588

George III silver wine funnel, London 1778, 4¾ins. high. £118

One of a pair of condiment funnels with cork, by William Hutton & Sons, Birmingham, 1906-7. £24

A silver wine funnel by George Lowe, Newcastle, 1824, 14cm. long. £105

WINE JUGS

Victorian silver wine jug with band of applied decoration, by Stephen Smith, London, 1873. £360

Victorian silver and silver-gilt wine jug by Stephen Smith and William Nicholson, London 1863, 35ozs. £345

Victorian Grecian-style engraved wine jug by SR/CB., Sheffield 1876, 33.25ozs., 14ins. high. £800

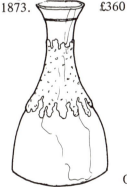

Silver decanter, 9ins. tall, weighing 28ozs. £115

One of a pair of George III silver wine jugs by Thomas Holland, London 1807, 168ozs., 14½ins. high. £3,000

Tapering hunting flask by Rawlings and Summers, 10ins. long, weighing 7ozs., complete with leather case. £240

WINE LABELS

Silver wine label engraved Madeira. £25

Silver vine-leaf wine labels. £58

Vine-leaf wine label by Hilliard and Thomason, Birmingham 1889, pierced for 'Gin'. £28

Queen's coronation wine label, London 1953. £45

Pair of silver wine labels, James Phipps, London, circa 1770. £52

Georg Jensen wine label. £25

Crescent-shaped wine label, by Phipps & Robinson, London, circa 1790. £26

Early 19th century plated decanter labels, Rum and Brandy. £10

Oval wine label by Joseph Willmore, Birmingham 1843, engraved for 'Rum'. £20

Claret label by Mary Binley, London, circa 1765. £30

Two of a set of nine George III wine labels of shaped design, made by James Hyde. £170

Victorian chased spirit label and chain, Birmingham, 1837. £14

Silver propelling pencil by Sampson Mordan, 1920. £15

Pen-holder by Sampson Mordan, 1825. £35

Late 17th century parcel gilt Continental table set, 250oz.
£5,000

Silver mounted writing set of letter opener, pen and knife, seal and two ink bottles. £23

19th century desk set containing pen, paper knife and seal, 8½ins. x 3½ins. £65

Indian silver quill pen. £25

Silver pen with two silver nibs, London, 1808. £78

A fine silver mace shaped penner, circa 1690, with slots for three quills, maker W.B. £250

Silver pen cleaner in the form of an artist's palette by Levi and Salaman, Birmingham, 1890. £6

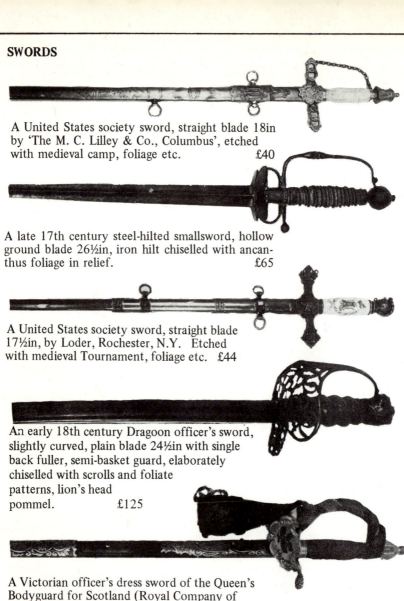

A United States society sword, straight blade 18in by 'The M. C. Lilley & Co., Columbus', etched with medieval camp, foliage etc.   £40

A late 17th century steel-hilted smallsword, hollow ground blade 26½in, iron hilt chiselled with ancanthus foliage in relief.   £65

A United States society sword, straight blade 17½in, by Loder, Rochester, N.Y. Etched with medieval Tournament, foliage etc. £44

An early 18th century Dragoon officer's sword, slightly curved, plain blade 24½in with single back fuller, semi-basket guard, elaborately chiselled with scrolls and foliate patterns, lion's head pommel.   £125

A Victorian officer's dress sword of the Queen's Bodyguard for Scotland (Royal Company of Archers), double edged blade 31in.   £82

A 17th century Schiavona, single edged multi-fullered straight blade 36in, with clip back point with traces of Andria Ferrara in fullers.£135

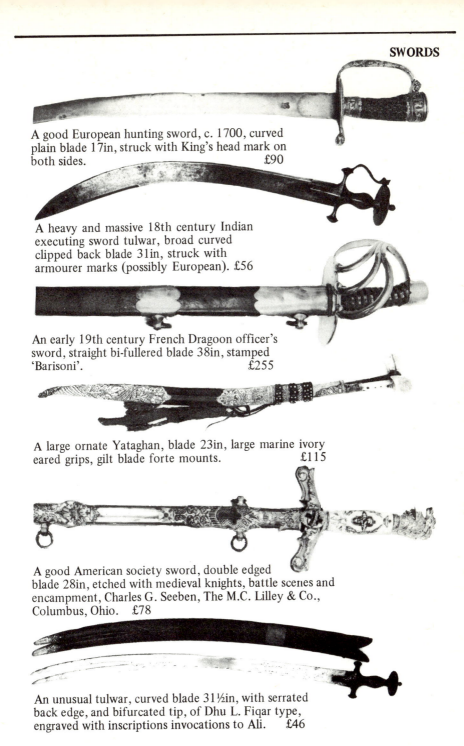

A good European hunting sword, c. 1700, curved plain blade 17in, struck with King's head mark on both sides. £90

A heavy and massive 18th century Indian executing sword tulwar, broad curved clipped back blade 31in, struck with armourer marks (possibly European). £56

An early 19th century French Dragoon officer's sword, straight bi-fullered blade 38in, stamped 'Barisoni'. £255

A large ornate Yataghan, blade 23in, large marine ivory eared grips, gilt blade forte mounts. £115

A good American society sword, double edged blade 28in, etched with medieval knights, battle scenes and encampment, Charles G. Seeben, The M.C. Lilley & Co., Columbus, Ohio. £78

An unusual tulwar, curved blade 31½in, with serrated back edge, and bifurcated tip, of Dhu L. Fiqar type, engraved with inscriptions invocations to Ali. £46

Set of a Boer War supply column by Britain.   £180

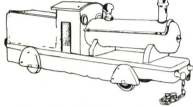

Unmechanical train, painted in
green and red.   £38

Toy horse and carriage made of
papier mache and metal, circa
1890, 33cm. long.   £140

A Tipp Co. clockwork fire engine,
circa 1930, 1ft. 7ins. long.   £80

1930's ice-cream salesman
on tricycle.   £26

Britain's South Australian Lancers, set of five in box, circa 1911. £110

Set of 14 Salvation Army band figures, made by Britain. £240

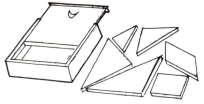

Victorian children's wooden puzzle in box. £1.75

A tin Lyons 1910 open delivery van. £60

Mechanical rickshaw made by German firm of Lehmann, circa 1912. £95

Victorian dapple grey painted wood rocking horse. £75

Britain's Royal Horse Artillery Team of lead soldiers. £75

Dinky open two seater, No. 22a. £200

Dinky Mayo composite aircraft. £35

Battery-driven model of a 1925 vintage car. £58

Heyde Roman display box. £130

Victorian dappled grey horse and clown toy. £130

Doll's house dated circa 1912. £130

Victorian mechanical clown toy. £130

A Lehmann's clockwork 'Also' car, circa 1930, 4ins. long. £38

19th century Noah's Ark complete with over 100 carved and painted figures, 26ins. long. £155

Dinky sports coupe, No. 22b. £170

Band of the U.S. Marine Corps. lead soldiers. £110

Early 19th century wind-up dog, which opens its mouth. £95

Victorian horse on a pusher, known as a cock-horse. £68

Late 19th century Guignol theatre, 81cm. high. £88

TRANSPORT

1933, 4½ litre Lagonda Sports Tourer.
£6,800

1901, Princeps 1¾ h.p. solo motor cycle.
£750

Ipswich made 19th century boneshaker.
£240

A James Starley Coventry lever tricycle
built by Haynes and Jeffy's, 1877.
£1,000

Victorian pram.   £20

Victorian penny-farthing cycle.   £120

English bicycle, circa 1880, with 52in.
diameter wheel.   £280

'Thalia' steam traction engine by John
Fowler & Co., Leeds.   £4,450

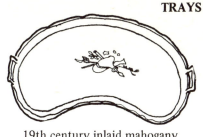

English black and gold papier mache tray, signed Jennens and Bettridge, approx. 30 x 22ins., circa 1830. £130

19th century inlaid mahogany tray with brass handles, 65cm. wide. £28

Victorian country made oak knife-box. £9.50

Mahogany inlaid oval tea tray with brass handles, 26½ins. £12

Victorian papier mache oval tray painted with flowers enhanced by mother-of- pearl 75cm. wide. £40

A square Japanese lacquer chamfered tray, 16½in. wide. £560

Butchers' boy's shoulder meat carrier, circa 1810. £48

Benares damascened circular coffee tray on a folding stand, 23ins. diam. £14

TRAYS

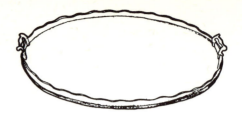

George III mahogany tray inlaid
with a conch shell. £16

Mahogany oval tea tray with
brass handles, 28½ins. £30

Mahogany and satinwood
oblong cutlery tray,
2ft. x 6½ins. £44

Stained circular revolving
table dumb waiter. £6

A superb gold lacquer and Shibayama tray signed L. Tsuru-
fune, 23¾in. x 16½in. £2,450

Victorian mahogany butler's tray
on a folding stand, 70cm. wide.
£20

An Oriental brass circular shaped
coffee tray, 56cm. diam., on
carved wood stand. £26

English Regency 'Pontypool' tray,
black with gilt decoration, approx.
25 x 18ins., circa 1810. £65

INDEX